W9-AQA-812

THE SOURCES OF
MODERN ATHEISM

ONE HUNDRED YEARS
THE OF DEBATE
OVER GOD
SOURCES
OF MODERN
ATHEISM

MARCEL NEUSCH

Translated by Matthew J. O'Connell

Theodore Lownik Library
Illinois Benedictine College
Lisle, Illinois 60532

paulist press new york • ramsey

211.8
N495aE

Originally published as *Aux Sources de L'Atheisme Contemporain* © 1977 by
Editions du Centurion, Paris. English translation © 1982 by The Missionary
Society of St. Paul the Apostle in the State of New York

All rights reserved. No part of this book may be reproduced or transmitted in
any form or by any means, electronic or mechanical, including photocopying,
recording or by any information storage and retrieval system without
permission in writing from the publisher.

Library of Congress
Catalog Card Number: 82-60596

ISBN: 0-8091-2488-2

Published by Paulist Press
545 Island Road, Ramsey, N.J. 07446

Printed and bound in the
United States of America

Contents

Preface

The following essays make no pretense at being a complete study of the problem of God or at bringing together all that has been written on the subject from the atheist viewpoint. They simply initiate a dialogue with some of the most qualified representatives of atheism and by so doing seek to achieve a better understanding of the modern age. Thus, while my historical survey may have a value in itself, it is in my own mind essentially a way of coming to grips with what affects us today: the unbelief of our own times. An author may be approached in two ways: the first is to review what he said (or meant to say), the second is to concentrate on what he has to say to us today. As far as possible, I have tried to combine the two approaches; as a matter of fact, when dealing with authors of no great antiquity, such a combination is not very difficult, because the gap between what they said and what they say now to us has hardly had time to widen.

The subject of the essays is contemporary atheism. Let me offer here a word of explanation on terminology. People speak sometimes of atheism, sometimes of unbelief, but these two words are not perfectly synonymous. Atheism is a conscious and reasoned rejection of God; it therefore presupposes a degree of theoretical reflection on experience. Unbelief, on the other hand, is a way of life that is characterized by indifference and a practical rejection of God; it is therefore primarily an existential attitude, whether it be accompanied by theoretical reflection or be a matter only of vague feeling. Until a fairly recent period people fought, sometimes quite fiercely, over the question of whether or not God exists; at the present time, however, we are entering into what has been called the post-atheistic age, an age, that is, in which people are resigned to the absence of God and are organizing their lives independently, for good or for ill, and without any reference to God.

We are thus in a new situation, in which atheism is making way for unbelief, the explicit denial of God for agnosticism, avowed warfare for an indifferent neutrality. If this be the case, then we can understand why the struggles of the past with their at times tragic seriousness should now seem a bit ridiculous and why, in the extreme case, they should become as unintelligible as the medieval crusades. How could anyone devote so much energy to a debate which seems of such minor interest to these contemporaries of ours? After all, a man had to have religious convictions in order to fight so passionately against God, and there is no doubt that the adversaries of God did in fact have such convictions no less than the defenders of God. We may find it hard today to imagine what was at stake in the struggle, but certainly for the atheists of the past the issue was, at best, God or man, and, at worst, God or absurdity. With the passage of time it seems that the non-existence of God is no longer traumatic for the human spirit. It may even be a source of amusement.

> *Hamm:* Let us pray to God.
>
> *Clov:* Again! . . .
>
> *Hamm:* (*to Nagg*): And you?
>
> *Nagg:* (*clasping his hands, closing his eyes, in a gabble*): Our Father which art—
>
> *Hamm:* Silence! In silence! Where are your manners? (*Pause.*) Off we go. (*Attitudes of prayer. Silence. Abandoning his attitude, discouraged.*) Well?
>
> *Clov:* (abandoning his attitude): What a hope! And you?
>
> *Hamm:* Sweet damn all! (*To Nagg.*) And you?
>
> *Nagg:* Wait! (*Pause. Abandoning his attitude.*) Nothing doing!

Hamm: The bastard! He doesn't exist!

Clov: Not yet.[1]

Are they calling it quits too soon? Should they stop or continue? Will the persevering effort of prayer perhaps be heard?
Can anyone say whether God may make his appearance in these
overheated minds? Samuel Beckett, at least, is convinced that
the game has been played . . . and that God has lost. His diagnosis, like that of the existentialists, agrees with that of Hume, a
century before Marx: religion is a number of wrong ideas produced by sick minds. The game has been a sham, and now the
cards must be put on the table. If religion survives, it will be simply as a vestige of a bygone age.
   Here we have a persuasion which, though not always expressed with the same power and/or the same artistic skill, is
nonetheless spreading. What will it lead to? Once God has been
crossed out by methods which I shall be examining in detail in
this book, once the game with God is over, what is left but human beings? Some, in despair or Stoic resignation (the characters of Camus or Sartre, for example), continue to play the game
in isolation or with other people: a heroic, absurd game, but the
only thing left that can give any stature to the human person.
Others, uplifted and rendered enthusiastic by the idea that at
last they alone are responsible for the future (the human person
according to Marxism, for example), devote all their powers to
the building of a more human world. Still others, finally—late-
comers these, the nomads of the modern age—find no fixed
point and feel doomed to wander. But in every case post-atheistic man regards the God-question as settled. God has lost his
case.
   But if God does exist? Then the case must be reopened. For
in the eyes of the Christian, according to Cardinal Marty, "the
God-question does not permit of compromise answers. One or
other of the parties must be mistaken. To be or not to be is indeed the question!" But I feel no great pressure in this book to
provide an answer to the question, although the final chapter
does suggest a procedure and presents the reader with a choice.
For the time being, however, I am exposing myself unprotected
to the guns of atheism. My primary purpose is to conduct a
search through what Henri Lefebvre calls "the kingdom of the

shades," and to flush out those "giants in the shadow" who forged the dogma of modern atheism and gave current unbelief its shape. I am seeking, then, to draw up a dossier and to examine, on appeal, the documents of a case that was terminated too hastily.

The results that can be expected from such an undertaking are many. To begin with, atheism will reveal its proper logic, which is neither weak nor anything to be ashamed of but rigorous and self-assured. It does, however, have its limits and its faults, and I shall not hesitate to emphasize these, but only after verifying the real solidity of the argument. There is need, then, of setting forth the atheist's arguments without trying to put them in the straitjacket of an alien mode of thought or treating them as answers to questions they did not ask.

We shall also find in this logic a noble urgency. Most of the time it can be seen that above and beyond its theoretical formulation atheism has practical goals. If it seeks the destruction of God and joyously smashes the ideologies that are the sociological supports for belief in God, it does so not in order to weaken the human sense of responsibility but rather to stimulate and underscore it. Once God is removed, human beings are solely responsible for the fate of the race. In many cases, in fact, the rediscovery of man proves to be the reason for the denial of God. The realm of action is, even more than the realm of thought, the place where atheism issues its challenge to Christians. The atheist is committed to a cause in which the human person is the stake. The Christian may not stand back, therefore, but must answer him in St. Paul's words: *Et plus ego*—I am more committed than anyone else!

But the essential question remains and cannot be put off indefinitely: Does God exist or does he not? Is the case lost for good? Beyond any narrowly practical stakes the issue is the meaning and destiny of the human person. It is on this spiritual plane—too often abandoned through indifference—that the debate must be reopened and the believers of our time must enter the fray once more. The debate has nothing academic about it, because it deals not with abstractions but with human beings.

What is the human person? It is on the answer to this question that the answer to the problem of God will ultimately depend. Is man a useless passion, as Sartre claims? Or a passion for the possible, as Kierkegaard thinks? While not immediately evident, the answer is nonetheless beyond doubt: in its hidden depths the human entity is a passion for all that has become possible in Jesus Christ. Without making any pretentious claims we must rediscover the line of clear-sighted thought that will set us on that path. Human words—or so at least I am convinced—are not utterly deficient in dealing with the existence of God.

1

God in Trouble

For almost a century now the notion of God has been under attack from atheism. Nietzsche proclaims that "God is dead," thus voicing with all possible brevity a view that has become ever more widespread among the masses. Where do things stand now? No doubt about it: God is no longer a habitual concern for human beings. Less and less do they call him to mind as they go through their days or make their decisions. Millet's *Angelus,* once a symbol of how God is present in even the most everyday activities, is now just a sentimental holy card. God has been replaced by other values: income and productivity. He may once have been regarded as the source of meaning for all human activities, but today he has been relegated to the secret dungeons of history. People undoubtedly do refer to him from time to time, perhaps at the "big moments," to use Sartre's phrase,[1] or as a routine accompaniment to some of life's stages (birth, marriage, funeral), but this kind of reference is hardly more than a sociological survival. God has disappeared from the consciousness of human beings.

In everyday life, then, atheism finds expression in the form of a growing indifference that through contagion reaches into every level of society. It would be an exaggeration to attribute this decline of God exclusively to the offensive led by men like Feuerbach, Marx, Nietzsche, Freud, and a few others whom we may call, with Ricoeur, the "philosophers of suspicion." These lyric singers of atheism have relentlessly harassed God and shown the emptiness of belief in him. If they have had the audience they have, it is because they have been able to express with clarity a state of affairs which many people experience. Their resolute and carefully argued atheism confirms an unfocused practical attitude that was waiting for its rationale.

7

I am saying, then, that while the past century has given atheism its anti-theologians, it did not invent, so to speak, the rejection of God. Contemporary atheism has, for example, socio-political causes originating in the eighteenth century. It is undeniable, however, that by developing a full-scale anti-theology these thinkers have supplied credentials for what had been only a latent tendency at the practical level or even a simple carelessness about religion. They have assembled an arsenal of arguments in which the individual can find justification for his way of life. In fact, the arguments to which appeal is made today are almost always drawn, directly or indirectly, from these thinkers.[2]

Before approaching atheism in the person of its most prestigious representatives I intend in this first chapter to take a more global approach to the subject, even if I must necessarily stick to generalities in so doing. Several questions call for our attention.

First of all, how did atheism compel recognition? What obstacles did it have to overcome to win public acceptance? What is the source of its strength? This first series of questions, which necessitates a short historical retrospect, is in my view indispensable. It will help me to show the slow development of atheism over the course of three centuries.

Then there is a second series of questions: From what angle does atheism attack the problem of religion? What intellectual strategies does it use in order to quash the God-question? With the aid of these questions we shall be able to familiarize ourselves with the most common procedures followed by atheism in destroying the idea of God.

Finally, in a third series of questions I shall try to summarize the present situation. What is it that allows atheism to win acceptance? What are the values that it defends? Then, after hearing how atheists justify themselves, I shall ask: Are they in fact justifiable?

A Freedom Won Through Struggle

It is a fact that increasing numbers of people live as if God did not exist. Their certainty is not always very firm. For many there is still a question mark: Perhaps there is something to the idea of God, who knows? Indifference is often accompanied at the level of reflection not by a denial of God but by an absence of any opinion, an agnosticism. In fact, the present age is marked by a high degree of non-combativeness on the part of atheism and by the coexistence of all possible opinions. But this is a recent phenomenon and due in part to the lack of resistance to atheism on the part of believers. Atheism is not only tolerated but is even accepted with a benevolent smile. It is accepted as an eccentric life-style but also as a stimulus to questions about the faith of believers. Controversy is out of fashion now. We are already in the "post-atheistic" age in which each person organizes his life according to his convictions but at the same time respects the convictions of others.

We are living, then, in a mass civilization, a civilization from which God is absent and in which atheism is no longer surprising. In fact, nowadays it is faith that causes the surprise; the atheist sometimes thinks of it as a kind of aberration or, most often, as a disconcerting type of possible life-style. Christians themselves have ceased to live their faith as though it were something obvious or as a way of life whose justification is now beyond argument. Being less and less protected by the social environment, they are realizing that faith is a free act and that it therefore shares in the oddness and insecurity which marks the growth of freedom itself. It seems, therefore, that in the contemporary situation the roles are reversed: atheism, which used to be problematic, is now taken for granted, while faith, which used to be taken for granted, is becoming increasingly problematic.

Is it really necessary to demonstrate what I have been saying? Well, we have short memories, and it is good from time to time to recall the past so that we may understand our present experience. I shall not try to describe the genesis of atheism but shall simply sketch some of the stages in its development. Anyone who reads his history knows that the triumph of atheism is a recent phenomenon.

A Clandestine and Unobtrusive Atheism

There was a time when hardly anyone called the existence of God into doubt. Or at least an atheist was well advised not to display his convictions. We need not go back as far as the Middle Ages when views that seemed to do violence to society were punished by the iron collar, the pillory, the plucking out of the tongue and, in the case of a recidivist, the stake.[3] But read for

example the testimony of a citizen of Paris who wrote in the time
of Francis I, between 1519 and 1530: "On Thursday, the 18th of
the same month of August, a young man was burned at the stake
in Grève, having been convicted of heresy as a disciple and fol-
lower of Luther's teaching. He chose to die unconfessed, saying
that the right thing was to confess to God alone and not to a
priest, who is a sinner like himself."[4]

Such executions for religious reasons were part "of everyday life in Paris." In the seventeenth century heresy took prece-
dence over atheism which continued to be, as it had been in the
preceding century, a rare and marginal phenomenon and one
that was relentlessly tracked down where suspected. La Bruyère
was still doubtful that anyone could really be an atheist: "I
would like to see a man of sobriety and moderation, of chaste
life and balanced mind, who would say there is no God; such a
man would at least be speaking without ulterior motives, but
you will not find him."[5] In short, no one could be an atheist with
impunity and without endangering himself.

It was essentially the libertines who were the atheists of the
seventeenth century. What explains their appearance on the
scene? A real understanding of them would require detailed historical analyses. As a result of the Reformation the religious life
of the time was rent asunder: shifts occurred; there were efforts
at achieving a new balance; rival churches were formed. In this
shattered religious world each group defined the truth for itself,
and religion sometimes became nothing but a criterion by which
an individual's place in the social spectrum was determined.
Some persons even separated themselves from all religion.
"The autonomy of each group (which turned at times into aggressivity toward other groups) became more important than
disputes over 'truths.' It led everywhere to a verifiable skepti-
cism; it also paved the way for (and already was, in embryonic
form) a *non-religious* type of certitude, consisting of participation
in *civil* society."[6] The striking thing about the seventeenth century is the rise of differentiated groups. While some continued
to develop within the universe of religion, with the line of division running between the orthodox and the new heretical
groups, others quietly moved out to the periphery of religion
and claimed independence of thought. This was an atheism that
meant a break within society, and it inspired no less distrust than
heresy did.

In consequence, we see a man like Bossuet doing battle on two fronts: against heretics ("those in error") who deny their membership in the Catholic Church, and the libertines, who live on the fringes of the Church and lead their own independent lives. In the libertine the Church saw a real "outsider" and a kind of "otherness" it had not hitherto experienced: the otherness of the pagan and the atheist.[7] How did the Church react when confronted with this phenomenon? Its most clear-sighted thinkers diagnosed indifferentism and an "increasing atheism."[8] And even if they did not think this atheism to be a real threat as yet, they did see the danger coming and did not regard it as negligible. Bossuet was not mistaken in his view. In his concern to safeguard the integrity of the Church and prevent contagion, he brought up his heavy guns: an atheist is "a man who indulges in rash curiosity" and "blasphemes that of which he is ignorant." Bossuet's critique is aimed at two points: the atheist is morally corrupt and intellectually weak. Bossuet thus accuses him, on the one hand, of being corrupt, "a slave of his passions," and urges him therefore to find healing of heart. This takes care of the moral perversity. On the other hand, he attacks the atheist's "weakness, ignorance, and stupidity of mind."[9] So much for the intellectual side.

This approach to atheism was fairly widespread, even if it was not always expressed with the same oratorical violence. But if such were the situation of the atheist, how was he to be rescued from his immorality and persuaded of his intellectual error? Somehow the atheist's influence had to be neutralized. Force was not always excluded. The atheist was, after all, a pervert or at least an unbalanced person who should be prevented from doing harm. The solution might be imprisonment. We should therefore not be surprised to find the atheists of the seventeenth century living in prisons or asylums (two institutions not greatly different from one another). Even executions "because of blasphemy" reappeared during this period of the Counter-Reformation.[10]

As a person suspect and threatened, the atheist had thus no reason for expressing his convictions. His passionate devotion to the truth was usually not strong enough to make him risk torture. Moreover, social pressure was often strong enough to dissuade him from any sharp break. It was better to live a hidden life. Everyone has heard of Abbé Meslier (1664–1729), the parish priest who succeeded in hiding his real views throughout his lifetime. This priest spent the free time left him by his pastoral duties in writing proofs for the non-existence of God. He said everything there is to be said on the subject, and our modern atheists have simply been plagiarists! But Abbé Meslier felt no call to be a martyr; he preferred to play out the comedy during his lifetime and to die peacefully in his bed. He did, however, take care to leave the text of his demonstration with a notary. Voltaire acted as Meslier's public relations man. This borderline case is clear evidence of social pressure strong enough to keep an atheist silent. The incredible case of Abbé Meslier also shows the risks a declared atheist ran at the end of the seventeenth and beginning of the eighteenth centuries, as well as the easiest course for him to follow.

But the age did not limit itself to ideological constraints and the power of the police in order to get atheists back on the right track. An appeal was also made to the mind of the atheist, in the conviction that reason is stronger than unreason and must win out. An effort was made therefore to convince the atheist by piling up arguments. From the standpoint of reason the atheist was regarded as having stopped halfway in the reasoning process. Pascal summed up this point of view: "Atheism indicates strength of mind, but only up to a certain point."[11] And Leibniz echoes him in this revealing text from his *The Confession of Nature against Atheists:* "Francis Bacon, a man of divine genius, has rightly said that casually sampled philosophy leads away from God but that, drunk more deeply, it leads back to him. This is confirmed in our own century, which is fruitful alike of science and of impiety."[12]

Because it was convinced that atheism sprang from unreason or from reason that was not exercised to the full, the seventeenth century refined its intellectual strategies for proving the existence of God; it multiplied its arguments and sought to knock the atheist from the ring.

A Flood of Rowdy Atheism

Tolerance reigned in the eighteenth century. Pierre Bayle, whose work was completed at the beginning of the century, defines with utmost clarity the spirit behind this tolerance. He bases tolerance on "the rights of an erroneous conscience," and shows that unless tolerance is shown, the world will become "a cut-throat place."[13] This is the century of the Enlightenment which took for its motto: *Sapere aude*—Have the courage to think for yourself. It was tolerant of the thinking of others and claimed for each individual the right to think for himself and the right to reject the tutelage of religion. Without being himself an atheist, Bayle established a new right to practice atheism and thought that a republic made up of atheists could survive.[14] In any case, atheists benefited from the new climate of opinion. They could henceforth live in the open and make their preference known. Atheism moved from a clandestine existence onto the public stage.

In what form did atheism show itself in the eighteenth century? In showing itself openly it also became militant, violent, and jealous. D'Holbach saw in religion nothing but a "source of divisions, madness, and crimes." The Marquis de Sade gave free reign to his destructive frenzy: "F . . . that witness yonder [i.e., God]; my greatest annoyance is that God doesn't really exist and that I'm deprived of the pleasure of insulting him in more positive ways." Religion was accused of being irrational. D'Holbach went even further and saw it as not only a tissue of absurdities but the source of moral and political evil. In addition, it was incapable of explaining the world. So widespread was this illusory thing called religion that the minds of people remained sunk in sleep and were unable to advance to the stage of science. Science must therefore take it on itself to dissipate the illusion:

> Let men and women stop looking outside the world they live in for beings who will obtain for them the happiness nature refuses them. Instead let them study this nature, learn its laws, contemplate its power and the immutable way in which it acts. Let them then apply their discoveries to their own happiness and submit in silence to the laws from whose action nothing can remove them.[15]

But why set oneself against such an illusion? Simply in order to lead people to the truth? Undoubtedly. But the real stake is rather different: the illusion conceals a political snare; it introduces confusion into the social life of human beings. God, who "was a sultan, a despot, a tyrant to whom everything was allowed," is in the service not of human emancipation but of despotism. This is why Helvetius regards the criticism of religion as so important: to demystify religion is to strike a blow at the reactionary state. Even though he does not yet see how the illusion is to be dispelled, he attacks it for the baneful role it plays. Here we begin to see the real reasons for the criticism of religion: if the eighteenth century carries on a struggle against religion, it does so in the name of a political ideology.

How do believers react to this much more virulent attack which atheists openly launch against religion? Some Christian preachers go on uttering the same old nonsense as they repeat their predecessors but add nothing new of their own. Ballet, for example, continues to link atheism and sin: "They [atheists] are unwilling to admit that it is the corruption of their own hearts that inspires their hatred of gospel morality."[16] He adds that all these "fine geniuses of our time" would not hesitate to "sacrifice their minds, were it not that they would also have to sacrifice their passions." Cambacérès is more prudent, though hardly more nuanced, when he cries out in an oratorical flight: "Therefore you are not unbelieving; you are only corrupt."[17] But he is forced to acknowledge that there are unbelievers who are also honorable people; he admits, therefore, that there can be exceptions to his rule, but even at this point he cannot keep from voicing a doubt: Isn't it likely that an atheist has some "secret" vice? He concludes that while individuals may be "upright without the help of religion," it must at least be granted that "they find it more difficult to be so."

These hesitations on the part of a preacher show that the thesis linking atheism and moral perversion is being undermined. People are accepting a fact that is becoming increasingly clear: men and women can deny God while remaining sensible and morally healthy. Atheists still, of course, do not get a good press, even among avant-garde intellectuals. Voltaire does not like atheists and regards them as dangerous monstrosities. Nonetheless he avoids connecting religious error with some moral defect or putting it in the category of madness. He tries rather to get at the causes of atheism and finds the religions themselves to blame, because they have travestied the idea of God; another cause is certain intellectual difficulties which have, however, always been a scandal to the mind. "Atheists are for the most part bold and misguided scholars who reason badly and, unable to comprehend the creation, the origin of evil, and other difficulties, have recourse to the hypothesis of the eternity of things and of necessity."[18]

While admiring these emancipated spirits who are in the vanguard of progress, Voltaire regrets their intellectual short-sightedness. He regards atheism as due to inadequate reflection; it is an intellectual error.

Admittedly, Voltaire also has recourse to more down-to-earth, even sordid arguments in order to reject atheism and justify religion. But if he defends religion, he does so not because it is "true" but because it is useful. Voltaire's need of a God is based on physics: If there is no God, how is the great clock of the universe to be kept going? He also needs a God for reasons of morality: What other bulwark is there against the weaknesses of human beings? Above all, he needs a God for social reasons. How else is order to be maintained in a world made up largely of the poor?

However, Voltaire is not very consistent. He rejects atheism, but he nevertheless keeps God on the periphery of his life; he is in practice an atheist. He turns Pascal's approach upside down: the real "diversion" (*divertissement*) is not life in the world but the escape into various forms of a world to come.

> In his view our task is precisely to develop our fully human interests, to arrange for ourselves a society that is comfortable and prosperous, and to make ourselves as happy as possible through trade and industry. What is the God who bids us forget all this? He is a *diversion*.[19]

The emphasis has thus shifted and Voltaire is a true witness to his times. He has not as yet intellectually crossed the Rubicon, but he has taken his stand outside of religion. He is comfortable with religion provided it does not inconvenience him. He settles for a kind of lower middle class practical atheism that creates no embarrassments for him. In this regard he shares an outlook that was rather widespread in his day: an outlook that is interested not in truth but only in usefulness. "All the religions contain principles that are useful to society," Montesquieu writes. "This rule has scientific status and a moral bearing; it shows what the elite seeks to make of the religions: something useful to society."[20]

Atheists thus had a difficult road to travel in the eighteenth century. But atheism was irresistible and finally won its civic rights. Its real founders will appear on the scene in the nineteenth century; we shall be turning to them in a moment. But let me say a word here about the view adopted by believers, a view that has been modified only recently. It is true, of course, that nowadays we do not lock believers up in psychiatric institutions; we leave that kind of special hospital for other forms of government to use. We do however have difficulty in freeing ourselves of the view that atheism is proof of moral perversity. Vatican II introduced a change in this regard. As Karl Rahner writes, the Council

> ignored the traditional Scholastic thesis which held that a normally intelligent man could not be a positive atheist over a more or less protracted period without moral guilt. One can go beyond that and say that the Council did not merely lay this thesis aside but that it put forward an *opposite thesis,* namely, that it is possible for *a normal adult to accept an explicit atheism for a longer period,* even till the end of his life, *without any proof of moral guilt* on the part of the unbeliever.[21]

The Council acknowledged in effect that while God alone can give a complete (*plene*) answer to existential questions, atheists can nonetheless live morally upright (*recte*) lives. The opportunity for salvation is given to them even in the midst of their atheism. Such an acknowledgment provides the dialogue with atheists with clearer presuppositions and a more favorable antecedent judgment.

Man the Creator of God

Beginning in the eighteenth century religion began to lose ground, especially among intellectuals. In the nineteenth century something new appeared: atheism won the masses, and in particular the most defenseless strata of society. Marx showed great shrewdness in describing this shift in the world of atheism: "It is remarkable to see how, contrary to what was the case in the eighteenth century, the practice of religion is now to be found in the middle class (*Mittelstand*) and the upper class, while the rejection of religion has on the contrary . . . made its way down into the French proletariat."[22]

But even more important perhaps than this social shift within atheism is another phenomenon that marks a decisive turning point: in the nineteenth century atheism acquired its great intellectual representatives. In the eighteenth century religion had lost all value in the eyes of intellectuals, who regarded it as justified solely by its usefulness; in the nineteenth century it came to be completely stripped of any meaning and rejected as harmful to society. "Behold the enemy: God!" would be the title of a book by H. Gaston at the end of the nineteenth century. Religion would now have hardly any defenders outside a Voltairean bourgeoisie that was stricken with belated remorse as it saw the value of having a parish priest who would act as a policeman: "Who is it that defends order and property in our rural areas? The parish priest. Priests are nowadays the representatives of order even in the eyes of non-believers." Thus is freedom of teaching justified in the eyes of a Montalembert (1850).

Atheism on the other hand is now justified not only in practice but in theory as well. Its theologians try to base it on truth and thus to validate "popular atheism." The latter did not derive its existence from the arguments of atheism's theologians; it sprang rather from reaction against a Church that was more and more clearly on the side of the bourgeoisie. Henceforth an alliance of minds between bourgeoisie and Church will be confronted by an alliance of hearts between the proletariat and an atheism that makes the interests of the proletariat its own.

In the subsequent chapters of this book I shall be sketching the portraits of the individuals who gave atheism the appearance it has in our day and won a definitive freedom for atheists. What are the main lines of their thinking? The questions they ask are often the very same ones that theologians ask, but, as we might expect, the answers given are diametrically opposed.

God Is a Product of the Imagination

The first of these questions is: What is God? *Quid sit?* as the theologians used to put it. What is the essence of God? After answering the question of God's existence, they used to exercise a good deal of imagination in thinking about his attributes and sketching a portrait of him.

The theologians may have shown some hesitation in this area, but the atheists were peremptory in their answers: God is an illusion, that is, a product of the imagination, a being that lacks internal coherence and is adorned with all the qualities proper to human beings. This is not a new answer, of course, but may be found in all the materialists of the past. After all, has any atheist ever had anything new to add to Xenophanes? Long ago this Greek with his critical and scoffing mind had seen the gods as nothing but a freakish notion of the human spirit. Everyone is familiar with the famous passages: "Mortals believe the gods to be created by birth, and to have their own [i.e., mortals'] raiment, voice and body."[23] "Aethiopians have gods with snub noses and black hair, Thracians have gods with grey eyes and red hair."[24]

Is God, then, really the Creator of human beings? That is what the Christian faith maintains, but—atheists ask—has it not in fact reversed the roles? Yes, comes the unanimous reply, it is man who creates God for himself.

This assertion has been repeated with hardly any variation ever since antiquity. The eighteenth century was delighted with the idea. When Voltaire read in the Bible that God had made human beings in his own image, he had a ready answer: Of course, because human beings had already made him in their image! Human beings (atheists say) project onto God almost everything they see in their human world, not only positive qualities but defects as well (anger, capriciousness, and so on). Believers will hardly trouble to deny this observation, but whereas they conclude to the need of caution with regard to every image and even every concept of God, atheists conclude that God simply does not exist. Believers undertake to purify their faith, but atheists simply jettison any and every religious belief. The former endeavor to refine their theology, the latter allow God only an imaginary existence: God is *nothing but* a human projection. The difference between believer and atheist is to be found in this "nothing but."

The question of God's nature thus immediately leads the atheist to inquire into the origin of God: How could human beings have developed this illusion? The category to which appeal is most frequently made in explaining the mechanism leading to the birth of the gods is "projection," the mechanism of which I have just been speaking. What is God? A human projection, that is, a manifestation of subjective states, these being given an independent existence and personified. The projection tells us nothing about God but it tells us a great deal about human beings, their desires, their aspirations, their hopes, and so on. In their gods human beings body forth everything which they are not but long to be.

Feuerbach dismantles the mechanism that accounts for this projection; Marx, Nietzsche and Freud provide a more searching theoretical explanation of it. In every case, however, the idea is the same: God is a projection or reflection (the latter term is frequently found in Marx). This means that some quality or situation which is part of human experience is transferred outside of human beings themselves and attributed (often in inverted form) to a hypostasized entity. Once the mechanism of projection is understood, atheism goes on to ask why human beings should execute such a projection and create a being distinct from themselves. More on this question in a moment. But atheism also asks: How are we to get rid of the projection? For the aim of atheism is liberation. It seeks to deliver human beings from this illusion. Nineteenth century atheism was not satisfied with vague attacks on God. It perfected a technique of liberation through knowledge.

God Is a Consolation to the Heart

Atheism does not explain only the how but claims to explain the why as well. *Cur Deus?* The question is of course not alien to theology: Why is there a God? Atheism, however, immediately changes the character of the question: Why have human beings invented God for themselves? Why do they want him to go on existing? Because they need him if they are to be able to endure life! In a world that spares them no sufferings human beings have recourse to God for the consolation that will enable them to get through life and have a hope even where there is no basis for any hope. Lamennais wrote in the last century: "The task of the human race is a long one, and the toil it must endure is harsh; to sweeten it God has given human beings two heavenly companions: the faith that sustains them and the hope that consoles them." This describes God's essential function.

Marx, Nietzsche and Freud are the thinkers who have been most insightful in analyzing the way of God's existence. Marx and Freud both see that the human person is overwhelmed by nature and frustrated in social relations; Marx looks to economic distortions for an explanation of these frustrations, while Freud seeks psychological explanations. Both men conclude that religion essentially meets a need for consolation. Marx will say that religion is "the sigh of the oppressed creature," the "opium of the people," the "heart of a heartless world," and Freud that religion is a "palliative measure" for use in a world that "brings us too many pains, disappointments and impossible tasks." Religion is the balm that enables us to put up with an unbearable life.

Religion thus has a compensatory function. In a universe that is lacking in logic, justice, and joy, it enables us to fight against absurdity, anxiety, and injustice by introducing a seeming balance. Religion is not primarily the result of intellectual speculation; it is the cry of a ravaged heart. As Augustine says at the beginning of his *Confessions*, "My heart is restless until it finds rest in you." Marx sees religion as a way of protesting against the distortions of human existence. It represents a refusal to be simply resigned, a breakthrough to a better world in which we hope that frustrations will be turned into joy. It makes no difference that the protest depends on an illusion; it is no less consoling on that account. Life would be utter despair if there were not a Creator God who is present in history, a providence that watches over the destiny of each individual. Human beings will not settle for being nothing but a "useless passion," and therefore they follow up their every Good Friday with an Easter Sunday.

The God to whom such thinking leads is not a very solid one and can hardly stand up to critical reflection. He answers a need in human beings; the trouble is that he has no reality save that given him by a sense of need that sees all deficiencies made good in his fullness. This "utilitarian" God who arises at the end of our reasoning processes and as the result of our anxieties and sufferings does not stand up to a serious examination. When we discover an infinite God who sustains finite human beings, we do not prove that God exists but only underscore the fact that human beings cannot adapt to their own finiteness. When we talk of a God who consoles, we say nothing about God but only come up against the fact that human beings cannot endure the anxiety they experience. When we say that God is all-powerful, we are not making a statement about God but only asserting that human beings cannot resign themselves to being crushed. Only in appearance do we "save God." God always appears on the scene at the extremity of human finiteness, anxiety and collapse, as the Being who makes up for a human lack. He is a "stop-gap" God who relieves human limitations, but whose existence depends on being a complement to human deficiencies.

Believers accept this criticism. In our day they are quite ready to do without this God of the gaps. The atheist however draws a more radical conclusion: he says that God does not exist at all. How could the atheist do otherwise? The only God he knows is this God who meets a "need," this God who is necessary for human life. He is ignorant of the God of "desire": the God who freely gives himself and, far from forcing himself on human beings, calls upon them to freely give themselves.

Religion a Curb on the Will

The third question raised by the atheist has to do with the effects of belief in God on the human will. When Marx said that religion is an opium he was saying that it lulls the will to sleep. "O Christ, eternal thief of energy!" Arthur Rimbaud cries. The criticism can be spelled out in detail. What, in fact, is the effect of religion on human activity? Here again the atheist's response is unanimous and unvarying: religion makes people childish instead of turning them into adults; it keeps them in a state of dependence instead of spurring them to rebellion; it turns them away from earth instead of giving them a taste for it; it paralyzes action instead of stimulating it. In short, religion acts not as a motive force but as a curb.

That is how all the atheists thought of religion—and with good reason! For what in fact did Catholics have preached to them? In 1848 Montalembert could sum up the social teaching of the Church in two verbs: "Abstain and respect!"—that is, abstain from theft and respect the property of others. "Accept poverty with resignation and you will be recompensed and indemnified eternally!" But atheists rebelled against this kind of religion, for they realized how harmful it was. To look for consolations in a supra-earthly life seemed to them disloyal, a betrayal of this world. They urged their fellow human beings to become autonomous, to rely on themselves, to shape their own lives, and to transform the earth in an imaginative and creative way. No one spoke out more forcefully than Nietzsche in denouncing this flight from the world and in preaching a return to the earth: "I beseech you, my brothers, *remain faithful to the earth,* and do not believe those who speak to you of otherworldly hopes! Poison-mixers are they, whether they know it or not."[25]

It has been said of a character of Julien Green that "everything not related to God bores him to death. He believes in God and in nothing else." But a human being forged by atheism believes in the earth and in nothing else. In language that is more sober but hardly different in substance from Nietzsche's, Marx offers the same view of the human person. "The philosophers have only interpreted the world, in various ways; the point, however, is to transform it."[26] The contemplative eye scans the surface of the earth, sees deficiencies there, and looks to God for a fulfillment that will make up for these. This is escapism. The "transforming" eye sees deficiencies as a challenge and task for the will—nothing more.

Against this background we can understand the atheist's aggressiveness. His relentless attack on the idea of heaven and on the hopes which this idea arouses has its positive explanation in his plans for the liberation of human beings and for involvement in earthly tasks. Those who refuse to expect anything from heaven are ready to set about transforming the earth without expecting help from any other source. Marx observes this phenomenon and concludes that it is imperative to get rid of religion: "The criticism of religion disillusions man to make him think and act and shape his reality like a man who has been disillusioned and has come to reason."[27]

Marx evidently thinks that human beings are unfit as long as they look to heaven. This is why the struggle against religion is not a merely subordinate matter; rather it is the "premise" of all criticism. As long as people have not stopped looking up to heaven, they will not turn their eyes to the earth.

In the atheist's view, religion is harmful for the basic reason that it withdraws people from action. It has the pernicious ideological function of supporting the status quo and of proposing that disorder is to be remedied by refusing to face it and looking instead for recompense in the next life. The atheist counters this ideology with a utopian vision which is critical of the badly organized present scheme of things and opens the minds of men to a truly human future. He substitutes an earthly future for the next life and mobilizes all human energies to make this future reality.

This kind of criticism is certainly relevant and a challenge to faith. Christian militants have realized this, as we can see from the life of Frédo Krumnow, a man who felt shaken in his Christian commitments by the Marxist challenge but who met the challenge by a life completely dedicated to militant action. He realized that no intellectual refutation can completely meet the Marxist criticism. Only by countering it with "the fire of life"[28] can it be given the lie. Krumnow's example is living proof of the limitations of a purely intellectual dialogue with atheism: argument is met by argument, but neither side can drive the other from the field. Atheism can be effectively refuted only on the field of concrete commitment. The Second Vatican Council understood this, for it wrote: "Atheism must be countered both by presenting true teaching in a fitting manner and by the full and complete life of the Church and her members."[29]

The conclusion to which atheism leads is clear. Atheists do not consider religion to be an error that can be refuted by an intrinsic analysis of its assertions (dogmas); they have little interest in the internal coherence of the faith. Nor do they regard religion as a lie; they do not look behind religion for a malicious will that seeks to lead others astray. Rather they regard it as an illusion, that is, the product of unconscious activity in human beings who are faced with impasses and who find in religion something of subjective value, a response to their anxieties, but who also experience it as a curb on their wills.

Atheism proposes two contrasting procedures as the way to rid ourselves of this illusion. On the one hand, it offers a genealogy of religion: it shows how the idea of God arises in the imagination, and undertakes to trace a "genesis or genealogy, to use Nietzsche's phrase, which consists in discovering in the hidden movements of consciousness the source of an 'illusion,' a myth-making function."[30] Then there is a second operation which tries to break down the idea of God and reduce it to a psychological or sociological or psychoanalytic basis. In thus analyzing the idea of God, atheism is able to point to the human realities onto which the idea has been grafted. The expectation is that the mere progress of knowledge will lead to the disappearance of religion.

We can look back now and gauge the distance that has been traveled. Until the dawn of the modern age the atheist stood in the dock: his obstinacy could only be due either to moral perversity or to inadequate philosophical reflection. Today, on the other hand, the atheist is among the prosecutors: religion springs from ignorance or a mistaken understanding of its human roots, and it can only corrupt the will. Atheism represents an effort on man's part to recover for himself all that is human, all that he took from himself and attributed to God.

Toward a Humanism Without God

Are we in a position now, after this brief historical sketch, to draw up a preliminary set of conclusions? In the course of time atheists have won their freedom; they are no longer banished by society. In addition, they now have a well-developed "theology"; they know what positions to hold regarding God and religion. For the rest, they accept life as neither greatly exciting nor unimportant, as a place of both routine and joy, but in any case to be lived without reference to faith and without evasion. For a long time atheism could be defined as a system of thought that was directed against faith; today, however, the face it shows is less sharply defined, more open. "Contemporary unbelief offers itself rather as a positive possibility of human existence, an integral way of being human without faith."[31] We speak nowadays of positive atheism, the aim of which is "to reveal man to himself, in his power of affirmation and creation of meaning. In connection with this undertaking, whether proximate or long-range, interpretation in its negative aspects is simply the ascesis through which human desire must pass before being restored to its own greatness."[32] The struggle against religion is always inspired by a particular concept of the human person and by the goal of liberation.

A Secular World

Not everyone will agree that there can be such a thing as "positive" atheism. In thus describing it we are acknowledging that atheism possesses values hitherto unsuspected or at least not hitherto recognized precisely as values. What, then, are these values? One key term sums them all up: the autonomy of the human. In order to grasp the positive significance of atheism we must go back to the time before the spread of atheism.

We can describe that earlier situation with the term "Christendom," that is, the unity of world, Church, and Jesus Christ. Think of each of these three as a circle. There was a time when the three circles were superimposed and their circumferences matched completely. Today they tend to move apart, like continents adrift: the Church is one such continent, the world a second, and Jesus Christ the third. They may still overlap but they are no longer completely coincident. The person who remains entirely on the continent named "world" and pays no attention to the other two is a "secularized" person. Atheists live in a secular world that no longer has any connections with the other two continents.

In the past there was an institutional link between the three spheres: the Church claimed to speak in the name of Jesus Christ (imperialism in regard to truth) and to lay down this truth for the world (triumphalism) in various areas. During the Constantinian Era (fourth to nineteenth centuries) it was taken for granted that the Church was indeed to be identified with Christ and that there was cooperation, if not an identity, between Church and world. The Church gave expression to God's will for the world and told the Western conscience how it was to think and live. The result was the formation of a "conventional" religion,[33] that is, a religion whose truths and practices were accepted not as the result of personal thought and decision but because we were told we should accept them, whether at home or in school or in church. In this kind of religion there was no place for questioning. Deviants and the erring were simply cast out. On the other hand, those who lived in harmony with the Church and thereby with God were rescued by the Church from existential anxieties.

This conventional Christianity is now dead. The world no longer gears itself either to the Church or to Jesus Christ but goes its own independent way. It has claimed self-determination and autonomy and chosen its own values and its own laws.

This process has had two consequences. The first is that the world is now a secular world. This means that human beings, now free of the tutelage of the Church and religion, no longer expect or accept guidance from these. Various names have been given to this phenomenon: "dechristianization," "paganization," and so on. But whatever the value judgment passed on, secularization now seems to be an irreversible development. It means that henceforth whole areas of society and culture are withdrawn from the authority of the ecclesial institution.

Secularization has occurred successively in different spheres: science in the seventeenth century, at the time of the Galileo affair; politics in the eighteenth century; anthropology and ethics in our day. In each sphere the break took place under the worst possible conditions. I need not remind the reader of the circumstances of Galileo's condemnation in 1633; an individual was condemned but science emerged the winner. The political order won its autonomy in a less brutal manner, but the Church did not fail to resist when it had to surrender its hold on the temporal power.[34] At the present time we are seeing the separation of Church from ethics. In this area secularization is affecting not only manners (the environing culture) but making its way into consciences as well. More and more individuals are thinking and acting without reference to religion. Ethics is gradually escaping from the control of the Church in such important matters as contraception, abortion, divorce, sexual freedom, and euthanasia.

The second consequence is connected with the dramatic turnabout that secularization has brought. Not only is the Church stripped of all authority, but its interventions are judged a priori to be anti-humanist. The values it preaches are regarded as passé; worst of all, it relies on principles that are judged to be dubious and outmoded, or on a hypothetical human nature to which it claims to have the key and which is patently adulterated. Until not long ago the Church had a monopoly on meaning (the meaning of institutions and of existence itself), but now it is in competition with other ideologies that all claim to preach a valid message about human beings. In any case, to talk to an atheist about a "revelation" seems as odd to him as to talk of "flying saucers" (Kastler). The atheist's motto is that of the Englightenment: Have the courage to think for yourself!

The Church evidently has been largely responsible for this ongoing process of secularization. Instead of promoting it, the Church resisted it with everything in its power. It is itself partly responsible for secularization having developed as a form of resistance to the Church. The Church must therefore learn a new presence to the world. Will it present itself as an authoritarian Church, as in the past, or will it become a Church of dialogue? In the past everything moved in one direction (the Church speaking to the world); today there is movement in both directions (the world in turn has something to say to the Church). Only to the extent that the Church undertakes a genuine dialogue will it once again become credible and be able to speak God's authentic word to the world.

The Reasons for Modern Atheism

Atheism was born in a particular cultural context in which dialogue was difficult. It introduced a new set of problems and carried discussion into the areas of politics, psychology, economics, and so on. It turned away from problems of ontology and tried instead to explain the meaning of religion as seen from these other standpoints. The result has been various hues of atheism. There is, for example, a "political" atheism that springs from the observation that the Christian religion has offered a justification for every evil—torture, slavery, oppression—and in the course of its history has most often been on the side of the oppressor. Is it possible to have any esteem for such a religion? Thus there are many "causes" of atheism.[35]

But all these causes are not sufficient to justify atheism, that is, they are not objective grounds for the atheist criticism of the idea of God. One may challenge the Christian religion without thereby eliminating the reasons for God's existence, if I may so put it. What in fact are the "reasons" which atheists adduce in their rejection of God. Not all of them are of recent origin; some were formulated long ago by St. Thomas Aquinas.[36]

The reason most often given for rejecting God is the problem of evil. Because evil exists, *God is morally impossible.* The existence of evil is a fact no one can help seeing. Everyone can see for himself that life is a flood of sufferings and failures. Neither good will nor technology can get rid of evil. Evil, especially the suffering and death of the innocent, is the great scandal; Camus made this the theme of his novel *The Plague.* But who is the guilty party? We cannot accuse man in this case. Must it not therefore be God, who is said to be responsible for the world? If he is all-powerful, how can he not spare human beings all these evils? If he really existed, the world would have to be a quite different place. Maurice Clavel discerns God in the "reins and heart" that are torn by suffering; Frankl believes he can perceive God's presence in the unconscious of his patients.[37] But our atheistic contemporaries interpret suffering as a sign of God's absence; they conclude that he does not exist, since it is impossible to assert the coexistence of God and evil.

The second reason is no less classic: God is *useless from the scientific viewpoint*. Science can do without the God-hypothesis and explain everything by natural laws. While a scientist like Teilhard de Chardin believes it possible to "sacralize" evolution, Monod does away with any idea of the sacred and explains all becoming as the work of chance and necessity. Nowhere does he see any trace of God. The world displays only the laws governing movement, the fall of bodies, and so on. The world can be explained without bringing in God, even if the explanation is still incomplete. In other words, the God-hypothesis serves no purpose. On the other hand, science can say nothing about God. If it rebels against the idea of God, it does so less for scientific than for epistemological reasons: God was simply a way of filling in the gaps in science.

The third reason is more modern in character, although in a hardly different form it is also to be found in antiquity: *God is intolerable to human beings*. How can human freedom be reconciled with God's existence? For Nietzsche and Sartre there is an incompatibility between a God who knows everything and a human freedom that is left to its own discretion. How can human beings be free if they are constantly being observed, foreseen, determined or "predestined" as the ancients used to say? Some individuals may say: "God exists! I have met him!" when they have been suddenly invaded by the presence of the invisible. But such an invasion by God is an intolerable interference by a stranger in the "private" affairs of human beings! That alone is reason enough to reject him—or, rather, to deny him. People today are tired of living under the eye of God. They reject this "privileged spectator" and prefer to live in freedom.

The fourth and final reason is found less among ordinary folk but does make the rounds in philosophical circles: *God is metaphysically superfluous*. Without leading directly to atheism, this reason does throw discredit on all objectifications, even the Christian ones, of God. How is this reason formulated? In the form of a question that undercuts all answers to the previous reasons and compels us to reintroduce the problem of God. Here is how Heidegger puts it: "Why is there something rather than nothing?" In the view of the ancients such a question would necessarily bring God into the picture as the only possible or conceivable foundation for the being of the world. But Brunschvicg in his day had already refused such a recourse to God: "We shall not explain the why of being simply by imagining a being without a why." According to Heidegger being is related only to itself; it is therefore useless to look for "reasons" why being is. If we say that God provides the foundation for being we are substituting for being a human representation (an "existent") that reflects the "tyranny of the logos" and does not respect being as it comes into existence ever new. When we are confronted by being, only one response is appropriate: wonder.

Nowadays believers feel unsure of themselves. They see new teachers coming forward who issue them a radical challenge. When they seek to defend the existence of God, they have a sense that the cause is already lost. The intellectual courage they need in attempting to prove God's existence has been shaken, as Merlau-Ponty observes:

> It is striking to find that today one no longer proves the existence of God, as Saint Thomas, Saint Anselm, and Descartes did. The proofs are ordinarily presupposed, and one limits one's self to refuting the negation of God. . . . Philosophy works itself out in another order. . . . The philosopher does not say that a final transcendence of human contradictions may be possible, and that the complete man awaits us in the future. Like everyone else, he knows nothing of this.[38]

This text says a great deal; it sums up the present situation. Christians nowadays are on the defensive. They have repudiated triumphalism. But philosophy too has become more modest, for it no longer believes in the triumph of science; moreover, after having rejected faith in the Christian Absolute, it is not about to put its faith in any other absolute, be it science or Marxism.

Where do the atheists stand? Despite the line-up of "reasons" which they regard as definitive, despite their well-polished stratagems, atheists do not think they now possess the whole truth. In any case, they no longer regard science as the new absolute that is to be substituted for the old. Scientism is outdated. Renan could still look to science for the revelation of the "real" world, of that "real infinite" that had hitherto remained closed even to "the boldest flights of fancy." But scientism—"science outside its proper domain," as Dumesnil defined it—is only theology stood on its head; like theology it has an answer for everything. After rejecting the Christian ideology, scientism has constructed a new ideology out of science and technology. People today, however, no longer look to science for salvation. They are looking for a knowledge that will bring meaning, a meaning which science will never provide.

Human beings never stop dreaming. They would like to stand at the center of history and have every perspective at their disposal. Theology and scientism alike used to promise them such a central standpoint from which everything would be explained. But Christians and atheists alike have learned from their shared enterprise that there is no "royal way" and that we make progress in life only by clearing a difficult road between fragile certainties and many uncertainties.

2

Ludwig Feuerbach
The Father of Modern Atheism

We live in a cultural environment in which atheism, both theoretical and practical, is becoming ever more widespread. How can we account for this phenomenon? The preceding chapter has shown the development of atheism in the eighteenth century, but atheism became a real force only in the nineteenth century with the appearance on the scene of a number of anti-theologians who tried to justify its dogmas. Among them Ludwig Feuerbach (1804–1872) stands out, not as a wide-ranging genius but as a man of a single idea. He has been called the father of modern atheism, and in fact he is evidently the source of the entire modern criticism of religion. He directly influenced Marx, Freud, Nietzsche, and others, and caught the attention of a good number of theologians who were either shocked or stimulated by his thinking.[1] He has even been, indirectly, the source of a renewal in theology, since his ideas led to the theologies of secularization, which are one way of adapting the Feuerbachian challenge.[2] Let me therefore try to situate this strange figure.

A study of Feuerbach is worthwhile on two counts. For one thing, he will provide an introduction to Marx, who was frequently satisfied simply to repeat Feuerbach. For another, he will help us to purify our own ideas. Nowadays we are better informed about Marx's criticism of religion than about Feuerbach's. This is not surprising. Marx is the source of a current of thought that is based on certain forces at work in society and has therefore become part of people's thinking. He is at the origin of the wave of atheism and secularism of which we are keenly aware today. But most of us are ignorant of the source of Marx's own atheism. As a matter of fact, Marx developed it under the egis of Left Hegelianism and the direct influence of Feuerbach who functioned briefly as a theologian and then, being converted to atheism, spent his time refuting God. Consequently, even though he was later eclipsed by Marx, it is fitting that we sketch a picture of him here. I shall have occasion to emphasize the impact of his criticism on theological thinking. At this point we can look to him for a more immediate service: if it be true that we are always inclined to make God in our own image and likeness, no one is better able than Feuerbach to help us become aware of this tendency and rid our picture of God of the distortions we import into it.

Feuerbach's Spiritual Journey

Feuerbach was attracted to theology at the age of sixteen. In 1823 his wish was granted: he began the study of theology at Heidelberg. He was soon disillusioned. Theology had made a poor recovery after the Enlightenment and was in a state of profound crisis. There were two theologies on the scene: an orthodox theology that was engaged in a battle against rationalism (a rear-guard action, doomed to failure), and a liberal theology that had no ties with the Churches, drew its inspiration from Hegel, and was seeking a reconcilation with the philosophy of the day, at the risk of passing into the hands of the barbarians. Feuerbach could not feel at home in either camp and soon abandoned theology for philosophy. In 1824, while still undergoing an interior crisis, he went to Berlin where he followed Hegel's courses for two years. Hegel proved to be his savior, and he would always think of Berlin as the place of his spiritual birth. "I have changed over from theology to philosophy," he wrote to his brother. "No salvation without philosophy!"[3]

A distinctive trait of Feuerbach's character is already evident: he is a man of a single idea. He rejects compromises and facile syntheses and opts instead for a strictly unified thinking. But unlike the unity of Hegelian thought, which absorbs everything and manages to harmonize it, the unity achieved by Feuerbach is attained by eliminating one of the terms of the problem. Hegel sought to unify Christianity and philosophy; Feuerbach rejects Christianity in the name of philosophy. In this sense, Feuerbach is not an "orthodox" Hegelian. His enthusiasm for the master will not last long. The (intellectual) break with Hegel comes in 1839. As Engels was to say: "He [Feuerbach] was incapable of disposing of Hegel through criticism; he simply threw him aside as useless."[4] Feuerbach celebrates Hegel as a liberator, but though Hegel is the weapon by which he is able to overthrow theology, he does not take him with him into the promised land of anthropology.

The break with Hegel had become an open one before the appearance in 1841 of Feuerbach's principal work, *The Essence of Christianity,* but this book still shows traces of Hegel's influence. Feuerbach would henceforth be the leading representative of a new philosophy that was openly at war with Christianity. The Left Hegelians immediately recognized this philosophy as their own. While the Right Hegelians continued to look upon Hegel as the St. Thomas of Protestantism, the man who effected a synthesis of reason and faith, the Leftists retained only the critical side of Hegel, the role of reason as destructive of faith. That was the function of reason which Feuerbach accepted: religion is the expression of feeling and imagination, and it is up to philosophy to get rid of it. Feuerbach was able to carry out this liquidation with some skill, and from this time on the Left will look upon him as its intellectual guide. In 1888 Engels wrote: "One must himself have experienced the liberating effect of this book to get an idea of it. Enthusiasm was general; we all became at once Feuerbachians."[5] In what did this liberation consist? In the simple statement that there is no God, and man alone exists. Moreover, man becomes fully human when he discards his religious illusions and devotes himself unreservedly to human tasks.

There is no point to saying much more here about Feuerbach's life. He lived quietly as the father of a family. His friends tried to get him involved in politics; he was elected a deputy but played an unimportant role and wanted nothing more than to return to the calm of the countryside. He was never to receive a university post. He was a kind of atheist monk, who spent his life refuting God and inventing atheistic man. He would revamp his strategy and launch new indictments of God, but he would never alter the judgment he had passed: God is a product of man's creating. The constantly repeated theme of Feuerbach's work can be summed up in the key statement of his *Principles of the Philosophy of the Future* (1843): "The task of the modern era was the realization and humanization of God—the transformation and dissolution of theology into anthropology."[6]

These words contain a program. Feuerbach's aim is to rescue theology from its self-inflicted blindness and adapt its content for modern man. He wants to rid it of its mythical character
and reduce it to an expression of human psychology. The point
is no longer "to posit the finite in the infinite," that is, to link
man to God, but rather "to posit the infinite in the finite," that
is, to reduce God to man.[7] Feuerbach subjects religion to a familiar process of reduction: religion is simply the mythical garb
with which man clothes certain human realities.

It would be unjust, however, to look only at the negative
side of Feuerbach's work. In addition to his critical attacks
Feuerbach can point to a positive result: the advent of man. Criticism reveals that the secret behind God is man himself, but the
revelation of this secret at the same time relieves man of his
fears and sets him free for those truly human tasks which require
solidarity with other human beings. The elimination of God
from the universe of the human imagination is a condition for
man's accepting responsibility for his own life.

People often think they have said everything about Feuerbach when they can summarize his teaching in some such formula as this: all religious ideas are projections of human needs and
desires into an imaginary other world. The formula is legitimate
as far as it goes, but it is indeed a very summary expression of
thinking that is complex and constantly evolving. Feuerbach
himself describes the stages of his development: "God was my
first thought, reason the second, and man the third and last. The
subject of the deity is reason, but the subject of reason is man."[8]
It is possible, then, to distinguish three periods in his life: a
theological period, of short duration; an idealist period, when
he was under the influence of Hegel; and an anthropological period, where he takes his stand and develops his new philosophy
in which only man is left.

Religion, Man's Earliest Form of Self-Knowledge

The ideal would be to follow Feuerbach stage by stage. I
shall, however, concentrate chiefly on his ideas about God. His
program remained the same throughout his life—to reduce theology to anthropology—but its execution required revisions and
corrections along the way. We find in Feuerbach's work no less
than three successive explanations of the phenomenon of reli-

gion. In a book that is still not outdated, Gregor Nüdling has provided an appropriate analysis of the three.[9] He shows how Feuerbach successively reduces God to the essence of man, then to the essence of nature, and finally to the essence of desire. I shall emphasize chiefly the first of these explanations, which is also the most accessible, since it finds expression in *The Essence of Christianity.*[10]

The Reduction of Theology to Anthropology

But first a word about Feuerbach's project. In what does this reduction of theology to anthropology consist? It consists in showing that the content of ideas about God is identical with the being of man himself, in recognizing that God is a projection of man and in restoring to man the reality of which religion has deprived him. The difference, then, between theology and anthropology is a difference not of content but of language. Feuerbach points to the real identity of the two when he says: "In short, my teaching is that theology is anthropology."[11] Or, in fuller and more explicit form:

> Thus in the first part I show that the true sense of Theology is Anthropology, that there is no distinction between the *predicates* of the divine and human nature, and, consequently, no distinction between the divine and human *subject.* . . . In the second part, on the other hand, I show that the distinction which is made, or rather supposed to be made, between the theological and anthropological predicates resolves itself into an absurdity (*EC,* xxxvii).

And yet there is a difference. The difference is not an essential one, however, since it has to do with form and not content. Theology transposes human reality to the sphere of the imaginary. Theology rules over an unreal empire, whereas the aim of anthropology is to understand the concrete human being and its real world. In Feuerbach's view, the difference between theology and anthropology reflects the opposition between reality and representations of it, with the latter being relegated to the realm of imagination and dream. Theology moves in a dream world that has no other content but the real universe and feeds upon human reality without realizing it. When theology transposes the real into dreams, it transfigures this reality and thereby renders it unreal. Dispel the illusion that accompanies every dream, and you will rediscover the human reality hidden therein:

> Religion is the dream of the human mind. But even in dreams we do not find ourselves in emptiness or in heaven, but on earth, in the realm of reality; we only see real things in the entrancing splendour of imagination and caprice, instead of in the simple daylight of reality and necessity. Hence I do nothing more to religion—and to speculative philosophy and theology also—than to open its eyes, or rather to turn its gaze from the internal towards the external, *i.e.,* I change the object as it is in the imagination into the object as it is in reality (*EC,* xxxix).

The criticism of religion consists essentially in dispelling appearances and bringing heaven back to earth. The task is not an easy one, because dreamers prefer their dreams to reality and resist anyone who tries to open their eyes:

> For the present age, which prefers the sign to the thing signified, the copy to the original, fancy to reality, the appearance to the essence, this change, inasmuch as it does away with illusion, is an absolute annihilation, or at least a reckless profanation; for in these days *illusion* only is *sacred, truth profane* (*ibid.*).

Here we have a clear statement of Feuerbach's project: to destroy the religious illusion and bring men back to their simple human reality. To reduce means to demolish, but it also means gaining possession once again of what has been alienated, which in this case is the human person. This recovery of the human, which the religions have refused to acknowledge, requires that we begin by demystifying the religions and showing that whenever they speak about God, they are in reality saying something about man.

This criticism of religion is not an end in itself. It is a roundabout way of helping man to become conscious of himself. This goal explains the title Feuerbach originally intended to give to his *The Essence of Christianity:* " 'Know Yourself': A Contribution to the Critique of Pure Unreason."[12] This original title already includes a value judgment: religion is "unreason"; but it also states a program: the attainment of knowledge of man by way of a critique of religion. How does Feuerbach carry out his program? *The Essence of Christianity* is a first version, which other works will complete.

Man, the Reality of God

What, then, is the reality of God? The content of "God" is reducible to the content of "man," with man being understood here not as the individual in its concreteness but as the human species (*Gattungswesen*). Feuerbach effects the reduction by writing: God = human essence. This reduction is a demystification. But before reducing God to man, we must describe how man invented God. How could the set of behaviors we sum up as "religion" have originated in the mind of man? We must first describe the *genesis* of the idea of God before moving on to its *reduction* back to man.

How, then, did human beings come to ascribe to another (God) what actually belongs to themselves, and thus make themselves prisoners of an illusion? Feuerbach's argument, the fallacy of which I shall point out later on, supposes the equivalence of the infinity proper to God and the infinity proper to the human species. The religions say that God is infinite. But the attribute of infinity, says Feuerbach, is in fact a property of the human species. He then uses this attribute as the middle term of a syllogism in order to establish an equivalence between the object of religion—God as an infinite being—and the object grasped by the human mind when it has reached its full development—the infinite human species. If this equivalence be accepted, then the conclusion is inescapable: religion simply takes the human reality and locates it in God. God is the human essence that has been alienated from man. But the externality of God in relation to man is only apparent; it is an illusion that must be dispelled.

Such is the result of Feuerbach's analyses. But how could human beings have imprisoned themselves in this kind of illusion? For an answer we must go to the definition of man. The thing specific to man is his ability to be conscious of himself. Unlike the animals, which walk in the darkness of instinct, human beings can as it were stand off and look at their own reality because they are conscious of it. They can represent their own essence to themselves and, insofar as they are beings with senses, they can relate themselves to their own essence via the whole gamut of feelings. That which touches them and stirs feelings is the thing that interests them and is "holy" to them (*EC,* 63). In other words, the human reality is not pure facticity but must be taken possession of by means of consciousness. Consciousness is man's innate power of representing reality, external and internal, to himself.

What is it that consciousness thus grasps? The human essence. But in what does this essence consist? In two things: the individual as restricted, finite, limited in temporal duration, and destined to die; but also the human essence which transcends individuals and survives them and which is infinite since the human species will endure. This distinction between individual and species is essential, for it is the point of insertion for the illusion we call religion. The reason is that while human beings are directly conscious of their individuality, only belatedly do they become cognizant of the species as a whole which outlasts them and represents the fulfillment of their own infinity. The consciousness of individuals may thus be fixed on the finite (the individual that is destined to disappear) or on the infinite (the unending adventure of the species). In the religious stage of human development individuals fail to realize that this infinity of the species is also their own since they belong to the species.

The mystery of religion is explained in these words of Feuerbach: "Man . . . projects his being into objectivity, and then again makes himself an object to this projected image of himself thus converted into a subject; he thinks of himself and is an object to himself, but as the object of an object, of another being than himself. . . . Man is an object to God" (*EC,* 29–30). We can put this statement in diagrammatic form:

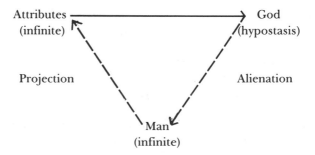

Feuerbach has thus dismantled the human machine for manufacturing gods. The psychological process has three stages: (1) The human essence has something infinite about it. But this infinity is not recognized as being a property of the human. Human beings are, so to speak, subject to attacks of vertigo when faced with their own essence. (2) They objectify this essence as a distinct and independent reality and confer on this new reality the status of a subject. "Religion immediately represents the inner nature of man as an objective, external being" (*EC,* 198). (3) But in this transfer human beings are alienated from themselves. They are impoverished in order to enrich another, imaginary being, stripped of their own substance in order to give life to a reality that exists only in dreams. But once this is done, this new entity acquires such a degree of solidity that human beings are henceforth unable to think except in terms of it, as though they were its attribute. They behave henceforth as "objects of God."

The whole secret of the religions is to have exploited this contrast between finite and infinite. The religions bestow substance on this infinity, but it is an illusory substance. Instead of seeing that the opposition of finite and infinite is immanent in human beings, they turn it into an opposition between two entities that are distinct from one another. Thus we can see that the religions simply project the human reality into a dream dimension. It is there that they have gone astray, since God is in fact simply a hypostatization of the human species. The success of Christianity is owing to the fact that it has been able to embody the whole rich reality of the species in a single individual, namely, God, and that in addition it has humanized this individual, thus showing what the real nature of this individual is.

The Demystification of Religion

This explanation of the genesis of the idea of God leaves a good many problems unresolved. Feuerbach explains "how" the transfer of human properties to God takes place, but he does not tell us "why" such a transfer should take place in the human mind. At the end of his demonstration he is convinced that God is a simple reflection of man. The religions enable man to see himself in God as in a mirror: "God is the mirror of man. . . . God is for man the commonplace book where he registers his highest feelings and thoughts" (*EC,* 63), the volume in which he

has recorded the best part of himself. If such is indeed the essence of all religions, that is, if their content is completely human, then it is important to destroy the illusion which the
religions keep alive and to recover the human heritage they have
alienated from us. Human beings must reappropriate what has
wrongly been taken from them. Here the philosopher will serve
as guide: "It is our task to show that the antithesis of divine and
human is altogether illusory, that it is nothing else than the antithesis between the human nature in general and the human individual; that, consequently, the object and contents of the
Christian religion are altogether human" (*EC,* 13–14).

    That is precisely the task which Feuerbach undertakes in
The Essence of Christianity. He takes each of the Christian dogmas
and examines it in order to find its anthropological meaning.
How does he go about this demystification of religion and this
liberation of man? He relies entirely on reason. He looks for religion to collapse as the result solely of the growth in consciousness; in the effort at explanation which he undertakes his aim is
to purify and heal. He gives an account of religion by explaining
the human behavior that had led to its establishment, and he
hopes that the awakening of consciousness will automatically be
therapeutic. He thinks that in order to penetrate the mystery of
religion and demystify it all that is needed is to subject it to a
rigorous analysis. Religion will then be seen to be "man's earliest form of self-knowledge," but an "indirect" self-knowledge:

> When religion—consciousness of God—is designated as the
> self-consciousness of man, this is not to be understood as
> affirming that the religious man is directly aware of this
> identity; for, on the contrary, ignorance of it is fundamental
> to the peculiar nature of religion. To preclude this miscon-
> ception, it is better to say, religion is man's earliest and also
> indirect form of self-knowledge. Hence, religion every-
> where precedes philosophy, as in the history of race, so also
> in that of the individual. Man first of all sees his nature as of
> *out of* himself, before he finds it in himself. . . . Religion is
> the childlike condition of humanity. . . . But the essence of
> religion, thus hidden from the religious, is evident to the
> thinker (*EC,* 13).

This text, which has for its purpose to explain the slow growth of self-knolwedge, outlines the progress of the human race through the ages. It points out, on the one hand, the progress made from one religion to another (Christianity took a decisive step here by humanizing God) and, on the other, the leap taken by philosophy. The religions represent stages of progress when measured by one another, but all of them are in error by comparison with the definitive truth which the thinker introduces. It can be seen that Feuerbach does not regard the religions as entirely lacking in truth. He invites his readers to sort out the religions and discern what is true and what is erroneous in them. The religions have in common that they confront man with his real essence, but only while at the same time turning it into a mystery:

> Religion is the relation of man to his own nature—therein lies its truth and its power of moral amelioration—but to his nature not recognized as his own, but regarded as another nature, separate, nay, contradistinguished from his own: herein lies its untruth, its limitation, its contradiction to reason and morality (*EC,* 197).

The original sin of the religions is to have separated what should have been united: God is not other than man, but is only his personified projection. This is why the relation which the religions would have man develop toward his own essence is an idolatrous, mythicized, implicit, veiled relation. In the religious stage (a stage of separation) man understands himself only imperfectly. It is for that reason that religions are linked to the human race's stage of infancy, unawareness, and primitive culture; the advent of reason will make that stage disappear.

A question still to be answered has to do with this twofold consciousness: a religious consciousness that does not recognize its object as human and instead projects it onto God, and a human consciousness which is a reconquest and reappropriation of this object by man. Why should consciousness be thus clouded over? Why such a passage through the religious stage? It must be admitted that Feuerbach, while offering a discerning explanation of the process by which consciousness manufactures its gods, remains silent on the causes which lead consciousness into this kind of alienation. Nor is he any more forthcoming on the forces which lead to a liberating self-consciousness and finally destroy the structure artificially built by the religions. Religious mystification and religious demystification alike remain mysterious.

It is possible to detect in the background of Feuerbach's thinking a conception of history that had been inherited from Hegel and was typical of the last century. Like most of his contemporaries, Feuerbach believed in ameliorative progress and in the perfectibility of human nature. He believed that history has an immanent teleology. This does not, as in Hegel, take the form of the unfolding of the Spirit that is on its way to its full development. History is rather the expression of human reason which is following a pre-determined itinerary in order to reach full self-knowledge. History is the progressive revelation of the essence of man. Religious history is the history of the progress of the human mind, the history of alienated consciousness that does not grasp its own essence except as given a form external to itself. In the religions we can see at work the law governing human progress: that which is closest to man (his essence) is also that which is furthest away from him and the last thing to come into his possession. But progress necessarily leads to the dissolution of this alienation and the full self-possession of the human essence.

New Approaches to the Essence of Religion

Feuerbach's explanation of the phenomenon of religion is developed at length in *The Essence of Christianity,* the best known of his books and the only one that really influenced his age. I have concentrated chiefly on the controlling idea of the book and not discussed in detail his criticisms of Christianity as such. Yet these criticisms are not without interest, since they illustrate Feuerbach's method and show in a concrete way the "anthropological" content which he finds in Christianity. At the end of his lengthy undertaking Feuerbach is able to claim victory:

We have shown that the substance and object of religion is altogether human; we have shown that divine wisdom is human wisdom; that the secret of theology is anthropology; that the absolute mind is the so-called finite subjective mind. But religion is not conscious that its elements are human; on the contrary, it places itself in opposition to the human, or at least it does not admit that its elements are human. The necessary turning-point of history is therefore the open confession, that the consciousness of God is nothing else than the consciousness of the species (*EC,* 270).

But this first approach to the fact of religion left Feuerbach dissatisfied. His definition of man as consciousness was abstract, and the reference to the species introduced an embarrassing dualism. For these reasons he attempted in his later writings to redefine the human person and began to speak of the concrete, sensible being. His *Das Wesen der Religion* [The Essence of Religion], written in 1845, is the product of this effort.[13] I shall limit myself here to some brief indications of its content, drawing chiefly upon Nüdling's book for my information.

Religion as Expression of Human Dependence

What is man? Feuerbach abandons Hegel for good and shifts the focus of his interest to human beings as they are: as sensible entities immersed in the natural world. As thus viewed, man is a "natural essence": he has a body and instincts. Feuerbach had previously taken interiority as his starting point and had defined man in terms of self-consciousness. Now, in *The Essence of Religion,* he starts with the exterior side of man. The result is an immediate change in his image of man: henceforth man is the limited individual who lives, enjoys, loves, and moves toward death. He is in his entirety bound up with other people and with nature; he depends on the environing world. There you have the key word: dependence. If we ask what is the most fundamental thing in the human entity, we always find that the answer is: the feeling of dependence. Moreover this feeling is not something abstract: "My feeling of dependence has eyes and ears, hands and feet." There is no longer any dualism of individual and species, finite and infinite, because the second term in each of these pairs has been eliminated. What interests Feuerbach from here on is the desiring, willing, feeling individual. "The only true point of view is that of the sensible being and of sense intuition. . . . Man is distinct from the animals only because he is the fullest instance of sensual life, the most sensitive and susceptible of all the beings in the world."

Feuerbach discovers this feeling of dependence at the source of all the natural religions. It constitutes what he calls the subjective principle of these religions. But dependence is always felt as a dependence on something, on some object. What is the original object of this dependence? Nature. Feuerbach therefore calls nature the objective principle of the natural religions. Here we have an explanation of religion that is strictly parallel to the explanation given in *The Essence of Christianity,* with this difference: that the explanatory principles have changed. In Feuerbach's earlier explanation the subjective principle was self-consciousness, the objective principle was the human essence; with this dyad as his starting point Feuerbach then showed us that the substance of God's being was in fact the essence of man himself. In Feuerbach's new approach to the problem, the subjective principle is the feeling of dependence, and the objective principle is nature. With this new dyad as his point of departure Feuerbach offers a reinterpretation of God. Once all the mystifications have been removed, God is seen to be nothing but nature hypostatized. Feuerbach can therefore assert: "Nature is the first and originating object of religion."

Feuerbach's thinking has evolved; he is aware of this and explains the change. He has come to see man as a concrete being that is closely bound up with nature, and this in turn has altered his vision of religion. Over against Christianity as a religion of interiority he sets another kind of religion, the religion of nature. In *The Essence of Religion* he shifts his attention to the natural religions which his earlier study of Christianity had caused him to neglect. He then asks himself a question: What is the explanation, in these natural religions, of the origin of the idea of God, an idea that cannot be totally explained in terms of man since God has some non-human traits? Christianity reveals a God with essentially human characteristics, but at the same time it offers a vision of God that is only partial and does not correspond to the one given in the natural religions. The God whom we meet in the natural religions has attributes whose origin can only be nature. "The theme or at least the point of departure of religion is nature; I abstracted and had to abstract from nature in dealing with Christianity, because the origin of Christianity is not God in nature but God in man."

In point of fact, the two theories of religion are not as opposed to one another as they might seem to be. Feuerbach has exercised his wits and harmonized the two theories by showing that each accounts for an aspect of God. The image of God is composite. Some of his attributes come from man (the moral attributes), others from nature (the physical attributes). God is pictured as a spiritual, personal, intelligent, loving, etc., being: these are attributes taken over from the essence of man; *The Essence of Christianity* develops a theory to explain the takeover. But God is also omnipotent, eternal, one, mighty, and so on; these are attributes derived from nature, and *The Essence of Religion* develops a model to explain this side of the picture. Not everything about the essence of God is explicable when man is taken as the starting point. God is a point at which human characteristics and qualities found in nature converge; each type of religion lays its emphasis primarily on the one or the other of the two aspects.

What are we to make of this new theory? Does it solve the problems left hanging at the end of the earlier explanation? No, it does not. We are left with the same perplexing questions: Why have human beings attached attributes of nature to God? What darkening of their minds has led them to project onto an alien being the attributes belonging to the external real world? Feuerbach is satisfied to assert, without explanation, that "that on which the life and existence of man depends becomes God for him." He had said something quite comparable in *The Essence of Christianity:*

> That which has essential value for man, which he esteems the perfect, the excellent, in which he has true delight—that alone is God to him. If feeling seems to thee a glorious attribute, it is then, *per se,* a divine attribute to thee. Therefore . . . man . . . believes only in the truth of his own existence and nature [*Wesen*] for he can believe in nothing else than that which is involved in his own nature. His faith is the consciousness of that which is holy to him; but that alone is holy to man which lies deepest within him, which is most peculiarly his own, the basis, the essence of his individuality (*EC,* 63).

On the one hand, then, God achieves reality only by a pillaging of human nature; on the other, he depends on borrowings from external nature. But why should God, an imaginary entity, be substituted for the human essence or for nature? Such a change remains unexplained. Feuerbach says that the imagination works the transposition; imagination is "the essential organ of religion." But is the question really answered?

Desire Gives Rise to All the Gods

The question receives a partial answer in a late work, *Theogonie* (1857). With unwearying patience and an uncommon stubbornness Feuerbach keeps at the question of God and tries to identify the anthropological fact that may offer an explanation of him. Feuerbach is really a man with only one goal in mind, as he himself acknowledges: "I am one of those people who have but a single aim in view and focus all their efforts on attaining it." His goal is to develop a consistent explanation of the religious phenomenon. *Theogonie* [Birth of the Gods] is more than a repetition or development of familiar themes. The method—the reduction of the gods to man—is the same as in the earlier works, but the conclusion which Feuerbach reaches is more drastic: the root from which all the gods spring is desire. Man is a being of desires, and the gods he provides for himself are only the "representatives" of his desires. He invents them as fulfillments of his desires.

But what is desire?

> Desire is a slave of distress, but a slave that wants to be free; it is a child of poverty . . . but of the poverty that is mother of the appetites and of love, not just in the sphere of sex but also on the objective level or the level of things. Contrary to what the propertied classes, so concerned with their own interests, believe, it was not modern communism or modern atheism that first instilled this longing into the poor. No, even the language of "sacred" scripture thinks and speaks of desire as identical with poverty.[14]

This longing which seeks to bridge the gap between desire and fulfillment is called self-centeredness. But we must not give this term moral overtones. Feuerbach understands it rather in a "metaphysical" sense. He will also speak of it as self-assertion, the will to live, the instinct for happiness, and so on. In short, self-centeredness sums up all the human energies and manifests itself fundamentally as a will to be happy. The desire for happiness is the deepest thing in man. Religions owe their success to the promise of happiness which they represent. What, after all, is the Christian faith but man's desire for happiness transformed into a hope of blessedness in the world to come?

This desire for happiness explains the birth of all the gods. "Where desires arise, there too the gods arise and make their appearance." "In every desire a god is hidden, but conversely behind every god there is only a desire." "A divinity is essentially an object called for by desire; it is represented, thought, believed only because it is demanded, called for, desired."[15] Desire makes gods necessary, because desire is a "child of poverty"; that is, it is the expression of a lack, an absence, a limitation, a deficiency. But because it does imply a lack, desire is a movement toward what can bring its fulfillment. From this point of view desire is an appeal, an aspiration, an exercise of freedom, a wish for fulfillment. God is simply the desire fulfilled. He represents the "half that is lacking to man," that is, the fulfillment of the desire. God fills the void which desire brings to light.

Here once again the secret of the religions is uncovered. This secret is not hidden in the impenetrable heavens. It is to be found in the human heart and its insatiable desire for happiness. The religions are simply promises that the desire will be fulfilled. They have no reality of their own but are simply exteriorizations of a human "optative" or wish.[16] The gods are projections of human desires; they are the dreams of a primitive who is crammed full with illusions. The gods owe their existence to the strategy followed by desire which projects its dreams into the empty space inhabited by the possibles and thereby provides itself with what it lacks.

This new conception of man and religion is, in Feuerbach's view, simply a clarification of this earlier thinking. When identified with desire, the subjective principle is given a broader psychological base, since desire has the feeling of dependence as one of its components. The objective principle is both extended and blurred, since desire, aided by imagination, does not feed solely on the attributes of the human essence and external nature. Desire is essentially inventive. It can lay hold of anything under the sun and derive gods from it.

But this new and more comprehensive view is not completely satisfying. It does indeed contain a large element of truth: the God whom we adore is often the God of our desires and has not a great deal to do with the God who is Spirit and truth. On the other hand, Feuerbach does not explain any more fully than before why man should try to fulfill his desires by inventing the spurious world of the gods. In Feuerbach's opinion, religions exist only because human desires seek fulfillment.

The Heritage of Feuerbach

Feuerbach's critique of religion is based on a single principle: man, who is the alpha and omega of his philosophy. If he sets out to reduce theology to anthropology, he does so in order to show that man is the sole real content of the idea of God and thus to save man from alienation. The task Feuerbach sets for himself is both simple and clear: to give back to man what belongs to him. Anthropology, the term that sums up his new philosophy, is simply "religion become conscious of itself, religion that understands itself." Is he successful in his undertaking?

The Weaknesses of Feuerbach's Undertaking

I must limit myself here to a brief critical judgment in which I shall stress the positive contribution of Feuerbach's undertaking rather than its weaknesses. It must be admitted that Feuerbach's anthropology is significantly less developed than his critique of God. And yet this anthropology was Feuerbach's real goal; it is also the thing in which I am mainly interested. As for his critique of the idea of God, I shall restrict myself to a few remarks on the validity of his procedure. The internal structure of the approach he takes is not without its defects.

Let me look first at the use Feuerbach makes of the idea of infinity. He says that divine infinity simply is a transfer to an imaginary hypostasis of an attribute that really belongs to the human species. He begins by defining man, i.e., the species possessing all the divine attributes, as God, and then maintains that man has erroneously conferred his own attributes on God, imagining this God to be an entity which is external and superior to him. He concludes that God is therefore in the image of man. But the whole argument is evidently fallacious because "infinite" is given two different meanings. As applied to the species Feuerbach's "infinite" refers to a virtual infinity: the species prolonging itself indefinitely in a gradual growth through space and time; this is Hegel's "false infinity." Can the infinity which is predicable of the species be applied also to God? Feuerbach unhesitatingly uses the same term, but, as everyone realizes, the infinity predicated of God is an infinity in act, an infinity that is already fully real. Feuerbach's infinity is still something finite, and finitude suggests at least one question: What is its ground? When does it derive its being, since it is incapable of explaining itself?

But Feuerbach has little real interest in questions of ontology. He shifts the focus of various questions and finds a new way of asking them. He does not ask "why?" which is a purely speculative question, but "how?" which is answered by explaining the genesis of concepts. His method is the one Nietzsche will make his own: the method of genealogy. Feuerbach shows how religion arises in the soul of man. He sees the idea of God as a "projection" outside of man or nature of properties belonging to them. "Projection" is a psychological mechanism that can be applied quite broadly and that achieved immense success once psychoanalysis gave it such a prominent place. In what does projection consist? In transferring to another entity, person, or thing qualities, feelings, and desires that exist in us but are not recognized as ours.

If this is Feuerbach's explanation, it is impossible to avoid asking the question "Why?" Why do human beings begin by projecting their own essence outside of themselves or projecting the properties of nature outside of it? At this point Feuerbach introduces the imagination. But is the question really answered by saying that God is nothing but an imaginative, poetic, sensible, and disguised form given to the human essence and to nature? At best, Feuerbach has offered a hypothesis.

Psychoanalysis is more explicit in this matter. It explains that it is easier for a subject to master a fear he has projected onto an external object than to control it when it is still in a diffuse form within himself. Projection is therefore a defense mechanism of the subject. But how valid is this explanation as applied to religion? Why this detour through an imaginary world instead of a direct grasp of the self and of nature? In what way does the attribution of human or natural properties to God represent a gain for the subject as compared with the simple acceptance of reality as it is: reality that is closer at hand and there-

fore also more easily understood and mastered than when
presented in the form of something dreamed? The psychoanalytic explanation is not to the point, since the projection by no
means makes possible more effective strategy for controlling
forces that transcend us.

As a matter of fact there is a prejudice at work in Feuerbach's whole approach to the problem. Like the entire age in
which he lived, he was convinced that error is located in the past
and truth in the future. History is the progressive emergence of
a truth that is maturing. Feuerbach thinks of his own role as one
of helping his fellow human beings to break loose from error
and to attain to truth, the truth being man himself.

The defects in Feuerbach's argument are of minor importance: they did not impede the success of his work. This is perhaps an indication that the critique of religion was not the real
substance of his work, even if it occupied the greater part of it in
quantitative terms. The critique is in fact only the reverse side of
a positive project, and it is this project that Feuerbach himself
emphasizes:

> Anyone who knows me only as an atheist does not really
> know me at all. . . . "I deny God"? Yes, but for me this
> means that I deny the negation of man; I replace the illu-
> sory, fantastic, heavenly state of man, which in real life inev-
> itably leads to the denial of man, with the sensible, real, and
> therefore necessarily political and social state of man. For
> me the question of the existence or non-existence of God is
> the question of the existence or non-existence of man.[17]

Feuerbach viewed himself as a new Luther. He felt called to
reform the religions and to redirect the thinking and activity of
human beings. He wanted to replace love of God with love of
man and to substitute faith in man for faith in God. He dreamed
of a new kind of human being who would no longer think of
himself as a pilgrim on earth, as Christians do, but would be
fully involved in time and in this world. For this change to come
about, man had to (in Feuerbach's judgment) abandon God for
man, faith for knowledge, prayer for work, Christianity for secular culture. Human beings must renounce their candidacy for
the next world and make themselves humble students of the
present world. That is the price of salvation.

Man Restored to Himself

It would be unfortunate were we to see only the negative side of Feuerbach's work. Despite the questions it leaves unanswered, his thinking has left a profound mark on the modern mind and especially on the course of theology. It is not surprising that atheists should have feted him, for he shows us that atheism can be a consistent, reflective, carefully argued position. The Left Hegelians welcomed him as an intellectual master and a liberator. Marx greeted him with enthusiasm and thought that this "antichrist" had struck a decisive blow at religion. He celebrated the liberative power of Feuerbach's thinking and recommended the reading of his work: "There is no other road for you to truth and freedom except that leading through the Firebrook [the *Feuer-bach*]. Feuerbach is the purgatory of the present times."[18] Feuerbach enabled atheists to polish up their weapons.

Above all else, Feuerbach gave his contemporaries a new vision of the human person, a new humanism. To him they owed "the charter of a religion focused on man."[19] His positivism, which is comparable in many respects to that of Auguste Comte, does not get rid of religion. Feuerbach rejects the old religion but he does not reject the religious act itself. Henceforth, however, this act will have man himself for its content. Religion as the service of God disappears, but it is reborn in the form of service to man. The relationship with God is replaced by a relationship with other human beings:

Love to man must be no derivative love; it must be original. [Only then can love be an authentic, sacred, and effective power.[20]] If human nature is the highest nature to man, then practically also the highest and first law must be the love of man to man. *Homo homini Deus est*—this is the greatest practical principle; this is the axis on which revolves the history of the world. The relations of child and parent, of husband and wife, of brother and friend—in general, of man to man—in short, all the moral relations are *per se* religious (*EC*, 271).

Human beings need only their fellow human beings. They owe their existence to nature, but they owe their existence as human beings to their fellows. Consequently, the unity of "I" and "Thou" will henceforth be their God. When the idealist says: "I myself am the truth," Feuerbach replies: "It is together with other human beings that I am a man."[21] Here you have the religious humanism of Feuerbach; it will be echoed in the young Marx.

This revolution in religion marks the dawn of modern times. Hegel had been still attempting to save religion through a reconciliation of reason and the modern age. He spiritualized religion but did not reject it; he simply stripped it of its mythical form. Feuerbach humanizes it and alters its context by ridding it of everything that is not human. At the end man and his world are left as the only sacral values for the future.

Feuerbach's thought has been claimed as the start of the secularization process. We can now understand the meaning of such a claim. He definitively cut all ties to religion, but he did not eliminate the religious sense; in addition, he made human beings responsible for their own future. Why this rejection of religion? Feuerbach emphasizes its incompatibility with the new humanism of which he is the prophet:

> Today we are still living in a situation of troublesome contradiction between religion and culture. Our religious teachings and customs are utterly opposed to our contemporary point of view in matters material and spiritual. . . . The elimination of this contradiction is an indispensable condition for the rebirth of the human race, the only condition, we might say, for the existence of a new race and a new age. . . . If there is to be a new era, there is need also of a new intuition and conviction regarding the elements and ultimate foundations of human existence; a new era calls for a new religion—if we want to go on using the word "religion."[22]

For Feuerbach, the spirit of Christianity is out of date, as is everything connected with it: theology, the Christian state. Its continued survival can only be harmful and delay the advent of man. "Secularization " implies the rejection of this spirit and the attempt to think and live with no other point of reference except man himself. Feuerbach's work is an assertion of radical human autonomy. It ushers in a new age.

It is not certain that people have always understood the dangers of such a choice. Moltmann has made it clear that this apotheosis of man is often accompanied by a descent into inhumanity. Feuerbach's aim was to rescue the human person from alienation into another world. But did he not open the way for an alienation of man by man?

> This antitheistic humanism leads unavoidably to anthropotheism, to the divinization of man, of humanity and those parties who claim to be a cadre representing non-alienated, divine humanity in the realm of alienation. If for this atheism "man is finally man's god," this may be morally fine in face of the situation where man is man's wolf. But a century's experience with such anthropotheism has shown that even these human deities can become man's wolf. If the consequences of Feuerbach's dethroning of God is that "the state is unlimited, infinite, true, perfect divine man," and politics becomes religion, then the history of atheism against theism returns to its beginning, and the old theism would have to be called relatively human. . . . If God is other than man, then a man can at least not play god over other men.[23]

Feuerbach, "Useful for Tactical Purposes"

Christians cannot simply be indifferent when confronted with Feuerbach's project. His explanations may often seem quite weak, but they nonetheless struck Christianity a heavy blow. Even if the man does not perhaps touch the true teachings of Christianity, he certainly represents an undeniable challenge to the Christians who live that teaching so poorly. Kierkegaard acknowledged that when seen from this angle Feuerbach exercises a purificatory function. He adds: "Feuerbach . . . is useful for tactical purposes."[24] As a matter of fact, Christians have responded to him in often quite contrary ways. Without making any pretense at a complete typology of the reactions he has elicited, I shall mention three.

Some emphasize the break which Feuerbach represents, and they take careful note of it. Karl Barth, for example, honors him for having shown, once and for all, that the gods invented by human beings are idols. But Barth also thinks that Feuerbach's criticisms really do not touch Christianity because the

Christian God is not a human projection; he is God as revealed
by God himself. I shall come back to Barth in my final chapter.
Here I shall mention only his judgment on Feuerbach. He sees
Feuerbach as having struck a mortal blow at all religions, which
are human inventions, and having thus shown the impossibility
for man of laying hold of the true God. Reason enables human
beings to grasp not God but their own shadows. The Christian is
urged to rely not on his human abilities but on faith.

What we have here is the now classic opposition between
religion (a human invention) and faith (revelation of God).
Christianity is a faith, not a religion. Feuerbach's critique may
apply to religion but it leaves faith untouched. Bonhoeffer goes
further. Whereas Barth uses Feuerbach to bring out the irreduc-
ibility of faith and to remove the latter in a definitive way from
the purview of human reason, Bonhoeffer falls into step with
Feuerbach and advances in the same direction. He sees secularization as an irreversible fact which Christians must accept. It is
Bonhoeffer's opinion that we too readily turn to the God-hypothesis in order to solve human problems in science, politics,
and morality. We must learn to do without it. Christians must
live in the world "as if there were no God," that is, they must
run the risks of being human and accept responsibilities which
are not forced upon them from outside, even by God.

Other theologians cannot accept such a gulf between human experience and Christian faith, but on the contrary try to
harmonize these two. The task is not an easy one, and the presence of Feuerbach on the scene is at least a challenge. How can
such a new harmony be achieved after Feuerbach? Approaches
diverge at this point. Some welcome Feuerbach's work but sort
out what they find in it; their judgment is that Feuerbach described only the "pathological" version of religions and pointed
out their "betrayals" but did not come to grips with "authentic"
religion. His critique is not without its value, since it forces us
on each occasion to be clear on what God we are speaking of.
"Theology must learn that after Feuerbach it can no longer utter the name of God without some explanation, that it can no
longer speak as if the meaning of this word were self-evident."[25]
Feuerbach's work should indeed lead to a good deal of circum-
spection in the use of concepts. At the same time, however,
Feuerbach must himself be corrected: because he identifies the
religious phenomenon with certain pathological manifestations

of it, he cuts himself off from an understanding of what is specifically "religious." These theological critics of Feuerbach then undertake to re-establish the truth and validity of the religious element in the human person.

Still other theologians, moving along the same line but with greater attention to the positive elements in Feuerbach, deliberately enter into a dialogue with him. They find in him an interlocutor whom they can listen to and even follow up to a certain point. They single out something that is fundamental in him, the "I-Thou" relation, and believe that this can be made the point of departure for a new theology, for they see it as providing the way to a specifically Christian approach to God. In Christianity the self cannot open itself to God in isolation; only through encounter with the neighbor can one encounter God. From this point of view, Feuerbach can be useful, since he establishes the anthropological basis for a kind of thinking that can claim, perhaps for the first time, to be authentically Christian. In this group of theologians we find Martin Buber, who develops his entire philosophy out of the "I-Thou" relation, Emmanuel Lévinas, who gives new life to the category of "the other," and the personalists, who wage war on individualism and regard relation to others as the fundamental category. In this way, Feuerbach, though an opponent of Christianity, opens up for the latter certain new ways which he himself should have followed. He teaches Christianity the dialectic at work in knowledge of God: in Christianity, only the mediation of the other makes possible true access to God.

Feuerbach's critique of religion portrays God and man as rivals: what is attributed to God is denied to man, and, conversely, what is given to man is taken from God. The God of Feuerbach resembles Caesar rather than the crucified Jesus. It is not enough to say that this is a caricature of God, because this caricature has a continuing existence in many minds. Once a person has experienced freedom and autonomy, such a conception of God becomes intolerable; and yet this conception, inherited from "Constantinian" Christianity, is not about to shatter easily.

What does Feuerbach propose to put in its place? A turning back to man, but to sensible, natural man whose autonomy Feuerbach thinks can be assured only if God is eliminated from the picture. But does not the true greatness of God himself consist in his respect for precisely this autonomy? And does not the greatness of man consist in acknowledging that this very autonomy is a gift of God? The turning to man also means an openness to others, an altruism. All the energies withdrawn from the other world and now available for us can henceforth become a revolutionary force and be put to work for the transformation of the world.

Feuerbach saw the goal of this "religious" revolution, but he did not show the means of reaching the goal. He expected the transformation of the world to come from a change in ideas. Marx will shift the revolution from this (idealist) heaven, where Feuerbach continues to reside, back to earth, for he realizes that only action or "practice" will transform the world. But if the humanization of the world, which is what Feuerbach wants, is to be fully human, must it not first change man himself?

3

Karl Marx
Religion, the Opium of the People

In the debate on the problem of God Marx has a privileged place because of the impact of his ideas on society. Unlike Feuerbach who owes his literary survival solely to the work of scholars, Marx is a familiar figure who lives on in the memory of millions of people. His thinking has been embodied in social reality and has become good news to the masses. But do people really know him? Have they an accurate grasp of what he said? As far as religion is concerned, his thinking is usually summed up in a formula that is known everywhere: "Religion is the opium of the people." But what does this formula mean for Marx himself?

It is all the more important to find Marx in his own writings because opinions about him are divided and often contradictory. Christians are far from unanimous in their views of him. Some think that Marx is radically opposed to Christianity and that this opposition is not simply dictated by historical circumstances but is essential to his thinking. According to this interpretation Marx made hatred of God the basis of his entire system, his vision of the human person, and his dream for society. This is the opinion of, for example, Maurice Clavel: "Marx's atheism, or rather his complete, existential hatred of God, is not just one factor or an accident or a result of his communism, but is rather its source and objective: yes, its final cause. It is from God, from God himself above all else, at every point, and after all else, that Marx wants to liberate us."[1]

For Clavel, then, the elimination of God holds first place

"in the order of Marx's real and deepest concerns." This would certainly be an important reason for rejecting any compromise with Marxism. But other scholars think the opposition is less radical and results from the historical conditions in which Marx lived his life. The atheism would in fact be alien to Marx's thinking at its most profound, not essential to his work, and secondary among his concerns. Such is the opinion of a Michel Henry:

> Marx was certainly an atheist, a "materialist," and so on. But even in dealing with a philosopher we must distinguish between what a man is and what he thinks he is. The important thing is not what went on in Marx's mind (of this we are ignorant) but what the written texts think, so to speak. What finds expression in them, in a manner no less clear than it is exceptional in the history of philosophy, is a metaphysics of the individual. Marx is one of the first Christian thinkers of the West.[2]

Could anyone ask for two more irreconcilable judgments? Temperament, of course, plays some part in these judgments. Clavel is a man of profound commitment, who judges Marx by the concrete Marxism of certain Eastern countries and by the descriptions in Solzhenitsyn's *Gulag Archipelago*. And the facts to which Clavel appeals certainly do exist. But can we make Marx's "teaching" responsible for them? Evidently not. If we believe Michel Henry, who subjects the texts to a patient scholarly rereading, Marx is closer to Christianity than he appears to be at first sight. His atheism is not really his own but is connected with the anthropology of Feuerbach which, for Marx, collapses after 1844. Marx's personal philosophy, which begins to emerge at this time, is wholly focused on the individual which it seeks to save and is, in this view, reconcilable with Christianity. If Marx had known Christianity from within, would he have fought it as he did? But we cannot remake history. The most important thing is to understand what he actually said.

A Christian Despite Himself

Marx was not completely ignorant of Christianity, since he was part of it as far as social statistics go. He was educated in Christian schools. Born at Trier in 1818, he grew up in a middle class family that showed French influence. His grandfather was a rabbi in the city. His father, Hirschel, was a lawyer. He was also a liberal-minded man—"according to his friends, a real eighteenth-century Frenchman who knew Voltaire by heart"—and not greatly troubled by religious scruples. When Prussia, which was founded on the principles of the Germano-Christian state, excluded Jews from public office (1815) and the liberal professions (1822), Hirschel did not hestiate at all. He was more attached to his profession than to his religion, especially since he regarded the Jewish faith as rigid, narrow, and intolerant. Acceptance of Protestantism seemed less of a compromise than conversion to the Catholic faith, and therefore he became a member of the small Reformed community of Trier. Beginning in 1824–25 his wife, Dutch by birth and likewise from a family of rabbis, and then his children followed in his steps.

Karl was the third of nine children. He grew up in a liberal, Francophile circle that did not at all like Prussian domination of the Rhineland. His childhood was a happy one, but we know little of it in detail. He entered the secondary school of Trier (1830–1835) and was a "good, though not brilliant" student. He had few friends there. Being younger, from a different background (he was middle class, whereas the other students were the sons of vintners or craftsmen) and a different religion (he was a Protestant whereas his fellow students were mostly Catholic and destined for the priesthood), he had few ties with this milieu.

From this period on he turned away from every form of dogmatism. The religion courses seem to have made no impression on him. At the end of his secondary studies, his essay on religion dealt primarily with morality. But his essay for German studies revealed his true ideal of life: "The master idea that should guide us in the choice of a profession is the good of human beings and our own fulfillment." On the other hand, can we really expect an examination paper to bring deeper thoughts to the surface? From this time forward, he seems utterly untouched by any religious concern.

In 1835 Marx left Trier for Bonn and began the study of law, but he felt drawn above all by literature and esthetics. Politics had little place in his life. He became secretly engaged to Jenny, who would become his faithful companion a few years later. At the beginning of 1836 he fell ill, and his academic year

was almost a complete loss. When the next academic year began
in October he went to Berlin. Here the environment was favorable to study. Marx now underwent the influence of Hegelianism, but more through the meetings of the "Doctors' Club" than
through his courses at the university. The club brought together
dissidents of the Hegelian Left whose main occupation was criticism of religion. As Engels would write later on, "at that time
. . . politics was a very thorny field, and hence the main fight
came to be directed against religion."[3] Strauss published his *Life
of Jesus* (1835) and introduced a new method of analyzing texts.
In his view, the Gospel narratives were simply myths that expressed the dreams and deepest yearnings of the Jewish people.
It was in this environment, in which criticism of religion was the
order of the day, that Marx lived during his years of study.
These same years led to his doctoral dissertation, the first important text in which Marx asserts his atheism.

There can be no question here of a complete study of the
religious problem in Marx.[4] The least that must be said is that
Marx's thought underwent development. Even if caution is
needed in accepting as fact what Althusser calls the "epistemological break" which he locates in about 1844–1845, there is no
doubt that Marx's thinking takes a new direction from this time
on. He increasingly abandons religious and purely speculative
problems and undertakes a deeper study of economic questions.
According to Michel Henry Marx's abiding concern, both in the
more philosophical studies of his youth and in the more eco-
nomics-oriented studies of his maturity, is the concrete person,
the living individual whom he seeks to rescue from all forms of
alienation: religious, political, economic. If Marx breaks successively with Hegel, Feuerbach, and the Left Hegelians, he does so
because their thinking remains at the level of abstractions. They
speak of the human person, but always in the abstract. Marx on
the other hand wants to reach this person as concrete individual,
as "worker in person." His philosophy is a philosophy of the individual who is rescued from that which negates him and is restored to mastery of himself.

Clearly enough, Marx's sole preoccupation is with human
beings. If he gradually moves away from the Young Hegelians, it
is because he sees the critique of religion as non-essential. The
real alienation of human beings is to be sought elsewhere. He
turns to political action, but very quickly realizes once again that

the deeper root of the evil is not to be found here any more than in religion. The real root is economic. But Marx does not study economics for its own sake. He is interested in it to the extent that its real subject is human beings. What is "the reality of economic reality"? He discovers that this reality is the human person, the living subject, the "subjectivity" whose capacity for work is exploited and whose aspirations are denied. The socialism of which Marx dreams entails a world in which human beings can freely attain to their own fulfillment, a world in which the individual is not subordinated to the collectivity but can achieve an autonomous fulfillment. Marx's concern is not with the abstract individual (the conscience, the "beautiful soul," of which the religions and the philosophies speak) but the human person who works, struggles, loves, lives, and dies. If Marx turns away from religion, it is because in his view religion neglects or even denies that human person.

In picking out some important texts of Marx I shall inevitably be giving his thought of religion the appearance of being more systematic than it really is. His thinking on religion developed chiefly out of his contact with the Left Hegelians; clearly then, it is to a large extent dependent on others. In the works which represent his mature thought he has little to say about religion. His theorizing on the problem of religion slackens and for practical purposes disappears after 1845, that is, from the time when he finds his real self.

Reason: A Land Where God Ceases To Exist

The atmosphere in which Marx worked out his first critique of religion was the atmosphere created by the Enlightenment. In his secondary school essay on a religious subject Marx imitates the eighteenth-century rationalists in professing not atheism but a "demythologized" Christianity in which only a lofty morality survives and faith and reason become one. This vague religiosity quickly disappears once Marx leaves secondary school and Trier. Through association with the "Doctors' Club" in Berlin he is introduced to new methods of thinking. Here religion is subjected to historical analysis and reduced to the status of myth (Strauss); it is stripped of all transcendence and reduced to its human dimension (Bauer); it is simply a picturesque kind of anthropology (Feuerbach). Marx's early writings are dominated by this reductionist tendency and the exaltation of the free and autonomous human being who needs no relation to God.[5]

God and Paper Money

This rationalist approach is evident in Marx's doctoral dissertation, begun in 1838 and finished in March 1841, on *The Difference Between the Natural Philosophy of Democritus and the Natural Philosophy of Epicurus.* Here Marx asserts, to begin with, the complete freedom of the philosopher, who need not render an account to anyone. He makes his own the Enlightenment motto: "Have the courage to think for yourself!" He takes Epicurus as a model in this respect, seeing in him "the champion of an unqualified freedom of thought." Like Epicurus, the philosopher must be free, accept no dogma from others, and exercise his critical powers while adhering to no standard except reason. There can therefore be no question of imitating Plutarch who "cites philosophy before the forum of religion."[6] On the contrary, it is "the theologizing mind" that must appear before the tribunal of philosophy. Like a king in his own country, philosophy is sovereign:

> Philosophy makes no secret of it. Prometheus' admission: "In sooth all gods I hate," is its own admission, its own motto against all gods, heavenly and earthly, who do not acknowledge the consciousness of man as the supreme divinity. There must be no god on a level with it.[7]

As a young man, then, Marx rejects all religious faith. He does so in the name of a certain ideal of the human person. Convinced as he is that faith is an obstacle in the way of freedom, he is determined to liberate the human race: "I want to increase the mind's freedom from the chains of religion." It is better for human beings to accept their misfortunes while retaining their freedom than to try to escape the misfortunes by surrendering their freedom to fear of the gods. "I would never exchange my misfortunes for that kind of slavery!" The only attitude worthy of a human being is not submission but struggle. Human beings must liberate themselves from their religious fears, take their destiny into their own hands, and live in freedom. Marx's ideal is thus a "humanism" without God.

What about the proofs for the existence of God? What significance do they have? Marx grants them no positive value but considers them rather to be simply products of the imagination. His manner of disqualifying them reflects a tactic carefully worked out by the Left Hegelians. It consists of reducing the idea of God to some aspect or other of the human person. God is simply an idea, that is, a product of the human mind. It is nothing but a "subjective representation" that demonstrates "the self-consciousness of the person" but enjoys its status as a reality exterior to the person only by grace of the human mind. In other words, it has no value at all. It can be compared to paper money, the value of which depends on people's confidence in it. Its value disappears as soon as confidence yields to distrust:

> Introduce paper money into a country unfamiliar with such a use of paper, and everyone will make fun of your subjective notion. Go with your gods to a country in which other gods are revered, and they will point out to you that you are subject to illusions. And legitimately so. . . . What a given country is in relation to certain sets of gods, the country of reason is in relation to God generally, that is, a country where he ceases to exist.[8]

Still to be explained is why human beings should invent gods. The reason is that they have not mastered their world and feel incapable by themselves of giving a meaning to their lives. Their wretchedness generates illusions and makes them look for alliances with, and consolations from, the imaginary beings we call gods. But, says Marx, it is absurd to look to God for meaning for man when God himself has meaning only through man. This way of acting is evidence of the obscurantism of the believer but not a proof that God exists.

Human beings should, like Epicurus, hate all the gods, for they are useless and even harmful. The human person should put trust in nothing but science. Religion and science are irreconcilable: attempting to harmonize science with Christianity is "like throwing the habit of a Christian nun over the exuberant body of the Greek Lais."[9] The only ideal worthy of human beings is the ideal of Prometheus, who becomes the noblest saint in the new calendar of philosophy. The only divinity left, in Marx's view of things, is human self-consciousness.

The Contradictions of the Christian State

In his dissertation Marx stayed with the subject of religion. If he rejected God, he did so in the name of a certain idea of the human person. But circumstances now forced him to turn his attention to politics. The reactionary people who exercised authority in Prussia regarded him with suspicion, as they did the entire Hegelian Left; this meant that Marx had no chance of obtaining a university professorship after defending his thesis. He therefore returned to Bonn and took up journalism, writing for the *Rheinische Zeitung* where he forged his first weapons. One of his early targets was the censorhip of the press by the government.

The excuse for speaking his mind was offered by an article of Hermes, editor of the Catholic newspaper *Kölnische Zeitung.* Hermes had upbraided the liberals for their "most unseemly attacks on Christianity" and for "spreading and combating philosophical and religious views in newspapers." He called for censorship, arguing that the state, based as it was on religion, had the duty of defending religion against its enemies. The Prussian state was officially Christian. It therefore had an obligation to assert God's will and see that this will was obeyed, since fallen man is incapable of achieving the good by himself. Such was the theology behind the concept of the Christian state.

Marx's reply appeared in the *Rheinische Zeitung* for July 10, 12, and 14, 1842, under the title "The Leading Article of No. 179 of *Kölnische Zeitung.*"[10] The dispute with Hermes provided him with an opportunity to point out the contradictions of the Christian state. The very notion of a Christian state is necessarily irrational, because religions are always local and limited (different countries, different religions), whereas reason, and it alone, is universal and can therefore alone claim to be the basis of a state. If a state feels a need of taking shelter behind a religion and basing itself on this religion, is this not a sign that this state is irrational? Recourse to religion is only a way of camouflaging the irrationality.

Now, the Prussian state claims to be a Christian state. Very well. But then it cannot escape the following dilemma:

Either the Christian state is "a realization of rational freedom"—but then it draws its inspiration from reason and not from religion; the latter is therefore useless, and if it lays claim to be the foundation of a state, it is at best usurping a role that belongs to reason.

Or the state does not embody this rational ideal—then the state is a bad one and can no longer claim to draw its inspiration from religion. Could religion possibly stand surety for a state that is contrary to reason and freedom?

Whichever of these two alternatives is taken, the state cannot really mean to base itself on religion. Reason alone, which is the interpreter of human rights, can supply the state with a valid foundation; reason must therefore in practice be the sole foundation of the state. Like the various sciences in the course of history the state must emancipate itself from religion and seize autonomy for itself. Insofar as a state is Christian, it is not based on an equality of rights but on religious privileges. Marx urges it to cast these aside and return to reason as its foundation.

At the end of this first approach to the problem, religion is seen as the triumph of the forces of unreason; Marx condemns it in the name of reason. It has no place in the life of the individual or in the state. Marx's condemnation is all the more passionate because religion prevents human beings from freeing themselves from alien control and becoming themselves. Like the individual, the state must find its "center of gravity" within itself, that is, in reason, so that when the individual obeys the state, he in fact simply "obeys the natural laws of his own reason, human reason."

Religion a Mystification

Such attacks by Marx could not go unnoticed. His newspaper was soon suppressed and he himself had to leave the country. In 1843 he settled in Paris. He began to move away from the Young Hegelians as he realized that the philosophical critique which satisfied them was in fact no longer adequate and that other forces had to be brought into play. He intended therefore to substitute "practical energy" for theoretical criticism and so to change reality itself: if the weapon of criticism was to be effective it had to be transformed into a criticism of weapons. But Marx was not urging a thoughtless activism. He knew that militancy was of value only if it was an enlightened militancy. His task would be to supply the theoretical help which the masses needed if they were to act effectively: "Material force must be overthrown by material force; but theory also becomes a material force as soon as it has gripped the masses."[11]

In Paris Marx founded the *Deutsche-Französische Jahrbücher* of which only one number was to appear (in February 1844). This Parisian period was extremely important for his thinking on religion. Until now his criticism had been of the rationalist type; henceforth he would take his stand on social reality. What is religion when seen from the viewpoint of society? It is an opium, a "spiritual aroma," that obscures reality, anaesthetizes the will, and therefore blocks the transformation of reality. Two texts in particular call for our attention: *Contribution to the Critique of Hegel's Philosophy of Right* (written 1843–44) and *The Jewish Question* (1843). The one offers us the general theory of religion to which reference is usually made in discussion of Marx; the other returns to his criticism of the state. In these texts, Marx is still under Feuerbach's influence. Like the latter he tries to show that religion is an expression of human reality but one in which this reality is alienated and obscured.

Man Makes Religion

I shall cite first, from the *Contribution to the Critique of Hegel's Philosophy of Right,* a text that is well known, but whose meaning needs to be brought out.

> For Germany the *criticism of religion* is in the main complete, and criticism of religion is the premise of all criticism.
>
> The *profane* existence of error is discredited after its *heavenly oratio pro aris et focis* [speech in defense of altars and hearths] has been rejected. Man, who looked for a superman in the fantastic reality of heaven and found nothing there but the *reflection* of himself, will no longer be disposed to find but the *semblance* of himself, the non-human [*Unmensch*] where he seeks and must seek his true reality.
>
> The basis of irreligious criticism is: *Man makes religion,* religion does not make man. In other words, religion is the self-consciousness and self-feeling of man who has either not yet found himself or has already lost himself again. But *man* is no abstract being squatting outside the world. Man is

the world of man, the state, society. This state, this society, produce religion, *a reversed world-consciousness,* because they are *a reversed world.* Religion is the general theory of that world, its encyclopaedic compendium, its logic in a popular form, its spiritualistic *point d'honneur,* its enthusiasm, its moral sanction, its solemn completion, its universal ground for consolation and justification. It is the *fantastic realization* of the human essence because the human essence has no true reality. The struggle against religion is therefore mediately the fight against *the other world,* of which religion is the spiritual *aroma.*

Religious distress is at the same time the *expression* of real distress and the *protest* against real distress. Religion is the sigh of the oppressed creature, the heart of a heartless world, just as it is the spirit of a spiritless situation. It is the *opium* of the people.

The abolition of religion as the *illusory* happiness of the people is required for their *real* happiness. The demand to give up the illusions about its condition is the *demand to give up a condition which needs illusions.* The criticism of religion is therefore *in embryo the criticism of the vale of woe,* the *halo* of which is religion.[12]

This text calls for several remarks. To begin with, it contains a theoretical definition of religion, one which is admittedly not very original: God is the "reflection" of man, but a magnified reflection that images forth man as completed and fulfilled ("superman"). But human beings do not see that such a transfer has taken place; it is obscured, because God seems to be an autonomous reality when in fact he is only a "reflection." The struggle against religion consists in showing this mystification for what it is. But this task has in fact already been accomplished. When Marx says at the beginning of the passage that "the criticism of religion is in the main complete," he is acknowledging that his criticism is not his own but is part of an ideological field developed by others: Feuerbach and the entire Hegelian Left. But Marx will be faithful to this definition as late as *Capital* (1867) where he writes: "The religious world is only a reflection of the real world."[13] The basic idea persists: religion is a "reflection" or, as Marx will call it later on, an "ideology,"

which has its roots in man himself—not however abstract man
"outside the world," as the Hegelians thought of it, but concrete
man, situated in the world and in a well-defined social context.

Marx thus follows Feuerbach in his understanding of the
genesis of religion, even though the starting point for the projection of God is now more precise and concrete. Like Feuerbach, he stresses the "illusory" nature of the man/God
opposition. The reflection is only a dream (a fantasy, a product
of the imagination) of what man does not possess but aspires to
possess. This reflection exerts a baneful influence because it
hides man's true reality from him and turns him aside from seeking his reality in this world and making his dreams of fulfillment
come true here on earth. The reappropriation of the human reality requires the criticism of religion, that is, the manifestation
of the illusory nature of religion. Religion must be reduced to
man, because "man makes religion, religion does not make
man." Because man is confused about his own reality in the
world in which he lives, he projects outside of himself an ideal,
imagined world in which he finds the fulfillment (although this
fulfillment is only a "semblance") that is lacking. That is how
God is "made."

Admittedly, Marx leaves unanswered an essential question:
Why do human beings refuse to live in the real social world and
transform it? Why do they seek an imaginary fulfillment that
brings only an illusory satisfaction? It is a fact that human beings
need to escape; they live in "a condition which needs illusions."
Marx does not tell us why they reach the point of trading their
real condition, difficult and frustrating though it is, for a condition which, though soothing and bringing fulfillment, does so in
only an imaginary way. He does, however, shed some light on
the function of religion. Its function is "consolation" and "justification." In a world that is too harsh for its inhabitants, religion
plays a practical role by introducing a seeming logic into a world
without logic (a topsy-turvy world) and making lavish promises
which the world is incapable of fulfilling.

Religion thus has two faces. On the one hand, it is the "expression" of real distress, the sign of a society gone wrong. If
everything were well in the world, human beings would not be-
take themselves to illusory worlds. On the other hand, religion
is also a "protest" against this distress, the denunciation as well
as the revelation of a heartless world. But the very denunciation

fosters illusion because instead of rousing human beings to transform the world it inspires them to take flight to a different world. This is why Marx can sum up his diagnosis in the lapidary formula: religion is the opium of the people. It is important to grasp the precise meaning of these words. Marx does not regard religion as an opium *for* the people, one that has been invented by a caste of profiteers (priests or princes) who want to keep the people in a state of oppression. No, it is an opium *of* the people, one that the people administer to themselves as a way of helping them put up with their distress and exploitation. But in Marx's eyes this kind of protest is ineffective because instead of promoting a struggle against an unjust world it organizes an escape into an imaginary world.

Such is the reason why at this stage of his thinking Marx regards the struggle against religion as an indispensable phase of the social struggle. He judges that human beings will in fact not be ready for a real struggle in the present world unless they have given up their illusions about another world. He writes: "Criticism of religion is the premise of all criticism." In a subsequent paragraph (just after the long passage I have cited) he explains what he means: "The criticism of religion disillusions man to make him think and act and shape his reality like a man who has been disillusioned and has come to reason." His thinking on this point will change: later on he will think that "reality" must be changed so as to eliminate the religious "reflection" of it. At the present point in his development, however, he is of the opinion that illusions must first be eliminated so that people may take an interest in the real world, since as long as they are fascinated by heaven they are useless for the struggle on earth. In other words, Marx is urging an awareness of religion as an illusion. To the extent that human beings get rid of the false image of themselves which religion offers them, they will become people of this earth and ready to seek the fulfillment of their lives here. They must therefore be stripped of their false hope of the next world so that they may develop an earthly hope and a revolutionary consciousness.

But Marx is not satisfied with the criticism of religion. He knows that such criticism has not resolved all problems. Other illusions are waiting to take over and continue the alienation of human beings. This is why he adds that once the criticism of heaven has been accomplished, all the profane illusions—right, the state—must also be tackled. The direct struggle against religion is indispensable, but there is also a further and more difficult struggle: "Once the *saintly form* of human self-alienation has been unmasked, [philosophy's task] is to unmask self-alienation in its *unholy forms*" (*ibid.*). I shall not stop to look at this new type of criticism. Marx is already shifting to another, non-religious level, namely, the political, to which the Young Hegelians paid no attention whatsoever.

Let me sum up this new development. Marx has the same goal as Feuerbach: to liberate human beings. But he sees that if this liberation is to be achieved, it is not enough to "become conscious"of man's self-alienation into religion, because the alienation is not simply religious but also, and more radically, political. The religious struggle must be followed by the political struggle. In Marx's view, the first criticism (dissolution of religion) has for practical purposes been completed, but the second (criticism of the earth) has hardly been begun. Feuerbach devoted his efforts to demystifying religion, but did not understand the importance of the political struggle. If a person simply rids himself of the religious illusion, he is not automatically capable of living his true life. The true life must still be won by changing socio-political conditions. The error of Feuerbach and the Left Hegelians was to think that human beings are emancipated once they achieve full consciousness. For Marx, their emancipation requires a transformation of the conditions of their existence. The text of Marx that I have been analyzing already signals a significant change of viewpoint: the criticism of religion gives way to a criticism of society.

Religion, Expression of a Defect

The Jewish Question (1843)[14] tackles the religious problem once again, but this time from a directly political standpoint. Written immediately after the *Contribution to the Critique of Hegel's Philosophy of Right,* this work of Marx is one of the most interesting for our subject. Once again, Marx shows that religion is a mystification, that is, a false expression of reality as an alienation, that is, it puts the fate of human beings in the hands of a foreign power. Above all, however, Marx emphasizes the shift of viewpoint which I mentioned above: religion is not the only form of alienation. The mere withdrawal from the universe of religion does not guarantee human beings the power to reach their fulfillment. Marx's goal is the full emancipation of the human person; "emancipation" is the reverse of alienation, the liberation of the human person from all his alienations. If emancipation is achieved through rejection of the world of religion, as Bruno Bauer claims—and Marx agrees with him—it is achieved at a more fundamental level through rejection of the oppressive state which while supposedly administering the common good is in fact at the service of the ruling class. Marx's thesis can be summed up thus: For human beings to become themselves it is not enough to separate Church and state and abolish the privileges granted to religion; the state itself must be denounced as a profane sphere of alienation.

Marx's study is a response to Bruno Bauer. What did the latter maintain? To understand his views we must recall the situation in the state of Prussia, a state based on the Christian religion. Because of their religion Jews in Prussia did not enjoy the same rights as Christians. (We may recall the case of Hirschel, Marx's father.) Jews could not hold civic offices or exercise political functions unless they renounced their religion. Their grievances were long-standing ones. They maintained that they ought to have the same rights as Christians in the Prussian state, without having to renounce their religion to do so. Bruno Bauer entered the debate, not in order to support Jewish claims but to demand a more general emancipation. In Prussia, he said, no one is emancipated; everyone is alienated at a fundamental level because the state is connected with religion. The emancipation of the Jews should be achieved not by their obtaining the same rights as others in an unchanged state, but by a transformation of the state which must renounce its allegiance to a religion.

In addition, Bauer added, Jews are in a poor position for demanding political emancipation since they themselves are unwilling to give up their religious particularism. How can they call upon the state to abandon its religious prejudice when they themselves remain attached to their particular religion? But Bauer looks beyond the Jews and calls for a general political emancipation. He wants a secular state that has no ties with any religion, because the religions represent a lower stage in the evolution of the human race and must now give way to "science" and the autonomy of the human order. Religion is at most a private affair. Bauer therefore demands of the state not that it grant religious privilege to the Jews but that it cut itself off from all religion. A state that presupposes religion is not a true state.

It is at this point that Marx enters the debate. He shows that Bauer goes only halfway. If there is to be freedom, it is not only religion but the state itself that must be attacked. Human beings are alienated not only by religion but by the Prussian state since the latter grants them no real freedom. The proof that a secular state is not automatically a place of freedom is the fact that even where the state is in practice independent of religion (as in the United States) people do not on that account feel free, for otherwise they would not take refuge in "private" religion. Such a flight into the religious sphere, even when the state is a secular state, is the sign of a basic defect in the state, the sign that something is missing:

> If we find even in a country with full political emancipation that religion not only *exists* but is *fresh and vital,* we have proof that the existence of religion is not incompatible with the full development of the state. But since the existence of religion implies a defect, the source of this defect must be found in the *nature* of the state itself. We no longer take religion to be the *basis* but only the *manifestation* of secular narrowness. Hence we explain religious restriction of free citizens on the basis of their secular restriction.... The question of the *relation of political emancipation to religion* becomes for us the question of the *relation of political emancipation to human emancipation*. We criticize the religious weakness of the political state in its *secular* constitution *apart from* the religious defects.[15]

In other words, Bauer blames all human misfortunes on the *Christian* state and fails to see that the state *as such* is to blame. He calls for political emancipation, that is, for a lay state, but does not understand that the real issue is human emancipation, that is, the freedom of the human person. Human beings are not emancipated if they are content to exchange religious alienation for political alienation. Human emancipation requires the rejection of every form of transcendence, sacred or profane, and the opportunity for people to achieve fulfillment autonomously. But no modern state gives them this opportunity. The modern lay state that emerged from the French Revolution does indeed guarantee abstract rights, the rights namely of a citizen (equality before the law, right to vote, and so on) but not real rights (the right to property, to employment, to freedom, and so on). The former, which are granted to all, are formal and lack any social content. The latter are real but only those who manage to seize them actually have them. The state guarantees individuals only certain formal rights and does not concern itself with whether or not these individuals are in a position to enjoy them. Like religion, the state itself offers human beings only an illusory fulfillment, a sham emancipation.[16]

The shift of focus is clear. Previously Marx had, like Bauer, attacked the "saintly" form of human alienation. In his mind, all the sorrows of human beings came from religion. Now, however, he intends to attack and "unmask self-alienation in its unholy forms," which means, essentially, political alienation. By comparison with Bauer, then, Marx has moved from one level of problems to another. He no longer calls for political emancipation, whether for Jews or others, but for human emancipation. This last will be achieved only through the elimination of the state or at least of the bourgeois state.[17] As long as religion maintains its hold on the hearts of human beings, this is a sign that while the state may be politically emancipated, it is still defective. For since religion is the expression of a defect, its existence is the symptom (the "phenomenon") of a defect in the state itself. As long as religion was present *in* the state, it was possible to be deceived about the nature of the state and to believe that religion was responsible for the lack of freedom. But once the state is *separated* from religion and yet human beings continue to be dissatisfied to the point of still taking refuge in religion, we have a sign that the state is suffering from some more radical defect. It is actually in the service of one class in its effort to dominate another.

As Marx sees it, then, the need is to emancipate human beings not only from religion but from the state as well. Only then will a real life become possible: not an egoistic life centered on the self, but a truly "social" life in which each individual is in harmony with himself and others. Marx's project is of an atheistic society that is completely immanent and has no reference to God.

Religion, One Ideology Among Others

From 1844 on Marx worked more closely with Engels, who roused his interest in questions of economics. His political activities caused his expulsion from France, along with a number of other Germans. He took up residence in Brussels and participated in several congresses; then, surprised by the revolution of 1848, he tried to play a part in it and returned briefly to Paris. Finally, he settled for good in London, in July 1849, and remained there until his death (March 14, 1883). His life was a hard one and marked by constant financial worries, since his only income consisted of fees from newspapers and subsidies from Engels. This was the period during which he worked out his own system of thought; the main focus of this thought was henceforth on matters economic. Several important writings show the shift in his thinking and the break with his philosophical past in which the influence of Feuerbach had been predominant. Little by little the new direction of his thought became clear; it was intended to be scientific thinking.

Religion, an Ideological Reflex

The *Theses on Feuerbach* (1845) are the action by which Marx took leave of a temporary teacher. Along with Feuerbach he has the whole Hegelian Left in mind as he points out the inadequacy of a purely speculative approach to the phenomenon of religion. He rebukes Feuerbach for not having really understood the genesis of religion: Feuerbach "does not see that the 'religious sentiment' is itself a *social product* and that the abstract individual whom he analyzes belongs in reality to a particular form of society."[18] Elsewhere Marx says:

> Feuerbach starts out from the fact of religious self-alienation, the duplication of the world into a religious, imaginary world and a real one. His work consists in the dissolution of the religious world into its secular basis. He overlooks the fact that after this work is completed the chief thing still remains to be done. For the fact that the secular foundation detaches itself from itself and establishes itself in the clouds as an independent realm is really only to be explained by the self-cleavage and self-contradictoriness of this secular basis. The latter must itself, therefore, first be

understood in its contradiction, and then revolutionized in practice by the removal of the contradiction.[19]

Feuerbach resolves the *religious* essence into the *human* essence. But the human essence is no abstraction inherent in each single individual. In its reality it is the ensemble of the social relations.[20]

In other words, the phenomenon we call religion is a set of representations (an ideology) closely linked to its social basis. It does not develop in an abstract way inside the heads of human beings but is a way of interpreting social reality. A practical consequence of this view is that it becomes impossible to criticize religion as though it were an independent entity. Since religion is a reflection of socio-economic structures, it can be challenged only indirectly. To struggle against it in a direct way is to fight with shadows. The real struggle must be directed to the material basis. But the struggle is then no longer ideological but material. "The philosophers have only *interpreted* the world, in various ways; the point, however, is to *change* it."[21] This is Marx's new conviction: religion is an ideology (this last term appears very quickly), and an ideology can be shaken only by changing the material basis from which it has arisen and which it reflects.

The German Ideology (1846), which is the joint work of Marx and Engels, is more substantial than the *Theses* and presents us with the authors' new outlook on religion. They look upon religion as lacking an existence of its own and as depending essentially on the economic basis. This is true of all ideological productions: the economic basis determines the development of social, political, intellectual, moral and religious life. The structure raised on this material basis is its ideological superstructure. The two authors are not sparing in their comments on those who think religion has an essence of its own. Here is their own view of the matter:

This means that we proceed not from what men say, fancy or imagine, nor from men as they are spoken of, fancied, imagined in order to arrive from them at men of flesh and blood; we proceed from the really active men and see the development of the ideological reflexes and echoes of their

real-life process as proceeding from that life-process. Even
the nebulous images in the brain of men are necessary sub-
limates of their material, empirically observable, materially
pre-conditioned, life-process. Thus, morals, religion, metaphysics and other forms of ideology and the forms of consciousness corresponding to them no longer retain their
apparent independence. They have no history, they have no
development, but as men develop their material production
and their material intercourse with it, they also change their
reality, their thinking, and the products of their thinking. It
is not consciousness that determines life, but life that determines consciousness.[22]

If religion, but also morality, law, and all ideological productions are only reflexes of real life, then two consequences
follow which the text emphasizes. The first is that ideologies
have no independent existence; it is therefore absurd to attempt
a linear, horizontal history of ideas that would focus on the links
between them. The only valid explanation of ideologies is one
that shows their connection with the material basis, the concrete
life of human beings, the economic situation, and so on. Religion is a social product that is to be explained by the state of
society at a given moment. The second consequence is just as
inescapable: there must be a reversal in the order of priorities;
the struggle against ideology is no longer the "premise" but
rather the result of transformation of the material basis. "The
real, practical ... elimination of these notions from the consciousness of man, will ... be accomplished by altered circumstances, not by theoretic deductions."[23] This is a point to which
I shall return.[24]

At this point several qualifications must be introduced although I cannot develop them at length. (1) The religious ideology is only one ideology among others. It is one kind of
distorted representation of reality, but other ideologies likewise
undertake, each in its own way, to reflect this same reality: morality, politics, and so on. (2) Although Marx uses the same
term, ideology, for all the productions of consciousness, he
nonetheless introduces a hierarchy among them. A classification
of ideologies in order of increasing density would be: science,
art, politics, law, morality, philosophy, and religion. Some ideo-

logies remain closer to reality than others. The religious ideology is the most ethereal, the one that obscures reality the most. It has absolutely no validity. (3) The production of ideologies is an unconscious process, as Engels notes: "The real forces that set the process in motion are unknown to the person, otherwise it would not be an ideological process."[25] (4) Dependent though ideologies are on their material basis, they nonetheless retain a certain autonomy that can assure their survival even when the material basis has changed, and that enables them to adjust to new situations. Some unqualified statements regarding ideology could suggest a mechanical connection between basis and superstructure. But in fact, while there is, "in the final analysis," a real connection between the two levels, it is not a rigid one. The Christian ideology in particular shows an almost unlimited capacity for adjustment to new circumstances. The Marxists have had to correct Marx on this point.[26] (5) Finally, it must be emphasized that "ideology" is an ambiguous idea in Marx. On the one hand, it refers to superstructure and from this point of view is a scientific concept that makes it possible to grasp a reality; on the other, it refers to something that is an error or illusion, since it gives a distorted interpretation of this reality, and from this point of view it is a philosophical category and a value judgment on the content which it conveys.[27]

The Struggle Against the Religious Ideology

Since an ideology is an error, how is it to be removed? Some statements of Marx and Engels suggest that they hope the religious ideology will wither away. Christianity, for example, was born in a particular historical context and therefore is destined to disappear through a "natural death." It has already ceased to exist for the majority of human beings: "For the mass of human beings, i.e., for the proletariat, these theoretic notions do not exist and therefore do not need to be dissolved, and if ever this mass had any such notions, e.g., religion, they have been dissolved long ago by circumstances."[28]

But Marx does not stop at this passive conception, which underestimates the resistance put up by ideologies. Reflection on the social function of ideologies leads him to adopt a more active attitude: ideologies must be combated. After all, what are the dominant ideas of an age? They are the ideas of the ruling

class. Like every social group, this class needs an ideology on
two counts. On the one hand, the ideology helps the group to
establish itself as a class, creates a common consciousness, and
causes the unconscious acceptance of the order it seeks to create. One function of the ideology is therefore to justify the
group. On the other hand, the ideas of the group must win acceptance from others. Every ideology, even though it is the expression of a class, seeks to be universally accepted. It therefore
serves to legitimate the existing order in the eyes of those whom
this order exploits. From this point of view, an ideology is a de-
vice for domination and enslavement.

Understandably, then, Marx did not remain indifferent to
the reigning ideologies of his day but sought to combat them.
He was undoubtedly convinced that an ideology was linked to its
material basis but he also knew that the material basis was in
turn constantly reinforced by the ideology which gave it legitimacy. This explains his vigilance and at times truculent aggressiveness. The essential aim of the mature Marx was of course to
effect a revolution in the economic and social basis, but he did
not hesitate on occasion to browbeat the Christian ideology by
showing the economic interests hidden behind the fine ideas.
Everyone knows the epigram he let fly at the Anglican bishops:
"The High Church of England will more readily forgive an attack on thirty-eight of its thirty-nine articles of faith than on one
thirty-ninth of its revenues."[29]

What does he have against the Christian ideology? That it
promotes a slave morality which degrades human nature and
withdraws human beings from action. On this point the reader
should go back to the pages of *The Holy Family*, which are as
spiteful as they are relevant.[30] Marx there tells the story of
Fleur-de-Marie, a young girl full of life and enthusiasm, whom
religion completely debases. The priests change her first into a
repentant sinner, then into a nun, and finally into a corpse.
Marx concludes that Christianity destroys all personality and
leads to servility. It turns the person into a "sheep" in the likeness of the Passover lamb.[31]

Marx especially dislikes Christian socialism. He sees in it an
effort to dominate a social situation of which it has lost control.
But what is Christian socialism but a nostalgia for the past or
"the holy water with which the priest consecrates the heart-

burnings of the aristocrat"?[32] As a matter of fact, for twenty centuries the social principles of Christianity have served to justify everything: slavery in antiquity, serfdom in the Middle Ages, the oppression of the proletariat. They have never sparked a rebellion or a revolution. They preach the submission of the oppressed class or at most utter pious wishes that the ruling class would show itself charitable:

> The social principles of Christianity transfer the consistorial councillors' adjustment of all infamies to heaven and thus justify the further existence of those infamies on earth.
>
> The social principles of Christianity declare all vile acts of the oppressors against the oppressed to be either the just punishment of original sin and other sins or trials that the Lord in his infinite wisdom imposes on those redeemed.
>
> The social principles of Christianity preach cowardice, self-contempt, abasement, submission, dejection, in a word all the qualities of the *canaille;* and the proletariat, not wishing to be treated as *canaille,* needs its courage, its self-feeling, its pride and its sense of independence more than its bread.
>
> The social principles of Christianity are sneakish and the proletariat is revolutionary.[33]

Christianity inspires only distrust in Marx. Its kindly words are suspect because they withdraw men from action. He sees Christianity as an ideology in the service of the ruling class and the prevailing order, and therefore as anti-revolutionary. Its every nook and cranny conceals "bourgeois interests." It is simply an obstacle to the establishment of communism. The coming of communism will signal the end of religion.[34]

After Marx

Marxism continued to develop and adapt. Its views on religion changed to fit circumstances and places, as did its practical outlook. As far as religion is concerned, Marx remained its point of reference but it also drew inspiration from Engels and Lenin. These two men, while repeating Marx, added nuances and sometimes a hardening of positions, for each of them bore the

mark of his personal experience and historical situation and acted according to temperamental bias.

Attacking Objective Causes

Friedrich Engels (1820–1895) was for most his life the fellow worker of Marx. From his youth he was more preoccupied
than Marx with the religious problem and kept coming back to
it, but his ideas are lacking in originality. He shows himself to be
rather a popularizer of themes developed by Marx, giving these
at times a formulation that is at once more simple and more rigid.[35] His personal studies are essentially an application of the
theses in *The German Ideology* to particular instances: the religion
of nature, Christianity, etc. His principle of interpretation, developed jointly with Marx, might be stated thus: "Each ruling
class makes use of the religion adapted to it, while the rising
class adopts a 'revolutionary religion.' "[36] Engels is therefore interested in sects, which represent so many rejections of religious
conformism and attempts to invent the revolutionary religions
which a new situation calls for.

What about Christianity as seen in this light? Its appearance
is to be explained by historical conditions favorable to it in the
Roman Empire. And the Reformation? It was the "ideological
garb" donned by the bourgeoisie at the moment when the latter
became conscious of itself as the rising class. Though Engels devotes many pages to the religious problem, he says hardly anything new. His practical attitude seems rather to be one of
tolerance. He sees no need to eliminate religion by a direct attack or police harassment or prohibitions. He does not even demand a profession of atheism from those who want to belong to
the workers' movement. Membership in the Internationale was
possible without presenting a certificate of atheism. The most
urgent need was to build socialism. Religion would die a "natural death" once the social basis is modified:

> Religion is prohibited. All religion, however, is nothing but
> the fantastic reflection in men's minds of those external
> forces which control their daily life, a reflection in which the
> terrestrial forces assume the form of supernatural forces. . . .
> Mere knowledge . . . is not enough to bring social forces un-
> der the domination of society. What is above all necessary
> for this is a social *act*. And when this act has been accom-

plished, when society, by taking possession of all means of production and using them on a planned basis, has freed itself and all its members from . . . bondage . . . only then will the last alien force which is still reflected in religion vanish; and with it will also vanish the religious reflection itself, for the simple reason that there will be nothing left to reflect.[37]

Contrary to the belief of Dühring (against whom Engels is writing here) it is not enough to prohibit religion for it to disappear. The effect of a prohibition may even be to revive it. Religion has objective causes which explain the varied forms it has taken at different periods of history. The most efficacious means of achieving the goal is to change the basis of which religion is the reflection. All of Engels' thinking is dominated by the "postulate of the non-specificity of religious phenomena," as formulated in *The German Ideology.* He believes that science is his best ally in the struggle against religion. For four centuries science has been winning the key victories over religion and has driven it from the main areas it had occupied. Science will finally eliminate religion from social life as well:

In the history of modern natural science, God is treated by his defenders as Frederick William III was treated by his generals and officials in the Jena campaign. One division of the army after another lays down its arms, one fortress after another capitulates before the march of science, until at last the whole infinite realm of nature is conquered by science, and there is no place left in it for the Creator.[38]

Priority of the Class Struggle

Lenin (born 1870) was more directly engaged than his predecessors had been in the revolutionary struggle, but he also determined the official philosophy of Soviet Russia on many points. He had been an unbeliever from the age of sixteen. As far as his views on religion were concerned, he often simply repeated Marx and Engels, making himself a defender of the strict orthodox Marxist doctrine. Thus he made his own Marx's theoretical position: "Religion is the opium of the people," and considered this formula to be the cornerstone of the entire Marxist conception of religion. For Lenin, then, religion was an illusion,

an anti-scientific vision of the world, but it was especially harmful at the social level, because it numbed men's wills. This is the
essential reason why Lenin calls it "the enemy to be overcome."

But how fight against it? Not every form of struggle is correct. The Marxist must "know how to combat it," that is, he
must know what he is about and choose the proper strategy:

> The struggle against religion must not be limited to ab-
> stract ideological propaganda; in no case must it be reduced
> to such propaganda. The struggle must be linked to a con-
> crete practice constituted by the class movement which
> tends to eliminate the social roots of religion.[39]

The struggle against religion is thus subordinate to the
class struggle, which is more essential. It is from the standpoint
of the class struggle that Lenin judges religion "in the final analysis." Religion is first and foremost a political problem, not a
philosophical problem. Each individual must be judged not on
his religious affiliation but on his place in the class struggle.

Such a shift in problematic is of very great tactical interest.
It means that a person is not to be forbidden entry into the Party
because of his religious beliefs. The real line of division among
individuals runs elsewhere. Religion continues, of course, to be
by its nature an illusion. In addition, it gets involved more in reactionary enterprises than in revolutionary ones. But it is precisely by its associations that the Workers' Party must judge it.
Everything else belongs to the "private" domain. Lenin even en-
visages the possibility of a priest asking for entry into the Party:
he is to be accepted not as a priest (that is his business) but as a
militant:

> If a priest comes to join us in the struggle and conscien-
> tiously carries out his role in the Party without objecting to
> its program, we can accept him, because the contradiction
> between the mind and principles of our program, on the
> one hand, and the religious situation of the priest, on the
> other, may under these circumstances remain a contradic-
> tion within him, a matter of concern to him personally.[40]

Religion is thus relegated to the "private" sphere. But this
must be properly understood, for Lenin introduces an impor-

tant distinction here. Religion may be a "private matter" but it cannot be regarded as an indifferent matter. To say that religion is a "private" matter means that the state must be a lay state and not use political or police pressures to bother people on account of their religious views: "Each person must be free to follow the religion of his choice." But this does not mean that the Party is to abstain from anti-religious propaganda and the education of the masses: "We require that religion be recognized as a private matter as far as the state is concerned, but we can by no means treat religion as a private matter from the standpoint of the Party."[41] If a priest asks for admission to the Party, he is required to remain silent about his religious views. He is to take no account of them either within the Party, where the only thing asked of him is to carry on the struggle according to the program (even against his ideas as a priest, should occasion arise), or outside the Party, where he is required to spread the Party's ideas, not his own.

Is such a hypothesis a contradiction? No: these reflections show us only that Lenin was intransigent at the practical level. In his view the fundamental line of division is not between religion and atheism but between dominant class and dominated class. To the extent that religion sides with the ruling class, it must be combated. To the extent that it takes part in the revolutionary struggle at the side of the oppressed, it will be tolerated, since it is regarded as a private matter. The conflict at this point is no longer a class conflict but a personal conflict between commitment to the struggle of the proletariat, which is objectively based on the materialist analysis of the world, and a religion which is considered to be simply a surviving illusion. Let the believer put himself in this absurd situation if he wishes! Lenin will not interfere; he looks only for militants who have no reservations and for an unconditional commitment to the class struggle.

Persecution and Outstretched Hand

It is impossible to review here in detail the history of the principal exponents of the Marxist tradition. Let us therefore leave aside these witnesses and their ideas and look for a moment at the real history of Marxism. We see in practice a reversal of trend. The struggle against religion, which Marx, Engels, and Lenin had gradually pushed into the background and regarded as secondary, becomes a major preoccupation of Communist regimes. Whereas Marx and especially Engels looked essentially to a revolutionary change in the social basis as the means of eliminating the religious ideology, the governments of the Eastern bloc have made this elimination a direct goal. The change of minds seems to them more important than the change in structures. That is the significance of the "cultural revolution" in particular: it is aimed at changing human beings first.

Can this about-face be explained? Why this struggle against the Churches? The reason is undoubtedly that the Churches exercise an influence on minds which seems in direct competition with the influence the Marxists mean to reserve to themselves. The existence of the Churches is an obstacle to the unconditional obedience demanded by the Communist regimes. This opposition between two powers which are irreducible and irreconcilable, because they lay claim to the whole person, is the source of all the open or tacit persecutions of Christians by the Communists. There is no need to stress the savagery of this persecution. Solzhenitsyn has given a poignant description of it:

> The root destruction of religion in the country, which throughout the twenties and thirties was one of the most important goals of the GPU-NKVD, could be realized only by mass arrests of Orthodox believers. Monks and nuns . . . were intensively rounded up on every hand, placed under arrest, and sent into exile. They arrested and sentenced active laymen. . . . True, they were supposedly being arrested and tried not for their actual faith but for openly declaring their convictions and for bringing up their children in the same spirit. As Tanya Khodkevich wrote:
>> You can pray *freely*
>> But just so God alone can hear.
> (She received a ten-year sentence for these verses.)[42]

These are facts. Can Marx's teaching be made responsible for them? It would be more accurate to make Lenin responsible. Now that the USSR has become part of the family of nations, these ideological struggles have been toned down. China has reproached the USSR for this, accusing it of tolerating the "madness called religion."

In France a different approach has been taken to the problem. At a very early date, in about the 1930's, the Communists launched a political offensive aimed at enticing Christians and promising them that the individual's convictions would be respected. This policy of the "outstretched hand" was inaugurated by Maurice Thorez and has now been urgently renewed by the French Communist Party. Is it simply a tactic geared to elections? The acceptance of a measure of philosophical pluralism? Probably both. The Communists are essentially proposing a concordat for the sake of action.

> Christians and Communists can cooperate in changing society. . . . We do not give priority to philosophical divisions over the common interests of the working population. . . . We do not seek to build a new society against the Christian working masses but together with them. . . . In short, we propose a contract.[43]

Is this not an approach similar to Lenin's? It does not eliminate the ambiguities we saw in Lenin himself.

On the other hand, it is true that the outlook of today's Communists is more nuanced. They no longer look upon religion as solely an "opium," an obstacle, an evasion, but recognize that it can become a dynamic source of life. "Today more and more Christians live their faith no longer as an individualistic, passive flight to the consolations of 'the next world,' but rather as the justification of their struggles against a society they judge to be badly constructed."[44] There is need, therefore, to distinguish within religion a dynamic nucleus, which is the faith, and the political matrix, which is the ideology. Communists acknowledge the value of religion when it takes the form of revolutionary action. They focus their attention on the social dimension and are unconcerned about the religious content, even though they themselves in no way renounce their own atheism. They claim that there is an irreducible "ideological" opposition between themselves and Christians, but, like Lenin, they regard this opposition at the theoretical level as secondary to the class struggle. If the faith turns into a revolutionary ferment, why should they be fastidious and not extend a hand to Christians engaged in the same struggle?

Marx's views are not impervious to criticism. But it is not my intention to disqualify his thought by an orderly refutation. That would be a barren exercise and one that rarely achieves the anticipated result. Isn't it more profitable to open ourselves fully to Marx's criticism and accept it for the powerful attack that it is? That is how Berdiaev looked at it: "Marx unmasks the idols; it unmasks a Christianity that has not lived the truth it professes."[45]

To what extent does this attack hit its mark, namely, Christianity? We may simplify somewhat and reduce Marx's criticism to two main points, one theoretical, the other practical. First of all, Marx constructs a general theory of religion which shows the Christian religion to be, like the other religions, a direct result of human behavior in a given situation. As such, Christianity is an illusion. This criticism, which shows the psycho-social genesis of religion, enables Marx to dismantle it and reduce it to its human dimension. This aspect of his thought is not very original. Marx depends on his predecessors and uses the arsenal of arguments available in his day. He pays hardly any more attention to the subject after his writings as a young man. If he had turned back to his critique in his later works, it is likely that the theory would be different from that which he actually left us.

The second aspect of his criticism is based on an analysis of the historical situation of Christianity. Marx looks at Christianity in terms of the function it exercises in society. From this standpoint he judges it to be a reactionary ideology. Christianity seems bound up with outdated social structures and in the ideological arena of the day represents an influence opposed to the rise of the proletariat. To what extent is this criticism justified? It must be acknowledged that in the nineteenth century the majority of Christians were not on the side of the working masses. Their lack of social involvement, the timidity with which they took part in the great struggles of the working classes, the hesitations and maneuverings of the hierarchy in taking positions: all provided abundant food for Marx's criticism.

This twofold criticism does in fact hit a certain type of Christianity that looks only for personal salvation outside of the present world. Marx judges Christianity by the manner of its presence in the world, and he finds that it is in fact absent from the movement of history. His criticism is aimed less at the spiritual attitude of faith, to which he pays no attention, than at the actual behavior, individual and collective, of Christians. For what does he reproach them? For being passive and too readily satisfied with their situation, for looking elsewhere for their salvation when in fact salvation is to be found only in history. In any accounting, Marx struck a deadly blow at religion conceived as an opium, as a refuge and consolation in misfortune. The religion he has in mind helps human beings to submit to history rather than to shape it. Marx rejects it because it promotes the virtues of slaves: servility, submission, compromise, illusory hopes. It lays no hold upon history but locates everything important beyond history (refuge in another world).

Marx did not understand that faith can be a life-producing dynamic, a power of "protest" and revolution. On this point the views of Communists have developed through contact with Christians whose faith does not withdraw them from action and does not lead to conservatism, timidity and laziness, but is a leaven of life and a motive for action. The Christian attitude need not be one of "transcendent egoism" (Berdiaev), of ethereal spiritualism; if it grasps the true meaning of the Incarnation it necessarily produces an acceptance of history and this with a view to shaping it and not just submitting to it. But, for the Christian, faith does not stop at this historical dimension. The Christian knows that the meaning of history cannot be fully realized within history, that there is something beyond the frontiers of history. Like the Marxist he accepts being fully within history, but he refuses to become a prisoner of history.

It is at this point that Marxism shows its limitations. There is no point to blaming Marx for what he failed to say. According to Althusser, Marx gradually broke away from all forms of humanism and after 1844 became an economist who gave human beings only an insignificant role in history. According to Michel Henry, however, the very opposite development took place. Far from rejecting humanism Marx gave it its true basis. If he goes in for economics he does so in order to show the unique place of man within economic structures. But the individual in whom Marx is interested is not the abstract person, the "beautiful soul," but the concrete person and its history. His struggle is a struggle on behalf of the person. He rejects Christianity but that is because Christianity is familiar only with man in the abstract and fails to come to grips with the real lives of human beings, with their sufferings, their struggles, their successes and failures.

We may accept that this is indeed Marx's perspective in approaching the human person. It remains true nonetheless that his humanism is closed to any transcendence. His is an atheistic humanism that leaves to man himself the task of bringing man to fulfillment. His ambition is to achieve control of nature and make human relations transparent. It is by succeeding in this twofold aim that man is reconciled to himself. Marx's socialism is not the collectivism that sacrifices the individual to the group. The substance of his socialism is the transparency of human relations and the full exercise of human freedom. But in Marx's view the individual can look only to this world for fulfillment. He will not find it anywhere except in society. If society were not corrupted by a defective economic system, the individual could achieve complete fulfillment and live in peace. This kind of "reduction" of the human person is heavy with consequences: it excludes all religious life, denies all transcendence, and closes itself off against any possible breakthrough of God.

At the same time, such a humanism excludes any question of ultimate meaning. Marxism is operative at the social level but is silent on such existential matters as love, life, suffering, failure, and death. The human person is the builder of his own future. He needs to put all his energies into building it. Such an outlook, limited as it is to the human horizon, will always judge religion to be useless if not dangerous. Marxism thinks of religion as directing part of man's energy to illusory ends and thus depriving this world of it. Socialism and religion can only be in conflict. But then it may be asked whether by closing off every spiritual avenue to man Marx does not imprison him into a new kind of alienation that is more tyrannical than that of the capitalist economy.

4

Sigmund Freud
Religion Is a Collective Neurosis

Freud always regarded himself as an atheist. "He went through his life from beginning to end as a natural atheist: that is to say, one who saw no reason for believing in the existence of any supernatural Being and who felt no emotional need for such a belief." Such is the judgment of Ernest Jones, Freud's well-known biographer.[1] Some people were astonished by this indifference to religion. Freud said he had no experience of an "oceanic" feeling which some described as a "sensation of 'eternity.'"[2] Consequently it is not to Freud's personal life that we must look for his views on religion, God, and immortality.

If we were to approach the question from that angle there would be little to say. The few events of Freud's childhood are insignificant in this regard. It happened indeed that his nurse visited churches with him, but the religious ceremonies struck him chiefly as a source of comic incidents to be related later on to the family. His parents were Jewish but observed only a few traditional practices and passed for "free thinkers." The atmosphere in Freud's family was "pretty much secularistic" and he experienced no special religious crisis. On the other hand, he had a good knowledge of the Bible.

It would be possible, of course, to undertake a detailed psychoanalytic reconstruction of his religious personality. This would be quite fair. The same kind of thinking has been done for his attitude to death, but not for his religious attitude. How might his personality be described in this regard? He was a Jew by birth, but did not undertake any practice and had no faith in God. Without ever denying his "Jewishness," he depicted himself to his friend, Pastor Pfister, as a "wicked pagan."[3]

But though Freud lacked any religious feeling, he seems to have fully respected the religion of his clients. In his psychoanalytic practice he showed tolerance; he was not temperamentally a fanatic, although he did give free rein to his waggish humor. When a convert felt utterly convinced of the existence of God and was sure that God would finally make the truth known to Freud as well, the latter answered mildly but with biting irony: "As for myself, God had not done so much for me. He had never allowed me to hear an inner voice; and if, in view of my age, he did not make haste, it would not be my fault if I remained to the end of my life what I now was—'an infidel Jew.' "[4]

This was in 1928. Freud's reply leaves no doubt about his convictions, as he formulates them without sparing his correspondent who was really far too pushy. But as far as we can tell Freud was not habitually aggressive in his dealings with believers nor did he work to undermine their faith. He claimed that psychoanalysis is a neutral tool in the service of human liberation, not a weapon of war against religious faith. In practice, he was even ready to acknowledge the therapeutic value of faith, as is clear from his correspondence with Pastor Pfister. He allows the latter to involve his patients with religion: religious sublimation can sometimes suppress an individual neurosis. But this is about all that can be expected from it.

Freud's efforts are devoted to the theoretical explanation of religion. He inquires into its origin and at this level he makes no concessions. His struggle with the idea of God is like Jacob's struggle with the angel, for it was an uninterrupted struggle that went on throughout his life.[5] Knowing Freud's personal attitude to religion, we may ask why he should have devoted so many pages to the phenomenon of religion, especially in the last years of his life. In fact, Freud was attracted by everything human and sought to know the secret hidden in it. His interest in the person of Moses in particular is probably to be explained, coming as it does during the period of Nazi persecution, by his curiosity about the origins of the Jews: What made this people what it is?[6]

I shall restrict myself here to Freud's theoretical judgment on religion, and shall follow his analysis step by step. I shall proceed from what is more evident to what is more hidden, from symptoms to underlying reality. Freud seems to regard one fact as certain from the outset: Unbelief is not surprising; it is faith that surprises him. Unbelief he regards as natural; it is faith, with its claim to a supernatural origin, that calls for explanation. Freud's own interior conviction on the subject was likewise acquired prior to any study of the matter. His way of looking at the world was that of the man of science who simply dismisses any appeal to the "mysterious . . . and mystically self-evident."[7] All of his energy is devoted to the scientific explanation of a phenomenon supposedly not accessible to science.

The Neurosis of the Human Race

When Freud inquires into the origin of religion, he sees in it nothing but a product of the imagination. Religious reality "is nothing but something psychological projected into the external world." But how is such a projection possible? The subject of this projection is a psyche that is ignorant of itself and transfers to a supra-sensible reality a content which in reality belongs to the psyche itself. Religion therefore hides no secret and is not impervious to analysis. As soon as one touches it, the idea of God disappears into the bogs of the human psyche. Despite further and more detailed study Freud's conclusion will remain unchanged: the gods "are the creation of psychic forces in man"; they all go under borrowed names. They are only supernumeraries; in the wings we always glimpse the figure of the father. Religious behavior is the socially established repetition of the son-father relationship.

The task Freud sets himself is to oust all the gods from the human psyche. What religion has constructed, science must dismantle. Science must "translate metaphysics into metapsychology," that is, it must translate theology into psychoanalytic terms. The task is an ambitious one, and in its formulation we recognize the language of Feuerbach (the reduction of theology to anthropology). It goes even further, however, when it aims at bringing to light the unconscious psychic foundation of religion. The dismantling of religion will therefore take the form of showing the psychic factors that played a part in its formation.

Analogy Between Neurosis and Religion

As soon as Freud turns to religion, he sees it as a form of behavior analogous to that of neurotics. The religious man resembles in many respects an obsessive. As early as 1907, in a short study entitled "Obsessive Acts and Religious Practices," he draws a parallel between the two phenomena and emphasizes the analogy. He does not say "religion = neurosis," but he does draw up a list of similarities and dissimilarities and try to build a bridge between the two terms. He writes:

> I am certainly not the first to be struck by the resemblance between what are called obsessive acts in neurotics and those religious observances by means of which the faithful give expression to their piety. The name "ceremonial," which has been given to certain of these obsessive acts, is evidence of this. The resemblance, however, seems to be somewhat more than superficial, so that an insight into the origin of neurotic ceremonial may embolden us to draw by analogy inferences about the psychological processes of religious life.[8]

Freud is struck by the quasi-religious behavior of certain patients as they perform the most ordinary everyday actions. They force themselves to follow regulations and rituals that have an obvious likeness to forms of religious activity. Their behavior is generally as rigid, lacking in spontaneity, and regulated in detail as a liturgy. For example, these people will not retire for the night unless they have placed their chair in a particular spot, methodically folded and arranged their clothing, and taken to their beds in accordance with a ritual that never changes and is psychologically codified and constraining. Others wash their hands a hundred times a day; they feel "compelled" to do it (a touching phobia); still others never feel morally clean (scrupulosity). Little Hans, who is analyzed in "Notes Upon a Case of Obsessional Neurosis" (1909), felt an insurmountable fear of horses and did everything in his power to avoid them. Compulsions, prohibitions, and fears of every kind poison the lives of these patients. If they change or omit anything they become deeply anxious. To the rest of us all this seems quite irrational, but to the psychoanalyst the behavior of the obsessed person is not without meaning. Its explanation is to be found in the unconscious: the obsessed person is trying to avoid or exorcise a danger that threatens him from within, a danger for which the horses, for example, are only a substitute.

Before naming this danger, we must develop the analogy between the two phenomena. In many respects the ceremonial which the neurotic observes is a stereotyped by-product of religion, its pathological reflection, "a tragi-comic travesty of a private religion."[9] But instead of handling it this way Freud reverses his direction and thinks of religion itself as a neurosis that is tolerated by society and even encouraged and promoted. After all, what is a religion but the observance of a strictly regulated ceremonial, a submission to prohibitions, the acceptance of codified rituals from which all whims and mistakes are excluded?

> It is easy to see wherein lies the resemblance between neurotic ceremonial and religious rites; it is in the fear of pangs of conscience after their omission, in the complete isolation of them from all other activities (the feeling that one must not be disturbed), and in the conscientiousness with which the details are carried out. But equally obvious are the differences, some of which are so startling that they make the comparison into a sacrilege.[10]

The only difference between the two types of behavior that really astonishes Freud is that religion is "universal" in character while a neurosis is "private." The similarities between the two phenomena lead Freud to hypothesize that they have a common origin, while the differences lead him to look for the root of neurosis in the individual psyche and for the root of religion in the collective psyche that was formed at the beginning of the existence of the race and passed on to all human beings.

At the end of this first approach to the phenomenon of religion Freud no longer has any doubt that the two are closely related not only at the level of symptoms but at the level of their cause as well. He has no hesitation therefore about transferring terminology and describing "obsessional neurosis . . . as a private religious system, and religion as a universal obsessional neurosis."[11] Each term may be substituted for the other without distorting the reality.

The Hypothesis of a Common Origin

The analogy between the two phenomena causes Freud to look for a common origin that would account for the identity of symptoms. The only way to get back to this common origin is through the psyche itself. What is it that we find at the root of human life? Urges which Freud calls instincts. These are essentially sexual in nature but can turn in different directions:

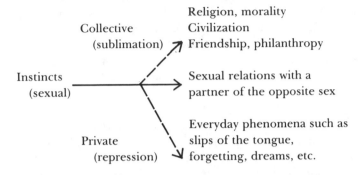

Religion, morality
Collective   Civilization
(sublimation)   Friendship, philanthropy

Instincts   Sexual relations with a
(sexual)   partner of the opposite sex

Everyday phenomena such as
Private   slips of the tongue,
(repression)   forgetting, dreams, etc.

Pathological phenomena,
among them neuroses and psychoses

When the instincts cannot find their normal fulfillment, they can do so indirectly. If some obstacle prevents the finding of the desired sexual partner, the instincts can either be sublimated in dedication to socially valuable and acceptable goals or be repressed and then reassert themselves indirectly in various forms of aberrant behavior. Both sublimation and repression are reactions to the oedipal conflict. These statements call for a brief explanation.

Let me begin with neurosis. As far as Freud is concerned, its secret is out: a neurosis is a sign of a conflict. Freud considers a neurosis to be a form of failure, a behavior developed by the ego in order to avoid a danger. The ego always finds itself in a precarious situation, since it must go its way while constantly avoiding two traps, one set by the id (a reservoir of instincts) and the other by the superego (the demands imposed by society). The ego is torn between the sexual instincts of the id which demand a maximum of immediate satisfaction, and the commands of the superego which represent the demands of reality and have all the force of law: the superego inhibits, prohibits, forbids. The ego has been compared to an honest bourgeois who is the unwitting victim of a confrontation between ugly ruffians (the instincts) and disagreeable policemen (the orders issued by the superego).

Caught in this way between contradictory demands, the ego

is constantly working out compromises. Neurosis is one kind of compromise, a pathological one which the ego develops to the benefit of the superego (the ego obeys its orders) and to the detriment of the instincts (which the ego desperately represses). Other compromises are possible, in particular the investment of psychic energy in certain forms of activity that are socially acceptable: art, literature, self-sacrifice, religion. In a neurosis the psychic energy of desire is used up in a way that is a simple loss. It is used up in a morbid struggle against the desire itself, without the ego ever reaching a satisfactory balance. In religion this psychic energy is usefully employed in dedication to a socially acceptable purpose. In this case the compromise can lead to a balance that is profitable to the ego.

This brief analysis suggests a key question, one indeed that is already suggested by the diagram drawn a few paragraphs back. What is it that causes psychic energy to be turned in the direction of sublimation, that is, investment in areas which the superego accepts as worthwhile, or, on the contrary, in the direction of repression, that is, its being pushed down into the unconscious, except to the extent that it emerges indirectly in deviant behaviors? This is a question that Freud does not answer. Nowhere, as far as I know, does he offer any proof of this bifurcation of psychic energy. What logic does the unconscious follow in this matter? Freud's explanations are not without their weaknesses and they evidently leave at least as many questions unanswered as answered.

The Oedipus Complex

But let us move in our examination of Freud's thought. The difference in the ways in which psychic energy is invested is not the result of a choice freely made. It is due rather to the pressure of forces that come into conflict and then manage to adapt to each other or to effect some eliminations or to reach a balance. Religion, like a neurosis, is the result of a compromise.

What is the conflictual situation that ends in the balance we find in the neurotic? Freud sees it as occurring in infancy; it is what he calls the oedipal stage. As everyone knows, at about the age of four or five, a child passes through a very violent crisis, the elements of which are an affective attachment to the mother and a hatred-inspired opposition to the father. At the moment when he awakens to the idea of love he turns quite naturally to the first available affective object, his mother, and claims this object as his exclusive property. The father then appears to him as a rival because the mother belongs to the father and the latter therefore becomes the target of a violent hostility. This hatred brings a real desire for the father's death: the father must be eliminated. But the father is a powerful rival who controls the child; the child must yield to him and submit to his will.

A normal development enables the child to emerge from this situation without having been excessively harmed. His desire will turn elsewhere, to an object other than the mother, an object not possessed by a third party. It is possible, however, for the child to remain imprisoned in the oedipal situation: he is unable to achieve a psychological detachment from the mother and he continues to resent the father's authority as dangerous to him. The father's repressive authority finally becomes a permanent part of the child's life in the introjected form of a harsh superego that traumatizes and paralyzes. It weighs so heavily on him that he can never give himself to pleasure and joy without feeling a sense of guilt. The ego is constantly on trial and never succeeds in freeing itself from this sense of guilt.

A neurotic is one who lives continually in this situation of conflict. He is in the unrelenting grip of a sense of guilt that is a source of anxiety and suggests to him the neurotic "ceremonial" which he will follow. His repressed desires are reborn over and over again, like the phoenix rising from its ashes. But the superego is keeping watch and immediately accuses the neurotic as soon as he makes any concession to these desires. The neurotic is an anxious person; his illness is one that affects his relationships. If we get to the root of his difficulty, we find that he is still a child dominated by his father. Whatever his age, a neurotic is a person with a distorted relation to his parents.

This explanation of neurosis may be open to challenge but it is the model Freud uses in order to explain the phenomenon of religion. At this point, however, a difficulty arises which compels him to broaden the hypothesis; it is a difficulty we have already seen. How does Freud's argument run? He argues that if the Oedipus complex is the source of the neuroses, should we not suspect that it is also to be found at the origin of religion? The hypothesis is an attractive one and Freud attempts to prove its validity. He has observed an analogy between neurosis and religion at the level of symptoms; he infers that there is also an analogy if not an identity of causes. He hesitates, however, to infer a simple identity. Why? Because of the universal character of religion.

The individual Oedipus complex seems to him to be too narrow a basis for explaining religion. It explains those "private" religions, the neuroses, but is inadequate to explain those "universal" neuroses, the religions of the human race. The universal character of the religions suggests to Freud the existence of a universal Oedipus complex that has left its mark on the human psyche. Is it possible to find in the childhood of the human race an event such as the one which the individual experiences in his early childhood at the time of the oedipal conflict, and which has traumatized the collective psyche of the race?

The Origin of Religion

Such an event did indeed take place at the beginning of human history. With the help of data provided by Darwin, Robertson Smith, and Atkinson, Freud attempts to reconstruct the psychological "fiction"[12] that gave birth to all the religions. What is it that we find at the beginning of the race's history? A murder. This murder created a feeling of guilt which human beings have never succeeded in sloughing off and which has led them to invent the religions as so many strategies for relieving themselves of it. Without going into great detail I shall sketch this explanation which appears especially in *Totem and Taboo* (published in 1913) and *Moses and Monotheism* (1939)

The Primal Murder

Up to this point Freud's journey back to the origins has seemed fairly coherent and logical, but he has still not moved beyond the limits of the individual psyche. There is indeed an identity of psychic structure in all individuals since the Oedipus complex has left its mark on all of them, but Freud refuses to argue from the individual psyche to the origin of religion. On the other hand, the fact of the analogy between religion and neurosis leads him to hypothesize, if not a single origin for the two phenomena, at least different origins that are identical in structure. That is, he believes that the Oedipus conflict is the source not only of neurosis but of religion. Since, however, the universal character of religion must be accounted for, he sets psychological observation aside and turns to ethnological data. He undertakes an historical investigation and tries to discover a collective Oedipus complex in the past history of the race.

He hypothesizes that something resembling the oedipal conflict occurred at the beginning of the human race. He then tries to shore up this hypothesis with facts so as to render it plausible. What do we know about the human race in its primitive state? According to Darwin, human beings originally lived in small hordes, each of which "stood under the rule of an older male, who governed by brute force."[13] The way of life was patriarchal: the father possessed all authority and kept a monopoly on pleasure. The sons possessed nothing and depended on the father's good will. As they grew up, the father drove them away so that he might have no rivals and might keep all the women for himself. (Such a state of affairs has, of course, been nowhere observed; the only primitive regimes which we know today are egalitarian.) The horde under the domination of a violent father was succeeded by the clan made up of brothers, "associations of men consisting of members with equal rights."[14]

A link is missing between the two ends of this change, that is, the authoritarian regime and the egalitarian regime. How did the one give way to the other? Here is where Freud slips in his personal hypothesis. Drawing on the works of Atkinson, he supposes that the sons, tired of having to submit to the father's authority and of being deprived of pleasure, formed a league against him and killed him. They "overpowered him, and together consumed the body."[15] This would be the origin of the totem meal which Robertson Smith had studied. The totem always represents the father; the totem meal is a feast celebrating the victory of the sons over the father: the sons celebrate their slaying of their father and through the common meal they appropriate his strength for themselves. Once the father had been slain, the sons had to organize their common life. To prevent any retrogression and keep violence at bay, they established rules for social life, especially the prohibitions of incest and murder. Thus did civilization begin.

If all these combinations of evidence are justified, the hypothesis of an Oedipus complex in which all human beings share is confirmed. The prohibitions of incest and murder enable us to infer the existence of such a complex. This twofold prohibition can be identified in the three situations which Freud wants to compare: the oedipal stage (repression of love for the mother and hatred for the father), neurosis (which is a fixation at the oedipal stage and a crystallization of this stage in the form of a complex), and primitive mankind (which found in this two-fold prohibition the only way of avoiding bloody confrontations and obtaining the circulation of women and the exchange of them among the members of the clan). The finding of the same elements in these varied situations suggests to Freud that the Oedipus complex is common to all three. The Oedipus complex which he has discovered in children serves him as the common bond in comparing the other two with the first.

Feeling of Guilt

However, the killing of the father was not pure gain for the sons. The murder made civilization possible but it also left a profound mark on human beings. The trauma inflicted left traces in the form of a feeling of guilt.

For Freud the feeling of guilt originates in the fact that the primal murder continues to weigh on the human conscience. The murder was the way of satisfying a desire, namely, the elimination of the father and the entrance into the promised land of pleasure. The father was eliminated; hatred triumphed. Henceforth desires could be freely expressed and satisfied without the father being there to disapprove. But in point of fact the expected sense of freedom did not prevail. Once the murder had been committed, filial love raised its voice in protest and the sons found themselves charged with murder. Guilt thus entered upon the scene. In this way the father took his revenge; he struck back at his sons by taking up residence in their consciences. In fact, "the dead now became stronger than the living had been."[16] The father's presence showed itself in the feeling of guilt which is an introjection of the slain father but as one transformed into an accuser. The eye in the tomb continues to accuse, and there is no way of evading its gaze.

It would be a mistake to treat these descriptions of Freud lightly, for they do have some foundation. Freud finds confirmation of them in certain clinical observations. Here again it is the guilt felt by some neurotics or by children that renders plausible the hypothesis of a primal and congenital guilt. We know, for example, that a child whose father has died at the time when the child is passing through the oedipal crisis feels a strong sense of guilt. After the death he often feels strongly that he is at fault; his unconscious is protesting and suggesting to him that his hatred may have been responsible for the father's death. The sense of guilt is an accusation leveled at the ego by the superego which blames it for not having repressed its hatred.

The result is that all the sons, who "hated the father . . . but . . . also loved and admired him,"[17] have "gotten" a feeling of guilt,[18] in the sense that one "gets" a cold. The strength of the feeling is due to the fact that it has absorbed the violence of the feeling of hatred which had initially been felt toward the father. There has been an inversion, a turning back upon the self of the hatred originally meant for the father. In Freud's view the superego therefore does not simply inherit the tyrannical authority of the father; it is also heir to the aggressivity which the child felt toward the father. Freud has little to say by way of explaining how this inversion of hatred and this transfer of its energy into the feeling of guilt take place.[19] The question is left unanswered by Freud.

The reader will undoubtedly ask: But how was it possible for the original sense of guilt, a psychological reality in the unconsciousness of the sons in the primitive horde, to be transferred to the later members of the race? How did the transmission and survival take place once the act was past that had given birth to the sense of guilt? Freud's answer is that the collective unconscious, which makes its appearance in this context, can be transmitted, but he does not explain the process to us. Once its existence in human beings is acknowledged it enables us to understand the birth of religions: religions are a way of counteracting the sense of guilt.

Birth of Religion

The psychological foundation of the religions now seems clear: they are in every case attempts to resolve an affective problem caused by the primal murder. The religions are attempts to exorcise the sense of guilt engendered by the killing and to manifest the repentance that act has inspired:

> The totem religion has issued from the sense of guilt of the sons as an attempt to palliate this feeling and to conciliate the injured father through subsequent obedience. All later

religions prove to be attempts to solve the same problem, varying only in accordance with the state of culture in which they are attempted and according to the paths which they take; they are all, however, reactions aiming at the same great event with which culture began and which ever since has not let mankind come to rest.[20]

The primal murder explains not only religion but the aggregate of social phenomena: religion, morality, civilization. In a striking summary Freud says:

> At first the brother clan has taken the place of the father horde and was guaranteed by the blood bond. Society is now based on complicity in the common crime, religion on the sense of guilt and the consequent remorse, while morality is based partly on the necessities of society and partly on the expiation which this sense of guilt demands.[21]

Freud believes that at this point he has reached an adequate understanding of the phenomenon of religion: all religions are attempts to resolve the same problem that was caused by the primal murder. Not all of the religions are equally successful. In Freud's judgment, the Christian religion has succeeded to a remarkable degree. It begins with an admission of guilt (original sin). It then strikes out along the only path that can lead to a real reconciliation with the father: the death of the son. Since the clan made up of sons is the guilty party, only the death of a son can effect a reconciliation. Through communion all the other members share in the act of atonement performed by one of their number. The sincerity of their repentance is shown, in the final analysis, by a radical renunciation of woman, because the latter had been the cause of the rebellion against the father.[22] Christianity thus completes the circle: the social revolution which led to an egalitarian regime is completed at the religious level by the coming of the religion of the son.

One may well debate the details of Freud's theory, since all of them are open to challenge. I shall be satisfied here to mention but one of the problems (it is one discussed by Paul Ricoeur) that are raised by Freud's argument; this one springs from the very logic of his explanation. Why were the attributes

of the primal father introjected in the form of the superego, thus
giving birth to morality, but also projected outside of the person
and transferred to a supra-terrestrial being, thus giving birth to
religion? This "bifurcation" of the father figure is left unexplained and mysterious.

In Freud's eyes there seems to be no doubt that God is
"nothing but" a transfigured human father. He is satisfied to repeat the theory of projection developed by Feuerbach, according to which religion is to be explained as the result simply of a
psychological projection into the external world:

> Psychoanalysis has made us aware of the intimate connec-
> tion between the father complex and belief in God, and has
> taught us that the personal God is psychologically nothing
> other than a magnified father; it shows us every day how
> young people can lose their religious faith as soon as the fa-
> ther's authority collapses. We thus recognize the root of re-
> ligious need as lying in the parental complex.[23]

An Illusion Without a Future

Freud believes that with the help of the Oedipus complex
he has gotten down to the archaic root of all religion. At the
heart of every religion, just as at the heart of every neurosis, is to
be found the "father-nucleus."[24] However weak his hypotheses
may be, Freud believes that he is now on firm ground, and he
will not budge from it. The forms that religion takes may vary,
but they all grow from the same psychological root. The questions to be asked now are: What role does religion play in the
lives of men and women? Is the role an irreplaceable one? What
future does religion have? Freud tackles these questions in his
book *The Future of an Illusion* (published in 1927).

In this book Freud seems to assign only a secondary place
to the involved explanations based on the hypothetical primal
patricide. He takes a much more commonplace approach to religion and looks at it primarily in terms of its function. He is thus
interested here much less in the deepest sources of the religious
outlook (these he regards as henceforth clear) than in what the
man in the street thinks of when he speaks of religion. What
does religion mean to the ordinary people? It means a belief in a

Providence which cares greatly for them and promises compensation in a future life for the privations endured on earth.

Need of Consolation

While Freud continues to refer to the hypothesis of a primal murder as the source of a religion that has for its purpose to help human beings gain control of the difficult relationship with the father, he nonetheless emphasizes above all the present function of religion which is to console people who suffer the harsh trials of life: "Life, as we find it, is too hard for us; it brings us too many pains, disappointments and impossible tasks."[25]

There is no need to dwell on the fact that life is too hard. People experience this harshness in three ways: they feel crushed by nature, doomed to death, and wounded by their relations with others. Religion tries to come to grips with this triple failure and thus to exorcise the harsh fate of human beings in this world: "The gods retain their threefold task: they must exorcise the terrors of nature, they must reconcile men to the cruelty of fate, particularly as it is shown in death, and they must compensate them for the sufferings and privations which a civilized life in common has imposed on them."[26]

What, then, is religion? It is an illusion, that is, a hope inspired by certain wishes. In order to make life bearable, frustrated desire invents the illusion we call religion: belief in a providential God and in immortality. Some people take refuge in sickness, others rely on drugs, still others seek amusement. Most people seek to neutralize the harshness of life by seeking consolation through the narcotic known as religion. By drawing its followers into a collective mania religion spares them the burden of an individual neurosis.

Today, of course, things are no longer quite so simple. In many areas science has replaced religion. Rarely do people any longer appeal to the gods to "exorcise the terrors of nature"; they trust rather in science and technology. It is more difficult for them to surrender the other two functions of religion, for they need the promise of immortality with which religion consoles them against death and assures them of compensation in the world to come for the frustrations endured in this life. The withdrawal of religion in favor of science does not yet mean the complete disappearance of religion. In the human person there always exists a child who needs to be comforted and who continues to call for the "sedative" that is religion.

The Ending of an Illusion?

Freud sometimes pays tribute to religion. It has rendered major services to the human race; for example, by giving its backing to morality it has contributed to the "taming of the social instincts." But it has also robbed human beings of the happiness that should have been theirs; it has not succeeded in "making the majority of mankind happy." It is therefore time to abandon religion and open ourselves instead to all the happiness available to us.[27]

Religion belongs to the infancy of the race. Just as infantile neuroses disappear in the course of growth, so too "it is to be supposed that a turning-away from religion is bound to occur with the fatal inevitability of a process of growth and that we find ourselves at this very juncture in the middle of that phase of development."[28] There should, of course, be no question of "trying to do away with religion by force and at a single blow."[29] Believers will perhaps continue for a long time yet to resist such a development, but the end is inevitable. The pace of the development will quicken once people stop being "conditioned" from their earliest years by religious education and begin to realize that religion represents a stage now past. Freud sees a kind of three-state law at work in this development:

> In the animistic stage man ascribes omnipotence to himself; in the religious he has ceded it to the gods, but without seriously giving it up, for he reserves to himself the right to control the gods by influencing them in some way or other in the interest of his wishes. In the scientific attitude towards life there is no longer any room for man's omnipotence; he has acknowledged his smallness and has submitted to death as to all other natural necessities in a spirit of resignation.[30]

Religion can only lock individuals into a stage that has been left behind and hinder their growth into the scientific age.

Human beings must be willing to become adults; the consolations of religion no longer deserve their trust. They must enter the scientific age and try to master the world, and for the rest, that is, whatever is forced upon them, they must be resigned. They must accept death, for one thing, as their inevitable lot. Is this too much to ask of them? No, for human beings have more resources than we think for confronting their destiny:

> Their scientific knowledge has taught them much since the days of the Deluge, and it will increase their power still further. And as for the great necessities of Fate, against which there is no help, they will learn to endure them with resignation. Of what use to them is the mirage of wide acres in the moon, whose harvest no one has yet seen? As honest smallholders on this earth they will know how to cultivate their plot in such a way that it supports them. By withdrawing their expectations from the other world and concentrating all their liberated energies into their life on earth, they will probably succeed in achieving a state of things in which life will become tolerable for everyone and civilization no longer oppressive to anyone. Then, with one of our fellow-unbelievers, they will be able to say without regret: *Den Himmel überlassen wir//Den Engeln und den Spatzen* ("We leave Heaven to the angels and the sparrows": Heine).[31]

The perspective adopted is austere and heroic. In Freud's judgment, no other attitude is worthy of human beings, and he himself adopted it without losing his sense of humor.[32] It is unlikely, however, that the majority of human beings will accept it: "It is painful to think that the great majority of mortals will never be able to rise above this [infantile] view of life [that religion offers them]."[33] Freud counts on such a development at least among the educated.[34] Science carries no promises in its pocket; it has only a task to set before us, "but an illusion it would be to suppose that what science cannot give us we can get elsewhere."[35] As Freud sees it, the religious illusion will increasingly lose its grip on the minds of men as time passes.

The Challenge to Freud

This kind of confidence in science has itself now become outdated. Freud's rosy optimism has been battered from every side. We cannot blame him, of course, for sharing the scientism of his time on this point; such optimism is quite understandable at a time when science was advancing in every area. The optimism has been shaken in our day because science has to admit its inability to introduce wisdom into our world.

More questionable is the cramped vision of the human person that Freud offers us. What is a human being? For Freud, it is a reservoir of instincts that constantly travel the same paths and with a wearisome monotony repeat the oedipal pattern. The Freudian unconscious is one-dimensional. Every human being resembles his patients in that its sufferings all come from unconscious sexual frustration. But do human beings not have other needs that are even deeper and more traumatizing, needs that come to the surface when men and women are faced with their own emptiness? Such is the claim of Viktor Frankl, a psychoanalyst who challenges the Freudian outlook as narrow and turns our attention to other horizons.

Frankl finds in the unconscious a dimension Freud had overlooked, a dimension in which it is the will to meaning and not the pleasure principle that is dominant. He calls this dimension "the spiritual unconscious."[36] Through his dealings with patients as well as in his own experience as a prisoner, Frankl gradually became convinced that human beings suffer not only from sexual frustrations or from inferiority complexes (Adler) but also from a lack of meaning which only the acceptance of God, who is "supra-meaning," can provide. The therapist therefore cannot be uninterested in the spiritual. Freudian psychoanalysis decrees that human beings can have within them only repressed instincts, but the decree is an arbitrary one that blinds the Freudian analyst to the fact that human beings also carry within them a repressed spiritual dimension. Frankl has developed a "logotherapy," which amounts essentially to a way of reorienting people's eyes and minds toward the spiritual. Logotherapy understands people to be alienated by blockages or their rejection of the spiritual; it aims to help them become free beings who are capable once more of a conscious, deliberate attitude toward God.

Frankl is convinced that the unconscious points to God, and he therefore opens it up in this forgotten direction. He does not hesitate to speak of "the unconscious God." The words may shock us. Is Frankl announcing a new proof of God's existence? Has he found the name or uncovered the face of some forgotten corner of the unconscious? Not at all. He is making no such claims. God cannot be localized, even in the unconscious. Then what does he mean by talking of "the unconscious God"? He is saying that the human unconscious speaks not only of unsatisfied instincts but of God as well and that, whatever the appearances, human beings always have an unconscious relation to him.

Psychoanalysis is not competent to decide the question of whether or not God really exists. We may even hesitate to follow Frankl in his hypotheses about an unconscious God (the terminology is at least ambiguous). The important point is that, contrary to Freud, Frankl refuses the reductionist approach which reduces the higher to the lower and that instead he respects the specific character of the spiritual dimension. He is convinced that the idea of God is more coherent than Freudian psychoanalysis is willing to admit. If religion were indeed nothing but a collective neurosis, then it ought to be eliminated. But it may well be that individual neuroses are simply expressions of a rejection of religion! If this is the case, how can the neurosis be eliminated if the person does not consciously reintegrate the religious dimension into his life? Frankl is convinced: if God haunts the dreams of his patients, sometimes to the point of obsession, he sees this as evidence less of a persisting illusion than of the struggle of the patient with the God he is rejecting.

Religion is not a trivial affair to be dismissed with a wave of the hand or deliberate neglect. Freud regards it as an extremely resistant psychological reality, against which he mobilizes all the forces of psychoanalysis. He believes he has analyzed the mechanism that produces it, and brought to light the psychological realities that can be seen behind the figure of God. Has he succeeded? At times he emphasizes the limited character of his discovery: "I have never lived anywhere in the house except on the ground floor and in the basement." But he then immediately yields to reductionism (religion is "nothing but . . .") when he adds: "I found a place for religion in my lowly little house once I discovered the category of 'neurosis of the human race.' "[37] After an initial modesty, an unshakable conviction: religion is a product of the psyche, and psychoanalysis has laid bare its foundations. Freud will not try to find religion another and more suitable dwelling place.

But the basis for Freud's understanding of religion is a nar-

row one; in addition, it is arbitrary. He burdens himself with suspect hypotheses that all lead to the formation of a "scientific
myth" which is relatively coherent but excessively strips down
the reality of religion. As Ricoeur observes, Freud had other
choices open to him but was unable to take advantage of them.
Instead of falling back on the murder of the father as explanation of the origin of religion, he could, in the framework of his
own presuppositions, just as logically have chosen a fraternal
covenant or eros as the origin. He would then have validated a
different type of religion, one closer to the religion of love that
he could have found in the Bible. But once he made neurosis the
sole point of reference in explaining the religious phenomenon,
the choice of patricide was inevitable.[38]

His choice entails an image of God as stern and repressive,
an image incompatible with that of the Christian God. Freud's
God is connected primarily with moral taboos and has an ideological role to play in society. His function is to strengthen social
cohesiveness and, secondarily, to console human beings in this
affliction. The image is in fact rather incoherent since this God
both frustrates and consoles; he takes away and he gives. This
kind of God fits in with human needs: he is required in order to
discipline the savage in us and to console the child that lives in
all of us. If such a God is ambiguous, this is because human beings are themselves ambiguous. What attitude can they adopt
toward such a God except trickery and infantile behavior: trickery to manipulate him, and infantile behavior to coax him? Such
attitudes are still too often found, but there is nothing Christian
about them.

As a matter of fact, Freud did not grasp the meaning of the
Christian faith. The aim of the latter is not to keep people at an
infantile stage but to bring our capacity for love to an adult level. There is therefore no other way of escape from the Freudian
criticism of religion than through an intensified witness of love.
"The only thing that can escape Freud's critique is faith as the
kerygma of love: 'God so loved the world.' "[39] A faith thus understood does not keep human beings in fear and submissive-
ness, it does not shelter them from dangers; on the contrary, it
demands that they take risks out of love. The Freudian critique
has this value, that it purifies and stimulates us to be constantly
validating our images of God and our religious behavior.

Freud was impressed by the survival of religion and its hold on the minds of people. In his last work he concedes, almost nostalgically: "How we who have little belief envy those who are convinced of the existence of a Supreme Power."[40] But he immediately gets hold of himself: his own studies prevent him from subscribing to such beliefs, which he regards as outdated beyond recall.

5

Friedrich Nietzsche
One of Christianity's Fiercest
Enemies

"Some men are born after their deaths," Nietzsche once re-
marked. Did he feel that he himself had been born too soon? He
may well have been. In any event, he could not have have been a
better prophet of his own destiny. For some years now Nietzsche
has been much touted, and his success, so limited during his
lifetime, is now immense. His thought has proved to be aston-
ishingly modern. What he foresaw—the decline of Christianity—
and what he predicted—post-Christian man—have become realities before our eyes. The compelling relevance of his thinking is undoubtedly what has made Nietzsche a favorite of many
interpreters.

Strangely enough, the more portraits we have of the man,
the more distant and impenetrable we feel him to be. This is due
in part to the personality of the man, which he deliberately tries
to hide from us, and in part too to his style. He is constantly
shifting perspectives; he continually changes his vantage-point
without warning us, continually varies the lighting on the stage.
His constant movement confuses us.

Not the least of the paradoxes about this ardent and ever
inquiring man is that although he was university trained and
taught philology, his books are written in a rather unprofessorial
way. He pulls his thoughts piece by piece from the depths of his
being and translates them into striking aphorisms, but then orders them in a way that is not always coherent. I am saying that
Nietzsche is a complex writer: his attractions leap to the eye, but

he is difficult to read. His interpreters are far from agreement on the overall meaning of his work.[1]

His thinking is, however, located within a specific horizon, namely, the Judeo-Christian tradition. It is within this horizon that we must reread his work.[2] Whether Nietzsche is doing battle with the philosophers—his contemporaries but also Plato or Socrates—or sketching the future, he does so with reference to or in contrast to Christianity. Nietzsche emerged from a Christian background and was unable at any point in his life to break loose from it.

A Relative of Priests

Without trying to explain the whole of Nietzsche's work by his life, as some interpreters do, we cannot simply ignore it. It is one key to his writings.

Nietzsche was born in 1844, the son of a pastor who died when the boy was still very young (1849). Nietzsche went mad at the beginning of 1889 and died at the beginning of the new century (1900). His many works were written during a very short period, like the outburst of a volcano.

His Christian Origins

Nietzsche never denies his origins and even states with a certain pride that he is a relative of priests. At times he pays tribute to the uprightness of Christian souls.[3] In any case, he acknowledges that from his father he received all he has of privileges, "*not* including life, the great Yes to life."[4] The qualification is important, for it sums up the essential fault Nietzsche finds in Christianity, that it has only contempt for life. The ideal which Christianity preaches and which his father has passed on to him is the ascetic ideal, which makes an ideal of death, since asceticism is a "kind of suicide," a "slow destruction of the body."[5] This was his negative inheritance from his father. Nietzsche will not really hold this against him because he believes that his father and all other Christians are the unwitting victims of a fate laid on them by centuries of history.

The ideal set before him in the Lutheran school at Pforta, where he received his early education, was no less rigid. Nietzsche was supposed to become a pastor like his father. He seems to have adapted without any great repugnance to the quite monastic discipline that prevailed at Pforta. A serious student who devoted himself wholeheartedly to his books, he left behind him the reputation of a pious scholar. But in fact he was already asking himself questions and sensing that Christianity would experience inevitable upheavals once the mass of ordinary folk realized that everything was based on conjecture: God, immortality, and so on. Nietzsche continued his studies at Bonn (1864) and, although enrolled for theological studies, he was interested primarily in philology and philosophy. He became increasingly convinced that Christianity was nothing more than a collection of family traditions.

He quickly drew a practical conclusion from this conviction: when his entire family attended services in order to receive their Easter communion, he refused to go with them. His father was long since dead, of course. His mother, bewildered by his attitude, did not have the "spiritual depth" she would have needed if she was to respond to his attack. He did discuss the matter with his sister Elizabeth, but his mind was made up: he had to reject these traditions that offered a false security, and embark on his own difficult quest. He wrote to his sister: "Here the ways of men divide. If you want to achieve peace of mind and happiness, then have faith; if you want to be a disciple of truth, then search."[6] Through all the vicissitudes of later life—teaching at Basel, journeys, friendships, disappointed love, the asylum— Nietzsche was never to withdraw from this choice.

War on Christianity

Ricoeur ranks Nietzsche, along with Marx and Freud, among the "philosophers of suspicion" who have most deeply shaken the religious faith of their fellow human beings. Beyond a doubt, Nietzsche caused a "wind that brings the thaw" to blow on the old Christian world, as he himself puts it.[7] The image that perhaps captures him best is that of a "breaker" or "smasher," for we see him "surrounded by broken old tablets and new tablets half covered with writing," like Zarathustra, the most famous figure in his books and his own mouthpiece.[8] As one of those who "have . . . outgrown Christianity and are averse to it,"[9] Nietzsche becomes one of Christianity's fiercest enemies.

His work has two sides to it: one is critical, as he takes the stance of a strict adversary of Christianity; the other is positive, as he endeavors to paint a picture of a new type of human being, one that is the antithesis of the Christian.

The critical side of his work is the one that is most fully developed. After all, Christianity cannot be eradicated with a wave of the hand. One may indeed mock it, but Nietzsche thinks that "Voltairean bitterness" is in bad taste here.[10] No, Christianity must be approached with full seriousness. If you want to strike it a deadly blow, your blow must cut to the root. It is to this task of destruction that Nietzsche devotes himself. What is the root of Christianity? There is no point in delving into the "archives": Nietzsche has an extensive knowledge of history but little interest in it. If you want to learn what the root is, you must remain in the present, see how Christians live, examine the intentions that motivate them, and sound the unacknowledged depths of these intentions. Nietzsche sets himself to reconstruct the "genealogy of faith." A real work of excavation takes him down to the will or intention that opts for faith, and there he detects *ressentiment.* There you have what lurks in the depths of the Christian soul; this is what explains religious belief.

The thing that is characteristic of Christianity is an "ascetical ideal": that is, a rejection of life and a projection of the meaning of existence into another life which is better than the first. Christianity is a "Platonism for the people": it looks upon the world as a prison from which we must escape, and it promises salvation, through faith, in an invisible other world. Christianity has shifted the center of gravity from the human person to God and thus introduced a division within the person who is now torn between a forbidden present world and an illusory next life.

The "No" to life that is characteristic of Christianity is to be blamed not on Jesus, who proclaimed a "gay message," but on Paul, the embodiment par excellence of *ressentiment,* who became the preacher of this "sad science." Of course, Nietzsche's judgment on Jesus is not always so benevolent; at times he criticizes him. But it is to be noted that he blames this development of Christianity toward an ascetical ideal chiefly on the disciples of Christ and on the Church that perpetuates the ideal. He even accuses the Church of betraying the message of Jesus. The Church has chained up this message; it has smothered it: "The Church is precisely that against which Jesus preached—and against which he taught his disciples to fight."[11] "The Church as a whole is a stone set over the tomb of a Man-God; the Church endeavors by force to keep him from rising again."[12]

In these remarks Nietzsche is not uninfluenced by prejudices. He is a victim of his times when without turning a hair he accepts the dissociation of Jesus, the "noblest" of men, who said "Yes" to life, from Paul, a frustrated individual who avenged himself by condemning our present life and exchanging it for another. Nietzsche's attention is focused primarily on the kind of Christianity (admittedly, the kind most widespread among the people) that ranks rejection and contempt as its major virtues and lives under the fear of sin. But this kind of Christianity does not represent the whole of the Christian tradition. It is however the kind that Nietzsche sees and fights against:

> I regard Christianity as the most fatal seductive lie that has yet existed, as the great unholy lie. . . . I reject every compromise position with respect to it—I force a war against it. Petty people's morality as the measure of things: this is the most disgusting degeneration culture has yet exhibited. And this kind of ideal still hanging over mankind is "God"![13]

The Three Metamorphoses

Nietzsche's thought is full of contrasts and even contradictions, and therefore difficult to interpret. Interpreters have at times chosen to reduce it to the rank of a "simple confession," although one that would indeed be quite incoherent. But Nietzsche himself asks us to take his thought more seriously: "I am one thing, my writings are another matter."[14] His work often shows traces of personal struggles, but it also contains insightful analyses that are a challenge to us. In what follows I shall try first to describe the general movement of his thought and sketch its trajectory in order to assign his criticism of Christianity its proper place within the whole. It is within this trajectory too that the well-known words "God is dead" will reveal their exact meaning. Finally, I shall attempt to pick out the traits of the new man as conceived and set forth by Nietzsche.

Nietzsche has often been presented as a nihilist, but if we look more closely, we find that nihilism is only one stage in the development of this thought. His thinking follows a dialectical rhythm, with negations located between affirmations. Nietzsche says as much himself in the famous parable of the "three metamorphoses" with which he begins his best known book, *Thus Spoke Zarathustra:* "Of three metamorphoses of the spirit I tell you: how the spirit becomes a camel; and the camel, a lion; and the lion, finally, a child."[15] This rather sybilline text is partially explained by Nietzsche himself.[16] Let us try to penetrate its obscurity.

Reverence

These three metamorphoses symbolize both the stages in Nietzsche's own development and the stages in the development of the human race. The camel-spirit means that the spirit devotes all its courage to accepting, in an uncritical way, whatever exists and is set before it. It accepts the heaviest burdens: those of religion and morality or the modern substitutes for these. Its essential characteristic is the attitude of docility that puts up with and reverences. It assumes a ready-made destiny; it does not create, it submits. It is an affirmative spirit in the sense that it submits to Christian values without questioning them. Its distinctive characteristic is reverence, and it makes no distinctions among the objects of this reverence. This accounts for Nietzsche's definition of man: "Man is a reverent animal."[17]

If reverence is the characteristic of certain kinds of spirits, it can nonetheless take different forms and find expression in many different areas. In the past, the spirit reverenced, above all else, religious values and the moral values associated with them. But these are now in a decline. Modern people have rejected Christian values, but they have not therefore become free and learned to create their own values. They simply accept a new set of burdens: secularized moral values and especially scientific values, with the scientist replacing the priest. They cannot do without a heaven, and so they hardly rid themselves of the one religion imposed on them before they invent another which is equally repressive. The scientist with his myopic subjection to the real world has still not become himself. He remains a docile spirit, a "camel-spirit"; he now adores a new and different set of objects, but at bottom he continues to be a man of adoration and reverence.

In short, the objects to which reverence is given may vary,

but it is still the nature of the camel-spirit (that is, of the majority of men, accustomed as they are to showing respect) to be reverent. "The ass [in Nietzsche's bestiary the ass is part of the same symbolic field as the camel] carries at first the burden of Christian values; then, when God has died, it carries the burden of humanistic values, which are human, all too human; finally it carries the burden of reality when no values at all are left."[18] Such a spirit, compounded as it is of respect and submission, is incapable of saying No and committing itself to the rebellion which is a condition for rising above itself. It can only say Yes, but it is a sterile Yes, comparable to the desert into which the camel journeys, weighed down by its heaviest burden.

Such is the Yes of Jesus, a Yes both heroic and painful. It causes the spirit to cleave only to all the values that are doomed to failure. The entire passage on the camel-spirit becomes clear if we render it more explicit with the help of references to the Gospel.[19] Jesus endured insults without rebelling; he stood aside without seeking glory; finally, he remained indifferent to success, although he could have reached out and taken it. This is why even though Nietzsche regards Jesus as the being who "took wing to the highest heights," Jesus remains the least in the Nietzschean kingdom. The Christian's Yes is of the same kind. The old pope in *Thus Spoke Zarathustra*[20] is unable to convert again to a new future and clings tightly to the old values, happy that there is still something left to reverence in this world. The spirit needs absolutes; it is ready to absolutize anything whatsoever in order to escape the giddying thought of an empty heaven.

Rejection

How is one to break out of this attitude of docility? Through rebellion. Rebellion becomes possible once values lose their absolute character. Therefore Nietzsche gives this advice: "Gather around you everything deserving of reverence and then let these values fight it out among themselves."[21] When thus confronted with one another, absolutes can only deny one another and thus become relative; they can no longer remain absolutes. Then, as soon as there are no more absolutes in heaven or on earth, the spirit is free and its only absolute will be what it decides to regard as absolute.

At times Nietzsche seems to ascribe this rebellion against values to simple fatigue. That is, the spirit will inevitably tire of its docility and will refuse to carry its burden any longer. Then it changes into a lion and responds to the dragon's "Thou shalt" with an "I will" that upsets all the categorical imperatives.[22] What is the lion-spirit? "The free spirit. Independence. The period in the desert. . . . Critique of everything one reverences. Attempt to overturn all values."[23] "The ass brayed: Yea-Yuh,"[24] but its Yes is only acceptance, not creation. Once the spirit has won its freedom it is capable of self-affirmation. Every regime of freedom begins with a rejection of the age-old values to which one has hitherto bent the knee.

The spirit must advance through rebellion; rebellion is a necessary stage on the journey to autonomy. "Those who would create must always destroy." Zarathustra, the prophet of a new world, begins by breaking the old academic chairs, and he urges his disciples to the same iconoclastic gesture: "I bade them laugh at their great masters of virtue and saints and poets and world-redeemers."[25] The lion-spirit refuses to be led. It wants to be its own teacher and live in its own space. The lion responds with a categorical No to all those who claim to be masters over it. It is a wild beast that roars, destroys, and tears to pieces everything men deem worthy of respect.

But the lion-spirit is not constructive; it sits amid the ruins it has made. The metamorphosis is still not complete. Such are the European nihilists: they rebel against their Christian heritage and ravenously tear at it, but they are incapable of guiding themselves to the creation of new values. They are a pure and simple No, reactionaries against a universe which they reject but are unable to make over anew. They are inspired by *ressentiment.* Nietzsche refuses to be identified with them: "Who are we anyway? If we simply called ourselves, using an old expression, godless, or unbelievers, or perhaps immoralists, we do not believe that this would even come close to designating us: We are all three in such an advanced stage. . . ."[26]

Such descriptions are still negative. Nietzsche immediately adds that this way of understanding him is incomplete and that he has already moved beyond nihilism. He is not satisfied with knocking down the "black scarecrows" that perch on "the tree of life";[27] he has devoted himself to the creation of new values.

He has no sympathy for the anarchists who want to overturn everything and do not succeed in building themselves. "They say: All this is valueless, and they refuse to create values."[28]

Affirmation

In order to become creative, the lion in turn must undergo a metamorphosis and be changed into a child: "But say, my brothers, what can the child do that even the lion could not do? Why must the preying lion still become a child? The child is innocence and forgetting, a new beginning, a game, a self-propelled wheel, a first movement, a sacred 'Yes.' "[29]

The child represents the person who is open to a new world, who has torn himself away from the old values and has decided to live from his own riches. He is no longer tied to any pre-existing world. He can therefore be independent in writing his own tablets, define good and evil as he pleases, and grasp with open hands the promises life offers. Zarathustra urges us to become children, that is, to shake off the somnolence of dogmatism and become creative. "Rise above yourself!": such is the only valid imperative. The decision must be made in utter simplicity: "The great decision: am I capable of a positive, affirmative attitude? Neither God nor man over me any longer. The instinct of a creator who knows to what he wants to put his hand. Great responsibility and innocence."[30]

Evidently, the child of which Nietzsche speaks is not to be identified with the child of the Gospel. The two are even diametrically opposed. The child of the Gospel knows nothing of rebellion and had not gotten beyond the stage of reverence: he is drowsy and submissive. Zarathustra rejects him as a companion. He wants nothing to do with these docile little children who sit with joined hands and crossed arms, full of love, folly, and infantile reverence, but lack the taste for risks and adventure. At bottom all they want is an easy life, a smug life that asks no questions.

Among these Nietzsche puts all believers, all the "canters" who "sit together long evenings and say, 'Let us become as little children again and say "dear God!" ' "[31] They are unsuited to this world because they heed the "cowardly devil" who whispers to them: "There *is* a God," and they keep their eyes turned to heaven.[32] Such people are deserters.

The child of whom Nietzsche speaks is quite different. His life lies on the far side of rebellion; he is ready to begin a new life that is an unreserved Yes to the earth and to himself. He does not rush toward values that have lowered over human life since time immemorial, but springs toward his own future which he receives from no one but himself. The child symbolizes the person who is completely self-created.

Having criticized the ascetical ideal of Christianity, Nietzsche replaces it with a different and opposed ideal, which is barely sketched out but the essential lines of which we can guess at, since they are antithetical to those of the old ideal. In defining this new ideal Nietzsche forges new concepts such as the overman, the will to power, and the eternal return. His interpreters have often misused and betrayed these new concepts because they try to reduce them to what they already know. What in fact is their content? It is not easy to pinpoint it, since the post-Christian man whom they define is still too much mixed up with the Christian man who is disappearing. Since the child is not a prisoner of a Yes said to God nor fixed in immobility or rejection but is free from all ties, he stands before an unforeseeable future and is ready to bring the "overman" into being. The "overman" is not a new model for humans; he is the human being that is self-created without a model and is condemned to innovate.

God Is Dead

Why does Nietzsche appoint himself a judge of Christianity and condemn it so violently? Is it simply because he suffered so much from it? Is it because of humanistic principles, in order to set free a race he regards as too much enslaved to religion? Is it a concern for truth, now that he has seen how radically in error Christianity is? These various motives may be mixed in together. At times Nietzsche gives the impression of being irritated at being called on to justify his rebellion. If he rejects Christianity, that is a matter of taste, he says: "What is now decisive against Christianity is our taste, no longer our reasons."[33] On the other hand, he spares no effort in gathering and fiddling with his arguments against Christianity. His rebellion against Christianity is not simply a matter of mood or taste; the truth is at issue.

The Death Certificate

Nietzsche records an undeniable fact: in our ancient Europe, so steeped in Christian civilization, God is already dead. Why? Because it is the lot of gods to die, and the Christian God is no exception. Nietzsche lists the signs of this death which not everyone has as yet realized. It will take time for the corpse of God to decompose completely in our Western civilization which had kept him alive for so long. Let us look again at the well-known passage in which Nietzsche, through the mouth of a madman, tells us the news of God's death:

> Have you not heard of that madman who lit a lantern in the bright morning hours, ran to the market place, and cried incessantly: "I seek God! I seek God!"—as many of those who did not believe in God were standing around just then, he provoked much laughter. Has he got lost? asked one. Did he lose his way like a child? asked another. Or is he hiding? Is he afraid of us? Has he gone on a voyage? emigrated?— Thus they yelled and laughed.
>
> The madman jumped into their midst and pierced them with his eyes. "Whither is God?" he cried; "I will tell you. *We have killed him*—you and I. All of us are his murderers. . . . God is dead. God remains dead. . . ."
>
> . . . "I have come too early," he said then; "my time is not yet. This tremendous event is still on its way, still wandering; it has not yet reached the ears of men. . . ."
>
> It has been related further that on the same day the madman forced his way into several churches and there struck up his *requiem aeternam Deo*. . . .[34]

Who is responsible for this murder? Sometimes Nietzsche says that God died of "old age," or that people got tired of putting up with him and in their weariness abandoned him. Here he offers a sociological explanation: the death of God was not the work of an isolated individual but of all human beings ("We have killed him—you and I. All of us are his murderers"). It was, then, a "collective murder," and those primarily responsible were not the atheists but Christians themselves. Without going into all the reasons Nietzsche gives for such a statement, we may say with P. Valadier that "it was the Christian tradition that pro-

duced atheism as its fruit; it led to the murder of God in the consciences of men because it presented them with an unbelievable
God."[35] Why is it that this responsibility lies primarily at the
door of Christians? Because they have not been able to present
God as a God of love but only as a repressive God who puts human beings in a moral vise. Those who formerly stood accused
before God have turned into his accusers.

The death of God is an event of key importance, but people
have not yet grasped its consequences. The event is far too recent and "too great" for its meaning to be grasped right off;
even Nietzsche, a "born guesser of riddles,"[36] does not feel capable of measuring its implications. But, unlike his nihilistic and
unconcerned contemporaries, he senses that the setting adrift of
a religion means also the setting adrift of an entire civilization
and that it poses the task of inventing post-Christian man. For
the moment, no one seems as yet to have grasped the urgency of
this task: neither believers, who cling to their old faith, nor
atheists, who do not fall into a panic but simply laugh at the
madman's confusion. The latter will have to accept the consequences of their action and pay the price for their nihilism.

For the moment let us stay with the statement of fact. Nietzsche speaks of God's death as an event that is still on its way and
not yet perceived by all. But he goes on to say that already "the
belief in the Christian God has become unbelievable" and that
the event of God's death "is already beginning to cast its first
shadows over Europe."[37] He is therefore not simply voicing a
personal opinion about the death of God. Rather he uses the
formula as an interpretation of "the fate of twenty centuries of
Western history."[38] In Europe the death of God has introduced
an age of darkness, nothingness, nihilism. Having lost their
Christian reference points, Westerners are no longer able to ori-
ent themselves. With the disappearance of the supra-sensible
world most people feel themselves all at sea, condemned to
wander through an infinity of nothingness, like that old man
who had devoted himself to his God until the latter's last hour
and now, finding himself "retired," is completely lost.[39]

Such is the shock that has resulted from God's death and
shaken the foundation of Europe. Few can endure it and be
ready to undertake a new manner of life. Nietzsche is therefore
obliged to grant that "Christianity . . . is still needed by most
people in old Europe even today."[40] Only the free spirit feels a

great thankfulness because at last he is in a position to set out on his own adventure.

This death of God, which is a verifiable fact of our civilization, raises two questions for Nietzsche. The first has to do with the very nature of God: If death thus attacks even the gods, is not the reason that they are human and share the fate of all things human? Like human beings, the gods cannot escape death. The second question has to do with the meaning of life. Since God is dead, there is henceforth no one up in heaven to dictate this meaning. The meaning is therefore not to be imported from outside us; it must be invented. Let us now turn to these two questions.

The Birth of the Gods

How was it possible for the idea of God and religion to sprout in the human mind and then take possession of all human beings? Nietzsche offers some particulars in regard to this question. He explains the origin of the gods by taking advantage of a psychological arsenal of well polished weapons. He then has recourse to sociology for an understanding of how religion spread among the masses.

The gods did not descend from heaven in full panoply; they originated in the minds of human beings and drew their own substance from them. Nietzsche sketches their "genealogy." He shows us the gods owing their existence "to a state of human intellectuality which was as yet too young and immature."[41] Men were bewildered by the forces surging up in nature or in themselves and looked for an explanation somewhere outside of nature and of man. Instead of assigning natural causes to the phenomena they experienced they attributed them to the arbitrary free choice of a higher power:

> *On the origin of religion.* In the same way as today the uneducated man believes that anger is the cause of his being angry, spirit the cause of his thinking, soul the cause of his feeling—in short, just as there is still thoughtlessly posited a mass of psychological entities that are supposed to be causes—so, at a yet more naive stage, man explained precisely the same phenomena with the aid of psychological personal entities. Those conditions that seemed to him

strange, thrilling, overwhelming, he interpreted as obsession and enchantment by the power of a person. . . . A condition is made concrete in a person, and when it overtakes
us is thought to be effected by that person. In other words:
In the psychological concept of God, a condition, in order
to appear as effect, is personified as cause. . . .
       . . . The naive *homo religiosus* divides himself into several
persons. Religion is a case of *"altération de la personnalité."*[42]

   The explanation given here is not far removed from Feuerbach's: projection outside the self of a psychological reality—
personification of this projected reality—understanding of the
self as dependent on the personified reality.
   According to this explanation, religion is a psychological
mistake or, more accurately, an illusion due to a psychological
confusion of cause and effect. The resultant religious behavior is
that of a naive person who is hoaxed by his own imagination.
Being unable to master the forces that control him, he establishes with them a set of magical relations that are modeled on relations between persons, and then deals with them as he would
with anyone else. "By imploring and praying, by submission, by
the obligation of regular taxes and gifts, by flattering glorifica-
tions, it is also possible to exercise an influence upon the forces
of nature, inasmuch as one gains the affections; love binds and is
bound."[43]
   The process by which the gods are created is the work of an
uncontrolled imagination and is pathological in character, a
form of frenzy. *Homo religiosus* is a sick person who invents his
own personal explanation of the world. He constructs a hypothesis which then lays such violent hold on his mind that he no
longer dares believe he is its creator. The happiness he feels is
so great that he attributes it to a cause outside himself, namely,
God. In other words, he ends up taking an invention of his own
mind as a revelation of God. He projects outside himself that
which comes from within him, by dividing his own personality in
two, as it were. Religion springs from a division within the human person.

   Religion is the product of a doubt concerning the unity of
the person, an *altération* of the personality: insofar as every-

thing great and strong in man has been conceived as super-human and external, man has belittled himself—he has separated the two sides of himself, one very paltry and weak, the other very strong and astonishing, into two spheres, and called the former "man," the latter "God". . . .

Religion has debased the concept "man"; its ultimate consequence is that everything good, great, true is superhuman and bestowed only through an act of grace.[44]

If the human person unconsciously plays this game of duplication, the reason is that it brings personal advantage. First, inasmuch as the person interprets something coming from himself as a revelation from on high, he secures his belief against doubt. Second, since he is compelled to face a life without joy, a life in which misfortune lies in wait at every corner, he provides himself with a means of escape; he finds consolation amid the harshness of life by living in hope of a life to come.

Religion thus has a psychological basis. On the other hand, it cannot be totally understood on so narrow a foundation. In order to account for the almost universal presence of religion, Nietzsche has recourse to sociology: every religion, to the extent that it is a form of mass behavior, needs a founder who develops its logic and forces this upon others. The founder really does not invent anything; he simply brings a category of people to an awareness of what they have in common. He is "a match versus a ton of powder."[45] His function is to give meaning to a style of life already in existence.

Jesus (or Paul), for example, found how small people lived in the Roman province—a modest, virtuous, pinched life. He offered an exegesis, he read the highest meaning and value into it—and with this also the courage to despise every other way of life, the quiet Herrnhut fanaticism, the secret, subterranean self-confidence that grows and grows and finally is ready "to overcome the world" (that is, Rome and the upper classes throughout the Empire). . . . To become the founder of a religion one must be psychologically infallible in one's knowledge of a certain average type of souls who have not yet *recognized* that they belong together. It is he that brings them together. The founding of a religion therefore always becomes a long festival of recognition.[46]

The founder of a religion is thus a man who by the trust and fanaticism he inspires is able to bring together people of a certain type whom he has chosen as his own. From this point of view, religions differ according to the category of people to which the founder addresses himself. A founder is able to lay hold of latent aspirations and give a religion its style. Nietzsche distinguishes essentially two kinds of religion: religions focused on "No," an example being Christianity, which directs its attention to negative values, and religions focused on "Yes," an example being the religion of the ancient Greeks, which divinized the animal side of human nature, and vitality, and youth, or, in a word, the positive values. The first type of religion emphasizes what is most base in man; the second type emphasizes what is most noble. Baseness and nobility are here measured, of course, by Nietzschean standards. But whatever the values accentuated in either type, the sociological process is always the same; we are dealing essentially with a process of consciousness-raising.

At Last, Man Is Free

The gods are born and die as human beings do. They sometimes have a strong hold on life by reason of the cultural importance they have acquired in a given civilization, but in every case their claim to immortality is given the lie sooner or later. The fortunes of Christianity are evidence of this truth. We have just seen how God came into existence. But why did he die at last? There are doubtless historical reasons, but above all there is the indifference of human beings who have grown weary of God. They cannot go on living with the eye of God always on them. From this point of view, God *had* to die in order that human beings might live. They had to rid themselves of all the prohibitions he imposed on them and the demands he made of them, so that at least they could live in freedom.

But he *had* to die: he saw with eyes that saw everything; he saw man's depths and ultimate grounds, all his concealed disgrace and ugliness. . . . This most curious, overobtrusive,

overpitying one had to die. He always saw me: on such a
witness I wanted to have revenge or not live myself.[47]

Such is the dilemma: either to submit, obey, and abdicate all
self-will, or to rebel, act freely, and assert oneself. Even little
girls understand this: when their mothers tell them that God
sees everything, they give a very relevant answer: that's indecent![48]

Now the death of God shows its true meaning: it is the condition for human freedom. As long as human beings live under
the eye of God, they cannot be free and enjoy life. Now that he is
dead, "Nothing is true, all is permitted."[49] They have nothing
more to fear and can give free rein to even their most dangerous desires: "At long last the horizon appears free to us again,
even if it should not be bright; at long last our ships may venture
out again, venture out to face any danger; all the daring of the
lover of knowledge is permitted again; the sea, *our* sea, lies open
again; perhaps there has never yet been such an 'open sea.' "[50]

Such is the meaning of the denial of God: a casting off of all
moorings and a setting out for a vast conquest. It is not enough
simply to break with the past. Nihilism by itself is a sign of weakness, the mark of a spirit not yet free, not yet able to create its
own values.

In the final analysis, the murder of God is an ambiguous action. It is possible that it may leave people in a destructive attitude of negation and reaction. As far as Nietzsche is concerned,
it should mean the end of metaphysical dualism and moral mani-
chaeism. No longer must we receive commands from outside
ourselves; we are confronted with a future which it is up to us to
fashion and which indeed we must fashion if we are not to per-
ish. "As soon as human beings no longer believe in God and in a
destiny in another life, they become responsible for everything
that they experience, for everything which, born as they are
amid pain, they are bound to suffer from life."[51] "Once God no
longer exists, solitude becomes unbearable; the overman must
set about his task."[52] "If we do not find greatness in God we do
not find it anywhere; we must either deny that it exists or create
it ourselves."[53]

Unlike the European nihilists who were content to live amid
the ruins, Nietzsche chose to create new values. He refused to
canonize the free and easy life. We must pay for the loss of God

with a constant victory over ourselves. " 'Dead are all gods: now we want the overman to live'—on that great noon, let this be our last will."[54]

Beyond the Death of God

What becomes of human beings who have rid themselves of the idea of God? Whatever they make of themselves. Nietzsche did not shrink from facing this question, but, taking "a position beyond good and evil,"[55] he attempted to formulate an ideal which he can oppose to the Christian ascetical ideal. No longer is there any prefabricated ideal which a person need only contemplate, copy, and carry out as best he is able. All that is left now is to grope one's way in a search for which there are no norms. The Christian ideal maps out the road in advance, but the Nietzschean ideal simply sends a man on his way without giving any directions. Each individual must determine his direction as he goes. "I am no seeker. I want to create for myself a sun of my own."[56] And he urges everyone to be a creator from now on: "Just as we no longer need a moral code, neither do we need religion. 'I love God,' which is the only primitive form of religious feeling, has been transformed in me into a love of my ideal and has become creative: nothing left now but human beings who are gods."[57]

Most people have not yet gotten so far. They forget to be creative; they need "teachers of the purpose of existence."[58] But their natures are perverted. Nietzschean man is a man who takes risks; he rejects every imposed finality and invents for himself the goals of his life.

We Want the Overman To Live

Where are we to go? How are we to get there? In answer to these two questions Nietzsche developed two concepts that have often been misunderstood: overman and the will to power. Contrary to what some commentators have claimed, "overman" implies neither self-idolatry nor self-exaltation; the "will to power" does not mean dominating or crushing others. We must dwell briefly on the true meaning of these two concepts, since they define Nietzsche's new ideal.

"Overman" sums up the new objective for human beings. It is an objective that is neither defined in advance nor written into human nature itself. It has been interpreted as the exaltation of a kind of superior man whose superiority would give him a privileged position in relation to others; Nazi racism appealed to it for justification. But Nietzsche himself anticipated such a misuse of his ideas, for he refuses "to participate in the mendacious racial self-admiration and racial indecency that parades in Germany today as a sign of a German way of thinking."[59] In fact, the term "overman" designates a type of new man, "a type of supreme achievement, as opposed to 'modern' men, to 'good' men, to Christians and the other nihilists."[60] It is not an exaltation of individualism or an exaggerated emphasis on self, race, or class.

When Nietzsche says that overman must will "himself," he means that he must have his center of gravity within himself. But he must simultaneously will the whole of reality and all other people with a will that respects their distinctiveness. "The context in which the idea of overman takes on a precise meaning (the contexts of friendship, maternity, marriage, individual and collective birth) suggests that acceptance of the other comes by way of acceptance of the self, but also that the creative act which the concept connotes has for its aim the creation of human relations in which the other is affirmed, and not a technological mastery of the world."[61] In short, overman is the child that has reached its full flowering, not in isolation but with others.[62]

"Overman" has to do with goals; the "will to power" is the means of attaining them. The will to power must assert overman, without reference to God and with no support from anything but itself. This will cannot rely on a moral code or a guide to the "purpose of existence"; it is pure movement of the self toward the self. Therefore Nietzsche's plan is to "replace morality with the *will* to reach our goal, and therefore to use *means adequate* to this end,"[63] including lying. Each person must thus develop his will to power as fully as possible.

The concept of the "will to power" has, like the concept of "overman," often been slandered. It does not mean a will to gain power at the expense of others (a reactive attitude) or to dominate others either biologically or politically. It excludes both violence and tyranny; the latter are rather what Nietzsche calls "the demon of power" or the "fanatical desire for power." The will to power is rather a certain quality of willing; it is "the existential depth inherent in the act of transcending oneself."[64]

"Will to power" does not mean "to will power"; it means rather that "whatever one wills, one must will it to the nth degree,"[65] a degree which it does not attain through barbarism but only through culture. It calls not for the unshackling of instinct but for self-mastery.

Masters or Slaves

Having reached this point, we must take the decisive step and ask about the origin of these two opposed types of human being. Over against the Christian, who is the victim of his God, Nietzsche sets overman, who invents himself and experiences all of his potentialities to the utmost. The former is chained to a pre-established ideal; the latter is open to a future that is not sealed off by values, for Nietzschean man invents his own values. He is no longer a "projection" toward an afterlife, but a "project," that is, transcendence in immanence.[66] The Christian, obsessed as he is with salvation, is driven by a will to truth at any cost and thus has his fixed point of reference in what already is; Nietzschean man is dynamized by his own will and is committed to a process of endless transcendence. The will to power is essentially a Yes to whatever is new. The difference between Christian man and Nietzschean man has to do with the quality of their being.

Nietzsche undertakes a psychoanalysis of religious man. The method he uses in tackling the phenomenon of religion is both retrogressive and genetic: retrogressive in the sense that it brings to light what is hidden under what is manifested, and this "hidden" reality is *ressentiment;* genetic in the sense that it shows us how Christian existence emerged from that hidden source. How, then, does Christianity emerge from the believing soul—psychologically, that is, rather than historically?

In order to answer this question Nietzsche looks around and sees two categories of human beings: masters and slaves. He is not speaking of two social classes but of two attitudes toward life. Masters are noble natures. They enjoy a pre-eminence over others that comes to them not from physical strength but from strength of soul. They are the true creators, who derive from their own inner depths their intensity of existence and the values they promote. Their Yes to life is not a form of reverence. It is rather like that of the child: an affirmation of a life that gushes up from the superabundant power and generosity of its nature.

Slaves are base souls: they are incapable of acting on their own and asserting themselves but can only "re-act" to their masters. They are "reactive," "spiteful" characters, individuals governed by *ressentiment,* more interested in taking from others than in affirming themselves. They long for power but succeed in getting it only by exalting their non-value as a value. Now at last they are in a position to threaten the very existence of the masters. Driven by the spirit of revenge upon the masters who are better than they, they claim equality. "The rise of Christianity is nothing more than the typical socialist doctrine," because it seeks to impose the same values on all and thus to humble the masters.[67]

Religion and morality have their origin in slave natures, that is, in the reactive type of person:

> In Christianity, three elements must be distinguished: (a) the oppressed of all kinds, (b) the mediocre of all kinds, (c) the discontented and sick of all kinds. With the first element Christianity fights against the political nobility and the ideal; with the second element, against the exceptional and privileged (spiritually, physically—) of all kinds; with the third element, against the natural instinct of the healthy and happy.[68]

The distinction between the two types could not be clearer. But, given that the distinction exists, what is to be the criterion of value? How are we to evaluate the actions of individuals? In Nietzsche the criterion for judging value is shifted: its point of reference is no longer a scale of values existing outside the person but the quality of the will that expresses and asserts itself. Every time a person appeals to certain values, we must ask: Who is it that speaks here? "Who is it that needs such values in order to live?"[69] The thing that will determine the value of a system or an action is the will that asserts itself therein: it is the will of a slave, a "reactive" individual, or that of a master, an "active" individual? Is it a will that has been taken in tow by the ascetical ideal, or a will that asserts itself by opening itself fully to the world? The former produces "illusory ideals," the other, noble values.[70]

It is rather easy to discern the rule that functions in the Christian ideal (a written rule, set down in the tables of the law); it is not a simple matter, on the other hand, to discern the rule that serves as point of reference in the Nietzschean ideal. Is it the will to power that acknowledges no norm, the fulfillment of the self by the self? But by what standard is it possible to admit or reject the actions of such a will? The ultimate criterion seems to be of an esthetic kind. The will to power is the will of an artist who makes his decisions in terms not of morality but of the beauty of the action: "Once we deny absolute truth . . . we must take our stand on esthetic judgments. . . . The reduction of morality to esthetics!!!"[71]

Nietzsche thus substitutes for a moral criterion an aesthetic criterion that perhaps finds its most adequate expression in the idea of eternal return. The child is a "self-propelled wheel," that is, it finds in itself both the source and the completion of its action. It must therefore evaluate its own action, and the only rule it can apply is a kind of "parody of the Kantian rule" that might be expressed thus: "Whatever you will, will it in such a way that you will the eternal return."[72] The eternal return is not the expression of a will to repetition, a desire for "the same old story." History is irreversible and goes its way without repeating itself. "Eternal return" has a spiritual meaning: it calls attention to the fact (which Sartre will use extensively) that reality is not fixed and that the will is not the prisoner of its own actions but contains limitless reserves and possibilities for the future. What the past may have been, the will can always return to it and move beyond it by giving it a new meaning.

The will thus has no other rule for its action than the eternal return. It is in no sense condemned to repeat itself; on the contrary, it is urged to keep transcending itself. The eternal return is an invitation to transcend the human all-too-human and make the overman its goal. The rule provided by the eternal return is a rule for perfection.

Conclusion

Nietzsche is all nuances. However, his attitude to Christianity is never neutral; it is often violent but never coarse. With rare perceptiveness he uncovers its influence everywhere. He sets himself to be an adversary of Christianity: "One should never cease from combating just this in Christianity: its will to break precisely the strongest and noblest souls."[73] For the Christian who is able to understand him, Nietzsche represents above all a challenge to faith. He is accurate in his criticism of the ascetical ideal that has been preached to excess by a Christianity exclusively preoccupied with morality and obsessed by evil. Over against this ascetical ideal which rejects the world and takes refuge in pre-established certainties Nietzsche sets another lifestyle, one open to life itself and the risks it involves.

When Nietzsche tries to show us how Christianity originated he does so in order to free us from its lies. All knowledge is liberating. Here Nietzsche shares the purposes of Freud and Marx. Freud dissolves religion by reducing it to its basis in neurosis, while Marx tries to explain it in terms of its economic basis and the social conditions this engenders. Nietzsche assigns religion to a certain quality of soul and thus undertakes the dissolution of Christianity in his own way, that is, in terms of its human basis. His courageous and clear-sighted diagnosis often strikes home and forces us to put some radical questions to ourselves. As one reads Nietzsche, one becomes convinced that he is far from outdated. He is perhaps the most contemporary of the critics of Christianity, the one who still makes the strongest impact on us.

On the other hand, can it really be maintained that the death of God is an accomplished fact which time will only confirm? Nietzsche himself was surprised to see Christianity still having an attraction for people: "When we hear the ancient bells growling on a Sunday morning we ask ourselves: Is it really possible! this, for a Jew crucified two thousand years ago . . . ?"[74] Is not this a sign that the message of Christ continues to be full of meaning for many of our contemporaries, despite all that has been said against it?

Of all the questions which a reading of Nietzsche raises I shall focus on two as I end this dialogue with him.

The first has to do with *Nietzschean man.* We spoke earlier of overman, and we know how ambiguous the term can be. Just how is this new type of human being to be described? Nietzsche told us that he engenders himself in a process of self-transcendence. But it is clear that this individual surpasses himself only in the direction of himself. He is condemned to be a *wanderer:* "*The* way—that does not exist,"[75] says Nietzsche in a chapter en-

titled "On the Spirit of Gravity". There is no way, but neither is
there any place on which to take a permanent stand. Overman is
also condemned to *madness,* since there is no meaning, or at least
no meaning determined in advance. Nietzschean man experiences *emptiness:* his ontological ground is nothingness. He is
urged to embark on a unique, personal adventure; for this he
needs courage. And yet Nietzschean man is not a pessimist: he is
an artist and plays the world's magical game.

The second question has to do with *Christian man.* Nietzsche
paints a negative picture of him, accusing him of being a despis-
er of life.[76] He confronts Christian man with an alternative: "Do
away either with all your forms of reverence or with yourself."
Nietzsche does away with the reverence practiced by Christians
and rejects the suicide of asceticism. Sometimes he looks on his
entire enterprise as a purification: "Utter indifference to dogmas, cults, priests, church, theology is Christian."[77] It would be
a paradox indeed to claim that his work is a defense of authentic
Christianity, but at least it can be called a harsh critique of those
travesties which Christians themselves must reject.

In the light of Nietzsche's criticism is it still possible to be a
Christian? Is Christianity not being irresistibly forced to enter
into the post-metaphysical age? What does such a new direction
mean? It implies at least that Christianity must overcome dualism and accept full responsibility for the world.

Nietzsche asks: What would be left to create if there were
gods? Christians must show by their rigorous thinking and the
active use of their freedom that the God of Jesus not only does
not suppress freedom but inspires and promotes it. Nietzsche
asks: "What is there left to create?" Christians must answer:
"Everything!"

6

Jean-Paul Sartre
A Cruel and Long-Range Affair

Jean-Paul Sartre's ideas were all the rage after the Second World War. They struck a chord in the soul of the period, marked as this was by a sense of existential emptiness. In a more or less watered-down form they made their way out into a broad public. Sartre's ability to get into the minds of his contemporaries was due not so much to the actual thoughts expressed as to the means he chose for conveying these thoughts: short stories, novels, plays. In fact, for the uninitiated reader his strictly philosophical books resemble cities that are off limits. Even the specialist experiences a kind of mental shudder as he makes his way into these vast and forbidding edifices. And yet he senses that here he will find the key to the literary works. If Sartre had limited himself to the philosophical treatises he would probably never have emerged from the precincts reserved to the specialists. It was his literary genius that enabled him to give a human face to ideas that are often quite abstract. This is the source of his appeal.

Unlike Nietzsche, who was obsessed with the idea of God, Sartre does not give God a central place in his work. In fact, he tackles the subjects in only a few works and in a marginal way.[1] His tone is also lighter than Nietzsche's, less tragic, less tense. It is all the more surprising therefore to find him saying: "Atheism is a cruel and long-range affair: I think I've carried it through" (*The Words,* p. 253). Does this mean that it was a difficult struggle for Sartre to rid himself of the idea of God and escape the grip of religion? But it does not seem that the removal was in fact a "cruel" process; the facts are rather different. From youth Sartre got rid of the idea of God in a painless way and quietly ceased all practice of religion. His atheism has never been of the militant kind.

The struggle which he "carried through" was not in fact a struggle against God, but a struggle in behalf of man. Whereas Nietzsche was a tragic victim of Christianity and could not speak of it without showing himself very aggressive toward it, Sartre never really entered into Christianity and he speaks of it with detachment. His struggle was the effort to think and live human life without God. Once God has been eliminated, human beings are condemned to freedom, and it is indeed a "cruel affair" to live this freedom to the full without reference to God and in complete responsibility for one's decisions.

A Missed Vocation

Sartre's arguments against the idea of God are often similar to those of Nietzsche. He does battle against God in the name of a particular idea of the human person. But before I explain his concept of God as this emerges from *Being and Nothingness,* there is a prior question that calls for our attention: How did Sartre himself become an atheist? The answer is to be found in his autobiography *The Words.* The pages in which he describes his religious development are as brilliant as they are detached.

A Prey to Saintliness

Like all children, Sartre was naturally religious. "I believed. In my nightshirt, kneeling on my bed, with my hands together, I said my prayers every day" (p. 101). This kind of fervor, which may seem exceptional nowadays, must have been taken for granted in a child living at the beginning of the century. It is joined to religious instruction that was the responsibility of generous souls who were never at a loss for good words. Sartre plays the game. He writes fine compositions, since he already has an unusual control of words. He understands the merits of religion and is quite ready to think of it as a necessity.

At this age religion satisfies a psychological need, for it serves as a guarantee. Sartre comes up against the fact of death and realizes the fraility of human existence. He understands that no one is spared; sooner or later death seizes everyone, with the sentence taking only seconds to apply. In the face of this experience of human fraility and contingency he feels what he will later on call "nausea": he felt "useless," "superfluous." This is the ground in which religion has its roots, and Sartre accepts religion because it gives life the justification it lacks:

> God would have managed things for me. I would have been a signed masterpiece. Assured of playing my part in the universal concert, I would have patiently waited for Him to reveal His purposes and my necessity. I reached out for religion, I longed for it, it was the remedy. Had it been denied me, I would have invented it myself (p. 97).

His afflicted heart did not have to invent religion; it only needed to accept it. Between the ages of five and seven he opened his heart wide to the religion that was offered to him. He carried within him two feelings which combined to make religion acceptable to him: sorrow of heart and confidence. As a trusting child, Sartre had no difficulty in accepting the religion that presented itself as filling the void in his sorrowing heart. In this religion he found his own justification and immediately felt at home, commissioned, chosen. He knew that he had a reason for existing.

We catch a glimpse here of an explanation of religion which Sartre will go on repeating throughout his work: Religion justifies an existence that lacks justification. In Sartre's view, God is simply a ridiculous answer to an inevitable question: Why am I here? Why do I exist? Taken in itself, existence lacks justification. After all, Sartre asks, what does it mean to exist? His answer is that of a man wielding a desperate sword:

> The essential thing is contingency. I mean that one cannot define existence as necessity. To exist is simply *to be there;* those who exist let themselves be encountered, but you can never deduce them. I believe there are people who have understood this. Only they tried to overcome this contingency by inventing a necessary, causal being.[2]

God is a way of overcoming this contingency. He is the justification that is tacked on to what is simply there without justification; he is thus a human invention calculated to hide the face of radical contingency. Filled with vertigo and nausea at their situation, human beings have invented all sorts of things: the "right to life," the "right to work," the "right to be respected," and finally the "right to immortality." But when they refuse to see their situation as it really is, they become prisoners of their bad faith.

Sartre followed a different course. At the outset, his sorrowing soul was "a choice soil for sowing the seeds of heaven" (*The Words,* p. 97), and he almost became "a prey to saintliness" (p. 100). He just managed to avoid such a destiny, being aided by the influence of his family.

My Grandfather Disgusted Me with It Forever

His fervor gradually disappeared, and the religious instruction he received from careful teachers was counterbalanced and finally rendered ineffective by the corrosive influence of his maternal grandfather, who was a Lutheran by religion and a Voltairean in outlook. "I was led to disbelief not by the conflict of dogmas, but by my grandparents' indifference" (pp. 100–1).

The environment in Sartre's home was not hostile to religion. The people there were sober and tolerant; they believed in God but did not talk about him. Atheism was even disapproved; the atheist was regarded as a "character" from whom some social scandal was to be feared, "a God-obsessed crank who saw His absence everywhere and who could not open his mouth without uttering His name, in short, a gentleman who had religious convictions" (p. 98). There were few such convictions in Sartre's milieu, and these were not dramatized. Neither did anyone boast of not having convictions. There was too much respect for society's conventions.

The predominant influence was that of the grandfather, who was a skeptic although he remained a Christian in name. For him "faith was merely a high-sounding name for sweet French freedom" (p. 99). He was an "actor" in spirit, and was not displeased to think that a "Great Spectator" was watching him; he did not, however, give this Spectator a place in his life. "He hardly ever thought about God except in big moments. As he was sure of finding Him in the hour of his death, he kept Him out of his life" (p. 99). In short, he avoided the cost entailed in a religious commitment, but he also refused to get involved in any fervent struggle against it: that would be too much trouble. Sartre was raised in this environment of indifference in which the grandfather played the dominant role. His mother, an affection-

ate and sentimental woman, had little influence. She had lost
her husband too soon and now had "her own God," a God who
consoled her in her sorrows.

Such was the family environment: not atheistic but indifferent. Religion was simply a set of social customs which no one
bothered to question; it was part of the family heritage and as
such to be respected, though more from conformity than from
conviction. "Christian certainties ... belonged to everyone.
They were asked to shine in the gaze of a priest, in the semi-
darkness of a church, and to light up men's souls, but nobody
had any need to assume them himself. They were the common
heritage" (p. 98). In short, people lived among these certainties
as they do among ancient mementos: through force of habit.

In order to grasp the place religion had in this family setting, we should reread an episode in the first act of *The Condemned of Altona*, where Leni places a Bible on a pedestal table:

Johanna:	What's that?
Leni:	The Bible. We put it on the table when we hold a family conference. (*Johanna looks at it, astonished. Leni adds, a trifle impatiently*) Yes, in case we have to take an oath.
Johanna:	There's no oath to take.
Leni:	You never know.
Johanna:	(*laughing to reassure herself*): You believe neither in God nor the Devil.
Leni:	That's true. But we go to church, and we swear on the Bible. I've already told you—this family has no longer any justification for living, but it has kept its good habits.[3]

In such an environment, where faith was now only a habit,
Sartre finally "thought of God less and less often" (p. 101). For
several years he still "maintained public relations with the Al-
mighty." But "privately" he "ceased to associate with Him" (p.
102). The religion that had been taught to him emphasized docility and submission to God; his grandfather's Voltairean outlook won the day over such a religion and caused him to live free
of its constraints.

The Accident That Separated Us

The religious indifference of Sartre's family had already had a profound effect on his faith, but the latter had not yet turned into unbelief. The event that caused the break was a very small one. Perhaps it did not in fact lead to the sudden decision which Sartre connects with it, but it does illustrate his most frequent grievance against God:

> Only once did I have the feeling that He existed. I had been playing with matches and burned a small rug. I was in the process of covering up my crime when suddenly God saw me. I felt His gaze inside my head and on my hands. I whirled about in the bathroom, horribly visible, a live target. Indignation saved me. I flew into a rage against so crude an indiscretion. I blasphemed. . . . He never looked at me again (p. 102).

The theme of the look is central in the philosophy of Sartre, and I shall come back to it. In this particular incident, it has the aspect of a personal experience, the psychological roots of which are readily perceived. There is an inevitable conflict between the child who is trying to find a way of avoiding punishment, and God who, he has been told, sees even the innermost secret places. The child can play tricks on his parents, but how can he escape this indiscreet being who can hold him in a bind no matter where he is? The only way out is rebellion.

Nietzsche had already attacked this shameless onlooker, this "indecent" fellow who violates consciences. Sartre in his return rejects this divine "indiscretion" which is unworthy of a human being and much more so of a God. He invents the only strategy that can save him in the circumstances: he shifts from accused to accuser. He gets good and angry and dismisses this God who has become intolerable to him. All the ties between the two are cut. Fifty years later Sartre observes somewhat regretfully: "He [God] vegetated in me for a while, then he died. . . . Fifty years ago, had it not been for that misunderstanding, that mistake, the accident that separated us, there might have been something between us" (pp. 102–3).

There was in fact nothing more, except for a few dramatic

or philosophical works written to explain to the world that this accident had been inevitable: it could not fail to happen. But apart from these bits of polemic, kept up for stage purposes, there was nothing more between Sartre and God. Atheism had become a "state of mind" in Sartre. There was no struggle: God had died of an accident; nor any real break: this final accident was simply the coup de grâce that finished off a God whose decline was already far advanced.

Sartre's biography is quite revealing, inasmuch as we find in it the same themes that stand out in his work. For Sartre atheism displays essentially its humanistic side, since it satisfies a need for being truthful about oneself: human beings have no reason for existing, and the desire to hide this fact by appealing to "God" is proof of nothing but bad faith. Atheism also is in keeping with a desire for seeing things as they are: society has long since ceased to believe in God, even though it still has a place for him, the place occupied by a dead person who is still remembered. To the extent that it does keep a place for a dead God, society is guilty of pretense and evasion; it uses a dead heritage as an excuse for not inventing a future for itself. Finally, atheism satisfies the demand for freedom: as long as we remain prisoners of God with his demands and taboos, we will not create ourselves.

There Is Nothing Left But Mankind

To what extent is *The Words* really autobiographical? Does it reflect experience or does it rather project into the past a thinking that developed only later on? It is doubtless both of these. One fact is certain: Sartre abandoned all religious faith at a very early period. He subsequently tried to turn what was initially a simple conviction into a full certitude.[4] In his literary work, especially in *The Flies* and *The Devil and the Good Lord,* he develops the same themes as in his autobiography. The characteristics of some of his stage figures closely resemble his own. Before formulating in an explicit way the reasons Sartre offers as philosophical justifications for his atheism, I shall for a few moments cultivate the company of the personages who incarnate these reasons.

A Holiness That Separates Us from Human Beings

Sartre's plays are always concerned with some philosophical idea, and *The Devil and the Good Lord* is no exception. It is in fact a real weapon of war against God. In addition to strongly worded pages against the Church Sartre offers in it an express statement of "the relations between man and God or, if you prefer, the relations between man and the absolute,"[5] and does so in order to demonstrate that there is an irreducible opposition between the two terms of this relationship. To take the side of God is to separate oneself from human beings; conversely, to choose man is necessarily to reject God.

The hero of the play, Goetz, goes through three stages: evil, good, and man. Initially he thinks only of burning and destroying everyone and everything: "Why should you want to do wrong?—Because Good has already been done.—By whom?—By God the Father. Me, I invent" (p. 46). Entering upon evil ways is not as easy as it might seem. Doing good, on the other hand, is quite simple: you need only copy what is written in the teacher's notebook. It takes genius to do evil, for you have to invent; you always end up wearying of the whole business and falling back on routine. "The boring part of Evil is that one grows accustomed to it—you need genius to invent" (p. 56).

Goetz is an absurd figure that illustrates one of Sartre's key ideas: man has no essence that precedes his existence; he cannot find the norms for his action by looking within himself. All he can do, therefore, is to create and freely bestow on his life the meaning he wants it to have. Goetz, moreover, does not stick to his initial choice, but this does not mean he is unfaithful to himself. He simply turns around and talks of being a saint (p. 64). This is just another challenge, or, better, it shows that the important thing is the choosing, no matter what the direction taken. Look at what happens to Goetz at this stage when he has decided to become a fanatic for God and seeks to do good to his fellow human beings. He distributes what he has; he shows the same extreme generosity in doing good as he had in doing evil. But to his great surprise goodness wins him as much if not more hatred than evil had done. He has chosen to pour out charity upon men and women, after having overwhelmed them with his hatred, but his only reward is contempt.

Theodore Lownik Library
Illinois Benedictine College
Lisle, Illinois 60532

Sartre sees two conclusions as inevitably flowing from all this, with each of the conclusions illustrated by one of the stages in Goetz's life. The first conclusion is that no invention is possible if there exists a God who is the Creator of values. Sartre, speaking in his own voice, formulates this concept elsewhere in very careful terms:

> If I have excluded God the Father, there must be somebody to invent values. . . . There is no sense in life *a priori*. Life is nothing until it is lived; but it is yours to make sense of, and the value of it is nothing else but the sense that you choose.[6]

Moreover, as for Nietzsche, so for Sartre this choice of values is located beyond good and evil. To a greater degree than the case of Goetz would suggest, Sartre proposes regulative principles for action in order precisely to avoid the kind of absurd choices that Goetz makes.

The second conclusion is that to choose God is inevitably to separate oneself from other human beings. One cannot choose both God and man. If one is to go to God, one must abandon one's fellows. After finding his love held in contempt Goetz believes that he sees the truth of this conclusion, and he decides in the future to remove this obstacle between himself and God: "Hide me from the sight of men!" (p. 125). If you are passionately in love with God, you must resign yourself to a life apart: "Ah! I should never have concerned myself with mankind: humanity is a nuisance, it is the brushwood that must be thrust aside in order to reach Thee. I come, Lord, I come" (p. 124).

Goetz's notion of holiness is a strange one, but in its own way it reflects the ascetical ideal which a certain kind of Christianity sets up as the model and which sees salvation as the fruit of a "flight from." Goetz embodies this outlook. Not only does he reject his fellow human beings, but he scorns everything human: the body, sexuality, involvement. "The body is disgusting" (p. 131). Like Nietzsche's camel-spirit, he calls instead for humiliation, destitution, and isolation. Only the contempt which other people show him will raise him above them and lift him up into the light. That is what holiness means: it necessarily separates one from other human beings. Sartre himself had almost become its "prey"; now he knows what the danger had entailed.

I Am on the Side of Humanity

Neither the choice of evil for evil's sake nor the ascetical ideal, which means rejection and flight, is Sartre's last word on life. The first of these two choices is absurd, the second is inhuman. Countering absurdity with absurdity is no more of a solution than trying to remedy absurdity by flying from it. In his indictment of the ascetical ideal, which had already been the object of Nietzsche's rage, Sartre does at least bring to light the persistent influence of Christian dualism which constantly springs back to life. The portrayal of the influence that is offered in Sartre's play is indeed grotesque, but it is not therefore the less relevant. The example of Goetz in the second stage of his development is the best illustration of the fact that God alienates us from our fellows. But if this choice, like the first, leads to an impasse, what alternative is left? One: the acceptance of all that is human!

Once again it is Goetz who illustrates this turning back to man. Having emerged from his mystical phase (which, like the earlier phase, exhausted him at last), he will live very simply as a man among other human beings; he will not try to control them either by evil or by good. He will bow to the facts: "I killed God because He divided me from mankind, and now I see that His death has isolated me even more surely. I shall not allow this huge carcass to poison my human friendships; I shall tell the whole truth, if necessary" (p. 147).

Hilda precedes him in this turning back to mankind, a turning which springs from a choice freely made in solitude. When Goetz tries to engage her in his own search for holiness, she resists him with all her strength. She is a realist and, when he says that the body is "disgusting," she answers: "The body is good. It's in your soul that there's rottenness" (p. 131). She herself has no doubt about the right choice to make: she will remain faithful to her fellow human beings: "I am on the side of humanity, and I will not desert my fellow beings" (p. 94). She rejects the idea of flight:

We shall not go to heaven, Goetz, and even if we were both to go, we would have no eyes to see each other, no hands to touch each other. In heaven, there is no time for anything but God. [*She comes to touch him.*] Here you are: a little flesh, worn-out, rough, miserable—a life, a wretched life. It is this flesh and this life I love. We can only love on earth, and against God's will (p. 125).

Anyone who thus chooses fidelity to the earth can only struggle against all that is opposed to it. This play is studded from end to end with Sartre's attacks, especially against the Church and the system of ideological servitude which the Church instituted. There is, for example, the famous scene of the sale of indulgences, one of the best and most ferocious scenes in the entire play (pp. 78–83). Sartre also denounces the Church for deluding and betraying the poor. His judgment is final: "Your Holy Church is a strumpet; she sells her favors to the rich" (p. 18). The Church's sway depends especially on the illusion it has managed to create or maintain. It fosters credulity but by that very fact it scatters the energies of human beings. It is all this that Hilda is attacking when, exasperated by an old woman with her rosary, she says: "Pray for us! Prayers are better than tears, they make less noise" (p. 92).

The complaints against religion mount up. Sartre sees in religion only a manifestation of fear-inspired servility that debases human beings by compelling them to bend the knee. To it he contrasts rebellion, which sets them on their feet: "Thou hast the power to let me die without confession and summon me suddenly before Thy bar of judgment; but we shall then see who will judge the other" (p. 94). Sartre sees in religion only a blind trust in God; but how can we believe in his goodness or even in his existence when we see children dying? (pp. 12–13). Nothing can justify God: if human beings are to live, then God must die. Those who have chosen the side of man can only reject everything that is opposed to human fulfillment.

The outcome of the debate is clear: one cannot choose both God and man; it must be one or the other. Goetz scorns human beings out of fidelity to God or, more accurately, to the wager he had made in solitude and in which he had deluded himself by making himself think he had heard the voice of God. Hilda rejects God and proclaims her fidelity to human beings whom she can see and touch. In the end she will rescue Goetz from his error and bring him over to her side. Finally, there is the case of Heinrich, a priest, who is convinced he can hold on both to God and to man but who in fact betrays both God and men. He plays a "double game," but he is a traitor (p. 21) and lost forever.

God Does Not Exist

I might cite many other harsh and offensive passages that attack religion as a mystification. Sartre can see only one aspect of religion: it alienates people psychologically and causes them to betray their human responsibilities. His conclusion is always the same: one must be "a man among men" and therefore categorically reject God.

Goetz belatedly realizes this. But when he does discover at last that God does not exist, he is filled with joy. Parodying Pascal, he exults before his friend-enemy, Heinrich the priest:

> I supplicated, I demanded a sign, I sent messages to Heaven, no reply. Heaven ignored my very name. Each minute I wondered what I could BE in the eyes of God. Now I know the answer: nothing. God does not see me, God does not hear me, God does not know me. You see this emptiness over our heads? That is God. . . . Silence is God. Absence is God. God is the loneliness of man. There was no one but myself; I alone decided on Evil; and I alone invented Good. It was I who cheated, I who worked miracles, I who accused myself today, I alone who can absolve myself; I, man. If God exists, man is nothing; if man exists. . . . Where are you going? . . .
>
> Wait, priest. I am going to make you laugh. . . . Heinrich, I am going to tell you a colossal joke: God doesn't exist. [*Heinrich throws himself upon Goetz and strikes him. Under the rain of blows, Goetz laughs and shouts.*] He doesn't exist. Joy, tears of joy. Halleluiah! Fool! Don't strike me! I have delivered us. No more Heaven, no more Hell, nothing but earth. . . . Farewell monsters, farewell saints. Farewell pride. There is nothing left but mankind (pp. 141–42).

Hitherto, Goetz had been asking what he could *be* (the emphasis is Sartre's own), and he had looked to heaven for the answer. He thought that he had a pre-existent essence, that his destiny was written down in heaven, and that he only needed to read it and then docilely carry it out. Now he understands that everything has to be invented and that he has carte blanche for the job. Will he return to his initial state when he had passed himself off as a hero of evil? No, for that too was an alienation. Now he must live with other human beings as one of them and be willing to be judged by them. His choices must be made without any reference either to the devil or the good Lord. Each human being is free, but each is also responsible to and for everyone else. And it is more difficult to be judged by one's equals than by an infinite being (p. 142).

Goetz has finally come to the truth. He realizes that his holiness was just a bit of comedy. Heaven is silent. God is only a vast corpse that poisons human friendships. We must get rid of him so that we can at last accept our human condition with its responsibilities and its risks. Commitments are necessary, but none of them are dictated to us in advance. The human person is "condemned to freedom." He comes on the scene without a mandate, journeys without a ticket, and does not know the goal. He is only what he makes of himself. He is unqualified freedom.

An Atheist in the Name of Man

Sartre has not presented his complaints against God in a systematic form, and we must not expect to find in his writings a treatise against atheism. It may therefore seem a bit artificial on our part to line up the reasons that led him to atheism. In any case, they can be summed up in a single word: man. That is, Sartre's denial of God's existence is based on a particular idea of the human person; his denial of God is always the result of his assertion of the human, since he does not think it possible to reconcile God and man. In his view the only consistent thing is to eliminate one of these two terms in the name of the other.

I am saying, then, that Sartre's criticism of God implies a particular idea of man but also a particular idea of God. I must therefore turn to a closer examination of these ideas in order to bring to light their anthropological presuppositions as well as the image of God that he is attacking. His criticism can be reduced to three specific grievances, of which the first two are of the psychological order (they start with a certain idea of the human person and on the basis of this eliminate the idea of God), while the third is based on ontological claims (it shows the idea of God to be contradictory but also brings out the human desire which the idea of God reflects).

It Is Impossible To Live Under the Eye of God

The first of these three criticisms is inspired by the model of human relations that we have already seen. This model which serves as point of reference in *No Exit* (a play in which occurs the well-known statement, "Hell is—other people!") also functions in *The Condemned of Altona,* in which the chief enemy of man is men. What does "other" imply? In Sartre's plays the relation with others is almost always one of conflict and estrangement. The other is one who judges and condemns; he is by nature an accuser:

> My client is tearing himself open with his own hands. . . . But I will tell you the secret of these multiple incisions. The century might have been a good one had not man been watched from time immemorial by the cruel enemy who had sworn to destroy him, that hairless, evil, flesh-eating beast—man himself. One and one make one—there's our mystery. The beast was hiding, and suddenly we surprised his look deep in the eyes of our neighbors. So we struck. Legitimate self-defense (*The Condemned of Altona,* pp. 177–78).

Encounter with the other does not release us from our isolation. For others, even those closest to us by blood or by love, look at us with an "objectifying" gaze that alienates us from ourselves. They immobilize us by locking us into the situation in which we were at a particular moment. They fail to recognize that our very being is a project, that at every moment we have the ability to make a new start and to move beyond ourselves to something new. Under the gaze of others, our freedom ceases to function; it seizes us, as it were. The gaze of the other enslaves us; it evokes fear and uneasiness; it is a source of danger. In fact, it is the most terrible of all dangers for us.

This tyrannical and corrupt reciprocity is doubtless not Sartre's final word on human relationships. In fact, he thought it advisable to offer further explanations and modify his earlier analysis by introducing the idea of solidarity. In speaking as he does in his plays of relations with others, he is not enunciating a

general law. Not all relations with others are necessarily poi-
soned. The point he is making is rather that "if relations with
others are distorted and vitiated, then the other can only be
hell. . . . Many people are in hell because they are too dependent
on the judgment of others."7 It is important to take note of this
correction if we are to identify Sartre with a formula which he
rejects in its unqualified form. But the correction changes nothing in his conception of God, for when he speaks of God, his
point of reference is the pattern of distorted human relations.

God's objectifying gaze makes him a burden to human beings. *The Words* accuses God of being "indiscreet"; Sartre had
been estranged from God because he could no longer stand being looked at. Goetz, in *The Devil and the Good Lord,* feels the
same discomfort: "Sleep with you under the eye of God? No. I
don't care for coupling in public. [*Pause.*] Oh, for a night deep
enough to hide us from his regard" (p. 133).

Lucien, in *L'enfance d'un chef,* feels the same way. He is out-
raged that the gaze of God should penetrate into the darkest
corners of his soul, and finally, like the young Sartre, he rebels:
"Lucien never knew what he did in the nighttime, but the good
Lord knew because the good Lord saw everything. Lucien knelt
at his prie-dieu and tried to be well-behaved so that his mother
would praise him after Mass, but in fact he detested the good
Lord, because the good Lord knew more about him than he did
about himself."8

The gaze of God brings about the fullest possible corruption of human relations, because here I am defenseless. Human
beings look at each other and may destroy each other, but in
these relations there is always alterity. The other objectifies me
and tries to imprison me within the limits of this objectification,
but I can always regain my position by nullifying his gaze with
my own and objectifying him in turn. The "omnipresent and in-
apprehensible" transcendence of others (*Being and Nothingness,*
p. 246) can be negated by a contrary transcendence. But what
about our dealings with God?

God is "the quintessence of the Other" (p. 208), "the concept of the Other pushed to the limit" (p. 242). The look he directs at men is an absolute look that no one else can relativize.
From the moment that I am faced with this "omnipresent, infinite subject" (p. 257), no dialectical dodges are any longer possible. At this point no escape is possible for the human subject.

Under the gaze of God, the person no longer has any secrets and is entirely foreseeable. This means that the whole game has already been played out. Becoming is an illusion, for the person simply follows a pre-existing plan. He thinks that by means of his freedom he invents, when in fact "freedom" simply carries out a program inscribed in the person's being.

We can see the kind of God against which Sartre is rebelling: God the spectator, the very God to whom his grandfather had adapted. But the grandfather had been an actor and loved an audience. Sartre is not that kind of man; he cannot stand being looked at. He sees God as an unconcerned judge who treats human beings as things. But then these beings automatically cease to be masters of their situation (p. 241). No restoration of the self is possible except through rebellion.

The image of God against which Sartre is rebelling is entirely dependent on the latter's analysis of a particular human perversion: the distortion of the look. Why is it, however, that after having corrected the model of human relations by admitting the possibility of healthy relations, Sartre did not introduce the same correction into his analysis of the idea of God? He simply chose, once and for all and arbitrarily, to use the model of distorted relations in understanding our relation to God. He could just as logically have appealed to a different model, but he did not do so. His tactics are clear: it is not his conception of man that determines his conception of God; on the contrary, his idea of God causes him to choose as a term of comparison the model of distorted human relations.

Once Freedom Lights Its Beacon in a Man's Heart

A second argument intersects with the first and in its structure follows the same logic. Sartre rejects the existence of God because he thinks it incompatible with human freedom. His argument represents in a sense a modern version of an ancient problem: the problem of predestination. If God exists, he knows everything, and he brings the entire weight of his knowledge and will to bear on the becoming of man. Becoming then no longer represents the welling up of human freedom, but is simply the unfolding of God's will. What becomes of human freedom under these conditions? In his play *The Flies* Sartre develops this contradiction by setting before us two types of people, the one being those who renounce their freedom in order to become slaves of the gods, and the other being those who reject the gods in order to remain free.

Sartre's thesis, then, is that to acknowledge the existence of the gods is to become their slave. The residents of Argos have slain their king. They expected this act to set them free, but in fact their slavery became only the heavier, because it simply shifted to within themselves. For, after their action, they are obsessed by their crime and tortured by remorse. More than ever, they grovel before their gods in the hope of winning forgiveness. They are slaves who ceaselessly perform expiatory rites in order to reconcile the gods to them. "What an ugly lot! Observe . . . their sallow cheeks and sunken eyes. These folk are perishing of fear. What better proof could we have of the effects of superstition?" (*The Flies,* p. 77). Here Sartre explains the origin of remorse and religion somewhat as Freud does; he uncovers an Oedipus complex that has not been integrated into the personality.

To this choice of alienation into the hands of the gods Sartre opposes the choice of freedom. Orestes is of a different stamp than his fellow Argives. He has shared in the crime but he fully accepts the consequences of his act and acknowledges no guilt. He is a free man. He even resists Zeus when the latter tries to make him bow to his law, but Zeus is forced to admit that the gods have no power over a free man: "Once freedom lights its beacon in a man's heart, the gods are powerless against him. It's a matter between man and man, and it is for other men, and for them only, to let him go his gait, or to throttle him" (pp. 104–5).

His sister Electra, an accomplice in the crime, does not have the strength to follow him in his rebellion. She stops half-way: she repents. A comparison of her words with Orestes' is enlightening: Orestes says to Zeus: "I shall not return under your law; I am doomed to have no other law but mine" (p. 122); Electra, on the other hand, says to Zeus: "I will obey your law, I will be your creature and your slave. . . . I repent, Zeus, I bitterly repent" (p. 124).

Here, then, is the dilemma: to submit to the gods and then live as a slave, or to rebel against the gods and enjoy freedom. Both attitudes are possible. Sartre suggests that the former of the two brings peace: the satisfied gods grant the submissive person a tranquil conscience. The other attitude brings anxiety: the person must accept the burden of his action, and no one else can carry it for him. Freedom is a risk which a person always takes alone and the consequences of which he must carry alone. Sartre resolves the dilemma without hesitation, although he does it more by banging his fist on the table than by reasoned argument: human beings escape servitude only by rebelling. Rebellion becomes the supreme act of self-assertion.

We are now in a position to see what is at stake in this debate. In the dispute about predestination, some people preferred to destroy human freedom rather than impose limits on the absolute knowledge and absolute power of God. Sartre prefers to reject God and deny his existence rather than destroy human freedom. In fact, he thinks that such a negation of God is implicit in the very assertion of human freedom. He criticizes Mauriac on this point. Mauriac had taken the omnipotence of grace as his starting point; Sartre speaks as the champion of man's absolute freedom and criticizes Mauriac for the way he treats his heroine, Thérèse Desqueyroux: "Even in her freedom, Thérèse is predictable."[9] Mauriac's God is outside of time; he is the "privileged observer" for whom nothing really new or unexpected happens under the sun. History cannot surprise him or change what he has determined beforehand in his eternal plan. Human beings are unwitting actors in a history created by another. Sartre rejects this approach, for if God has completely determined the meaning of my life in advance, what meaning can freedom have?

Once again it is clear what kind of God Sartre is rejecting: God the workman who fashions human beings for a purpose external to them and imposed on them as an inevitable fate. They thus become in God's sight mere things, objects, docile instruments in his hands. Nothing that they do can be contrary to his wishes. It is in this sense that we are to understand such Sartrean texts as this: "The conception of man in the mind of God is comparable to that of the paper-knife in the mind of the artisan."[10] As conceived on the model of the action of a workman or industrialist, divine creation assigns every thing and every being a place or role that is determined in advance. If the human person is of this kind, then he really can "invent" nothing, but at best plays a part he cannot refuse. Sartre makes no effort to reconcile God and man. On the contrary, he deepens the gulf between them and emphasizes the estrangement. If God exists, he cannot but pre-determine a destiny for man (so Sartre thinks), because there is no room in God for the unforeseeable. But, we may ask, is there not another type of relation possible in which God is no longer conceived as setting limits to man but rather as crowning his development?

God: A Contradictory Notion

Not only can the existence of God not be reconciled with human existence; it is also an inherently contradictory notion. Sartre's argument here is rather specious and cannot be understood except within the framework of his ontology as a whole. In order to show the contradiction he claims, Sartre starts with a distinction between two levels of reality: the in-itself and the for-itself. The two terms require explanation.

What is the in-itself? The term, which is Hegelian in origin, means for Sartre the brute being of things; the being, for example, of a pebble: opaque, solid, dark, sunk in the immediacy of its "being there," lacking any possibility of reflection on itself. Sartre defines the in-itself by the principle of identity: it is the perfect coincidence of self with self. Nothing can be said of the in-itself except that it is; our only reaction to it can be nausea, the typically Sartrean feeling one experiences in face of the gratuity and absurdity of things (and of human beings as well) which are simply there, without explanation, "*de trop* for eternity." The in-itself is "full of itself, and a more complete totality is unimaginable. There is not the least emptiness within this being, nor the least crack by which nothingness might slip in" (pp. lxv–vii).[11]

With man another type of being makes its appearance: the for-itself. What is man if not the being for whom the world of consciousness and freedom opens up (the terms consciousness and freedom are almost synonymous with the "for-itself")? Unlike the in-itself which is defined by relation to itself, the for-itself is always defined by relation to something other than itself: an object seen, imagined, thought, and so on. The for-itself is defined by relation-to: every consciousness is a consciousness of something, says Sartre following Husserl. "It [consciousness] never exists in the pure state; it exists only because it thinks of a tree, of the face of Peter. . . . It never comes into existence except by representing something different from itself; consciousness is natively focused on a being that is not itself."[12] In other words, the in-itself and the for-itself are not symmetrical terms, since one is defined by itself while the other is defined by its relation to something else and depends on the other. One may think of the in-itself without reference to the for-itself, but the converse is not true.

If such is indeed the ontological status of consciousness, then in regard to the latter the following two apparently paradoxical statements may be defended. On the one hand, it can be said that consciousness *is* what it is not: it is this table, this object sighted in the spatial world, this representation of myself or another; and it cannot claim an inwardness independent of the things within its purview. It always reveals a being that is not itself. On the other hand, it can also be said that *it is not* what it is, for consciousness is not anything of the things to which it is related. If objects are excluded from consciousness, consciousness is nothing.

Such, then, are the only two modes of being that Sartre acknowledges. But if we apply these two categories to the idea of God, the latter immediately shows itself to be internally contradictory, for the idea of God would in effect be "the impossible synthesis of the for-itself and the in-itself" (p. 66). "Is God not a being who is what he is—in that he is all positivity and the foundation of the world—and at the same time a being who is not what he is and who is what he is not—in that he is self-consciousness and the necessary foundation of himself?" (*ibid.*).

But such a being is inconceivable or, more accurately, is simply the embodiment of a dream. Either the idea of God incarnates the solidity of the in-itself—it has the same fullness as things—but then it lacks consciousness and freedom. Or it is a for-itself, that is, consciousness and freedom, but then it is affected by nothingness since it shows the non-coincidence of the self with the self and is therefore imperfect. Moreover, if God is a for-itself, he must depend on an in-itself, which is independent of him, in order to be himself. We are thus confronted with the dialectic described above. It must be said of God that, on the one hand, he is what he *is not* (i.e., he is related to something other than himself) but also that he *is not* what he is (i.e., he is located beyond all the fulfillments that the realities to which he is related can bring to him).

This argument against the idea of God is fallacious, for such validity as it might claim comes solely from the application to God of formal concepts that have been elaborated to fit the field of human experience and that function therein. Thus the dialectic at work gives the impression of being purely verbal. Nonetheless Sartre's analysis is revealing and has a twofold critical application. First of all, it asserts that the idea of God corresponds to a dream of human beings. What, after all, is the human person?

> Human reality is a perpetual surpassing toward a coincidence with itself which is never given. If the *cogito* reaches toward being, it is because by its very thrust it surpasses itself toward being by qualifying itself in its being as the being to which coincidence with self is lacking in order for it to be what it is. The *cogito* is indissolubly linked to being-in-itself . . . as a lack to that which defines its lack (p. 65).

God is the fulfillment of this dream, the transformation of this lack into a hypostasis. He represents the fullness of what is found in human reality in the form of a lack; he is the impossible synthesis of the in-itself (the dream of rest and repose) and the for-itself (the dream of dullness). This dream also has its place in interpersonal relations: when confronted with the other, each person desires to be an all-embracing consciousness and pursues the ideal of "a being who looks at" but can never be looked at (p. 399). Here again, God is the fulfillment of the dream of totality which for human beings remains only a dream. In short, the idea of God is nothing but a dream of the human person, "an absolute totalization of itself and of *all* Others"(*ibid.*). It thus contains a psychological truth.

Sartre's argument also has its theological side, for it offers a criticism of the idea of God that can only be of profit to a Christian. The argument holds against two equally questionable representations of God: one that turns God into an object and conceives of his fullness as resembling that of things which are full of themselves and free of all empty spaces, and one that as it were vaporizes God by imagining him as a vast and all-pervasive subject who leaves no room for development outside of himself. This criticism, as I said, is really a service to the Christian. It forces the man of faith to move beyond "a theodicy of the infinite Object or even a theodicy of the solitary Subject."[13] Such an infinite Object is a projection into the beyond of the fullness of the in-itself; such an infinite, solitary Subject is a totalization of the meaning of man and history that leaves no room outside itself for the freedom of other subjects.

But the trinitarian God is not subject to this twofold criticism. On the one hand, it is not an object: its fullness is of a different order than the fullness of poverty which the in-itself represents. On the other hand, while it is a subject, this subject is not solitary nor is it totalitarian after the manner of the for-itself so as to be in a privileged position in relation to all others. It is peculiar to God that he is not solitary but relational, and that this relationality does not impoverish him but brings him his perfection, for it is an expression not of divine limitation but of the divine fullness from which we can all receive.

Throughout these pages I have undertaken a dialogue with Sartre in which I have endeavored to assess the impact of his criticism. The idea of God which he attacks is indeed open to criticism. I would be making things too easy for myself were I to object that Sartre sets up straw men which he can then without difficulty throw into the fire. In fact, the God whom he attacks does exist in the behavior of Christians and at times even in the minds of the most prudent. This is a God who paralyzes more than he liberates, who arouses fear rather than love, and who alienates human beings by keeping them in attitudes of submission.

The rejection of this idea of God is inspired essentially by a certain conception of the human person. If God exists, how can man be free? He will always feel himself to be an "object" or "thing" in the hands of a God who manipulates him without his being aware of it. He cannot help but have the feeling that no matter what he does he is only carrying out a plan fixed in advance from all eternity. Sartre fights against such an idea of God to the extent that he sees it as contradicting his own conception of man. What is God? A free being who looks for slaves to serve him. What is man? A free being who wants to be "his own lawgiver." How can the two be reconciled? They cannot, and Sartre's atheism is the consequence of his assertion of human freedom, that is, a freedom that refuses to acknowledge any limits. If Sartre rejects God, it is because he sees him as the unqualified negation of human freedom. Absolutes are reciprocally exclusive.

Is God really dead? Sartre notes that he has been slain a

hundred times but always rises again from his ashes. Why? Because human beings cannot do without him. "God is dead, but man has not therefore become an atheist."[14] This is the "major concern" of our time: God is silent, but, with few exceptions, men and women continue to call for him. This is a sign that human beings do not yet fully assume their human condition with its absurdity, its purposelessness, its irrationality. They need reasons for living. To get through life they need a promise that will sustain them. This need is the source of all the forms of bad faith.

Faith in God is one instance of this bad faith. People find it difficult to accept the fact that there is no foundation, that they must be a foundation without having a foundation in values. Their freedom is a source of anxiety to them. They want to see themselves as necessary, justified, "given a mandate," "chosen." What a lucky find "God" is! He puts an end to the anxiety and the questions; he assures them of rest and peace. He is the supreme justification of the unjustifiable. That is how the idea of God originates: it meets a psychological need. But it is at the same time a trap for freedom. Its truth is the truth of a dream, and therefore it presents an evasion which a responsible person has no choice but to reject. "Existentialism is not atheist in the sense that it would exhaust itself in demonstrations of the non-existence of God. It declares, rather, that even if God existed that would make no difference from its point of view."[15] And in fact if God exists, the human person is no less free. Sartre's mistake is to conceive the relation between God and human beings as one of rivalry. In the Christian vision of things, however, God founds human freedom but he does not substitute his own for it; he does not obstruct its operation by pulling the strings from behind the scenes; he does not predestine it or trace out in advance the precise paths it must follow. Nor does he chain it to its past, as the human gaze does.

If Sartre were simply to change his idea of God and look upon him as neither artisan nor spectator nor exclusive totality but rather as love, perhaps his existentialism would then have room for God. And who can tell? Perhaps even freedom as he conceives it would find therein its real justification.

7

Roger Garaudy
Socialism and Religious Faith

Roger Garaudy has had a strange career. We might say of him what Sartre said of Paul Nizan: "An isolated communist is lost!" Garaudy was isolated when he carried on his fight with the French Communist Party, and he is isolated today in his position within Christianity. Although he was a member of the Party for thirty-six years and in leadership positions for almost twenty, he is today criticized, rejected, and cast forth into the outer darkness. He is alone, living his political commitment outside of any party and his Christian faith outside of any Church.

What does the French Communist Party have against him? That he spoiled the fine show of unanimity and set himself up as a judge; that he sought to introduce a spirit of freedom that was incompatible with united action, and even criticized the Soviet Union. Finally, he pushed his fellow members too far, and at the Nineteenth Congress (1970) the leaders of the Party put an end to his political career. They did not, however, manage to put an end to his fight. They isolated him but could not silence him. On the contrary, he now has complete freedom to speak out. He is bitter about his expulsion, but he also lets us in on the insight this occurrence gave him:

For the first time in my life I was tempted to suicide. I despaired because I saw what this Party, to which I had given the best years of my life, did to these two thousand human beings. These were people whose courage and honesty I knew from other situations, yet they allowed themselves to be manipulated to the point of not daring to say a word—not one of them! I know now that a party, whatever its character, is a machine for confiscating the initiatives of the membership.[1]

Since that time he has stood above the Party and has addressed himself directly to the vast majority, convinced as he now is that socialism will be built from below, not from above. Since he no longer has the support of an apparatus or fellow militants, he has chosen writing as the most effective way of spreading his ideas.

Roger Garaudy's books have been published in quick succession. They seem to resemble each other and yet each in turn has been a surprise. Whatever the material he deals with—socialism, art, religion—the same themes crop up and the same formulas recur with wearying insistence. And yet each book adds nuances and contains something unexpected. Among them there is one that represents a real synthesis of Garaudy's thought on all the essential points; that book is *Parole d'homme.* More even than the others it follows the pattern of repeating familiar themes, and yet it is a book unlike the others; strong, attractive, written at a single stretch, and of great literary beauty. It is also a book in which after long suspense Garaudy for the first time declares himself explicitly a Christian.

Why do I include Garaudy in this gallery of portraits, since he now seems to reject the atheism of which he was at one time convinced? True enough: he is an outcast from his Party and often suspect in the eyes of Christians. But he is of special interest on two counts. Not only is he the tireless prophet of a new kind of socialism which many Christians find undeniably attractive, but he is also a key figure in the Marxist interpretation of the Christian religion. He played a special role in the French Communist Party's dialogue with Christians, since he was for a long time the Party's delegate for dealing with Christians. He followed closely the development of ideas and positions within the Church and ultimately formulated a new interpretation of religion. The Party is largely in Garaudy's debt for its new attitude to Christians.

The second thing that is of interest in Garaudy is his personal position. After having asserted himself as a convinced atheist, he now calls himself a "Christian." As a young man he had been alienated from Christianity because he thought that it estranged him from the working class. Today he sees another side of Christianity and realizes its irreplaceable contribution to socialism: without the Christian faith the historical hope which Marxism awakened hardens, degenerates into totalitarianism, denies the person, and destroys itself. Faith, as Garaudy understands it, becomes a dynamism within socialism; it is an openness to the impossible. Does it also open out to God? This question is left unanswered.

Although Garaudy's work deals with many subjects, it has three main focuses: socialism, esthetics, and faith. But we quickly become aware that these are not three separated areas of concern. The three focuses lead to the same center, socialism. Faith and esthetics are of concern to Garaudy less because of their intrinsic content than because of their relation to socialism. Each plays a symbolic role as it proclaims a new manner of being and expresses this in a utopian or prophetic form, that is, in anticipation of its full realization. For this reason, it behooves us here first to give a brief description of Garaudy's socialism and then to discuss the role that esthetics and Christian faith play in relation to this socialism. After that we will be in a position to say something about Garaudy's faith.

Socialism with a Human Face

It was his conception of socialism that brought Roger Garaudy into conflict with the French Communist Party. The dispute broke out in connection with the crisis of May 1968. It found expression, on Garaudy's side, especially in his book *The Crisis in Communism*.[2] This was an explosive book, one that might have given the appearance of a treatise on political philosophy but was in fact a fully orchestrated attack on the French Communist Party and the Soviet Union. In it he calls for a "drastic 'rethinking'" and blames the Party and the Soviet Union for authoritarian methods, a lifeless bureaucracy, and an utter lack of dialogue with the membership. He also blames the Party for its unconditional alignment with the Soviet Union, and he blames the Soviet Union for imposing, in an authoritarian way, even if not by military force, a socialism that is outdated and for not scrupling to eliminate "rebels": in Yugoslavia (1948), in Germany, in Poland, and in Hungary (1956), in China (1958), in Czechoslovakia (1968). Thus both the Soviet Union and the

French Communist Party give a distorted picture of socialism and act only to stifle initiative.

Distorted Models of Society

Is Garaudy calling for a return to capitalism? By no means! Before exploring new ways for socialism, Garaudy draws up a balance-sheet and puts both the United States and the Soviet Union in the box. In the former we see the triumph of capitalism; Garaudy is critical of its "expansion for expansion's sake," its lack of human purposefulness, its victory won at the cost of profound human alienation. But despite these contradictions capitalism is not about to collapse. In the Soviet Union we see "the dictatorship of the proletariat," which is only a caricature of socialism. Both, then, are distorted models of society. Without indulging in utopianism but also without yielding to a resignation that amounts to connivance, Garaudy analyzes the modifications required to gradually render the systems more human. I cannot here repeat the details of Garaudy's discussion,[3] but I can at least sketch its main lines.

An analysis of the American "model" shows where the real resistance to social change originates. The thing that hinders any development in the direction of socialism is the appropriation of the means of production by the private sector. Those who control the means of production can also decide the course of the economy and set its goals. But when the owner is an individual, he cannot but make profit his aim. The American model is alienating for human beings, because its sole aim is not the person but growth:

> Seen in this light, the objectives of the economic apparatus are objectives of growth and expansion. The growth, the efficiency of the apparatus, become ends in themselves. The only criterion of value is the criterion of performance. . . . Hence there grows up a religion of means and a cult of growth.[4]

The basic error of this model can be summed up by saying that in it the person is at the service of growth instead of growth being at the service of the person. Human beings are subordinated to the economy.

By taking control of the means of production the Soviet

Union has also taken effective hold of the economy. But while the appropriation of the means of production by the state is a necessary condition for the development of socialism, it is not a sufficient condition. In becoming sole owner of the means of production the Soviet Union has secured the indispensable instrument, but its socialism nonetheless remains incomplete, for it has not given the economy a human purpose nor has it given the masses a share in the determination of the main directions to be taken by the nation.

The Soviet Union has in fact created an economy which is simply a replica of the American economy. Like the latter it pursues an out-and-out industrialization and growth and thus subordinates human beings to economic goals. In addition, it has excluded the masses from the important decisions that affect them. The result is a centralized bureaucratic socialism in which everything is decided at the top. Lenin had tried to eliminate this danger by establishing workers' councils; he wanted a socialism that would be built up by the masses. In 1920 he wrote: "By reason of bureaucratic distortions of our government, in which rule is exercised not by the masses of the people but by an 'elite' that claims to speak in their name, we are building not a socialism *by* the people but, at best, a socialism *for* the people."[5] The final words were to provide Garaudy with his slogan: a socialism *for* the people but also *by* the people.

The object of Garaudy's attack, whether in American or in Soviet society, is the separation of economic development and human development. In both societies, the only goal is growth; a real cult of growth has developed. The individual is valued only for his economic accomplishments. Garaudy likes to repeat John Kenneth Galbraith's sally: in his country "it is as if Saint Peter, deciding who was to go to heaven or hell, asked this one question, 'What did you do to increase the gross national product?' "[6] Productivity has become a dogma and the whole of society's life is subordinated to it; the result is a "one-dimensional man," whose aim, freely accepted or forcibly imposed, is growth and who is himself persuaded that there is no other way to salvation.

Today we face an urgent question: Are we to keep on making human beings the slaves of productivity, or has not the time come to make productivity serve human beings? In a system based on private property the latter kind of reorientation is

practically impossible, since profit is the universal goal. The reorientation requires a redefinition of society's goals. And yet, as
the analysis of the Soviet model shows, the transfer of ownership to the state will not automatically redirect the economy.
The masses have to be brought into the picture. A real change
in society will not come about until the masses begin to determine their own destiny.

Struggle for Socialism

Control of the means of production by the state is a necessary condition for the advent of socialism. On the other hand, as
the example of the Soviet Union shows, this control can be used
to serve ends other than the human person. There is need, then,
of inventing a new model of socialism, one that is not a copy of
the Soviet model and one that will not be prescribed in advance
for the individual country, since each nation must construct the
model while taking into account its past, its political conditions,
and its cultural traditions. Each must also choose the means, violent or peaceful, for bringing about the change. Yugoslavia has
given us an example in this matter:

> The workers themselves decide their production policy and
> thereby become the effective heirs to the actual rights per-
> taining to owners of the means of production. The sole
> "rule of the game" is that they may not destroy the means
> of production (unless it be to replace it with a better one)
> and that they may not, as a group, exploit other workers—
> anyone joining an undertaking enjoys all the rights of those
> already employed there.[7]

Such is the principle to be followed. Unlike the United
States, which shows extreme favor to private ownership, and unlike the Soviet Union, which recognizes ownership only at the
top (state ownership), Yugoslavia has established collective or
social ownership: the workers themselves are the owners of their
tools. This new situation opens the way to a true socialism.

According to Garaudy, socialism is a human project that
seeks to put all means at the service not of some alone but of the
entire community. This means, for society, a change in the rules
of the economic and political game. Each individual should be
able to share directly in the exercise of responsibility, whether

for the running of economic enterprises or for political life. In business, everything routine should be done by machines. Today it is possible to give due place to the human person who is the "subjective factor" in production: to imagination, responsibility, decision-making. In political life the masses must take their own affairs in hand, not through delegates but directly. It is difficult to run such a "direct democracy," but as long as we do not have it, the role of the citizen is limited to choosing a ready-made program; he will continue to be a consumer. Ideally, as Engels used to say and Garaudy likes to recall, "every housewife should be able to govern the state!"

It is the responsibility of all to create or invent the future: this is the thought that torments Garaudy. Such an attitude may indeed inspire evasion, but for him personally it is the very opposite of disinvolvement. Nowadays he commends this "project hope" to the general public, to all and sundry.[8] But we must emphasize the precise character of the project. Garaudy is opposed both to the utopians, who are cut off from reality, and to the positivists, who are so immersed in present reality that they are shortsighted with regard to the future. In order to avoid these ineffective extremes, Garaudy aims at the concrete utopia that is socialism.

"Socialism" has been made to cover almost everything under the sun, but Garaudy is far from sanctioning this variety. As we saw above, he has no patience with the models of socialism offered by the East. He is equally strong in his condemnation of both capitalism and present socialism, although he acknowledges that the second is better than the first. But if the only choice were between "the individualist jungle" and "the totalitarian convict-gang,"[9] we would have to despair. However, it is possible to look beyond these two "poles of oppression,"[10] which amount to almost the same thing, and imagine relations among human beings, relations based on community and love. Garaudy is drawn to the basic communities; he sees in them a first realization of the model of self-management.

Autogestion, or self-management! Everyone talks about this, but neither the bosses nor the "socialist bureaucrats" want it. They denounce it as "pernicious utopianism." Their resistance to it is understandable, inasmuch as it implies a redistribution of the centers where decisions are made, a taking from the top to the benefit of the base: "Autogestion is another name for the kind of socialism that cannot be created *for* the people but on the contrary exists only if it is created *by* the people. Not from the outside and from above, but from within and from below."[11]

In our present world this socialism has to be invented. But either it will represent the victory of love or it will not exist at all. "An individual or a society can function without love, but they cannot exist without it. A socialist revolution will be a victory not of science but of love."[12] If socialism throughout the world showed this attractive a face, there would be no room for hesitation; we would have to rally to it. The Christian would recognize himself in it because he would find there an ideal close to the Gospel. Every undertaking by Garaudy is an effort to give socialism this kind of face. His struggle, carried on in solitude and misunderstood, is in fact clear in its aim: "My task as a Communist is to give socialism this face which is that of human fulfillment."[13] Is this a lyrical illusion? But Garaudy is not proposing a ready-made model. "Everything, after all, remains to be done"; the essential thing is to create "a spirit."[14]

Another Side of Religion

Garaudy's socialism represents a refusal to alienate the human person into any system whatsoever, as well as an unshakable confidence in the ability of human beings to build their own future. His rejection of the Party and his criticisms of the Soviet Union are inspired by his ideal of an open society that excludes anathemas and gives each individual room for self-fulfillment. Using another image, Garaudy says that socialism is "an organization of economic, political and cultural relations that allows any child with the genius of a Mozart to become a Mozart."[15] Even while he was still a member of the Party, Garaudy was facing the problem of which living forces might be mobilized for this socialist struggle. With Gramsci he has spoken of a "new historical bloc" which would include more than the working class and the peasantry.

Above all, he has practiced the politics of the outstretched hand and endeavored to bring Christians into the struggle. His attitude to the latter is inspired by something deeper than political opportunism. While he has no pity for what he regards as reactionary positions, he has nonetheless come to see in Christianity signs of development which in his eyes were intitially only signs of hope but which then became a call for him to rally to it. He sees Christians as traveling a path of profound change, especially since Vatican II.[16] Despite the mistakes that have been made, the development seems to him to be irreversible. Furthermore, he understands that Christianity by its nature is not opposed to but rather in harmony with socialism.

According to *Parole d'homme* Garaudy owes his new vision of Christianity to Dom Helder Camara. At a meeting the latter said to him:

> The next step for us Christians is to proclaim publicly that capitalism, and not socialism, is "intrinsically evil" and that socialism is not to be condemned except in its corrupted forms. And for you, Roger, the next step is to show that the connection of the revolution with historical materialism and atheism is not essential but only historical and that the revolution is, on the contrary, of the same substance as Christianity.[17]

At this point, Garaudy was in a position to overcome his "dogmatisms" and "sectarianisms." He would now open himself in a decisive way to Christianity, although not without sorting out the contents of Christianity and distinguishing between religion as ideology and religion as faith, the former being harmful, the latter constructive. This key distinction enables him to reread with new eyes both the history of Christianity and the Marxist critique of religion.

The Historical Role of Faith

Christian history can be divided into three periods: the prophetic (or apocalyptic) era, the Constantinian era, and the postconciliar era, the last-named being a return to the prophetic era. The three periods show that two spirits are always at work in Christianity: one is prophetic or apocalyptic and shows itself in protest against the established order, a refusal of compromise with it, and a hope of another kingdom; the other spirit is the Constantinian, which cultivates close connections with the classes in power and preaches resignation and submission to the prevailing order.

Until recently, the Constantinian tradition had the upper

hand in the Church. How is this tradition to be defined? "The Constantinian tradition has consecrated all class domination—slavery, serfdom, the salary system—and has associated the Church with itself."[18] The Church has always tended to sanctify historical situations favorable to it as willed by God, even if in these situations human beings exploited one another. From the date when the Christian religion became a state religion (in 381 A.D.), it lost its power to challenge:

> The Bible would no longer be read as challenging the prevailing order but rather as contributing to the establishment of its legitimacy. Faith, the ever living seed of challenge to the prevailing order, would become instead the focal point of integration into this order.... Constantinianism is the tendency, present in the history of the Church from the fourth century to our own day (a tendency adopted by the hierarchy and the majority of Christians) to form human beings who submit to the established order.[19]

The Constantinian era is not dead and gone; many traces of it survive in the Church. The Church has an inherent tendency to be on the side of the most powerful, and when it does concern itself with the weak, it does so—as Juarès pointed out a long time ago—when the weak become a force to be reckoned with. The Church's positions are dictated less by justice than by political calculation.

Over against this massive and prevailing trend in the Church there has always been another trend that is more critical, more given to challenging the status quo. Although never completely neutralized in the past, it has most often been a current that was "marginal, represented by a minority, and suspect of heresy."[20] This is the prophetic or apocalyptic current (the names vary). In the past it inspired the rebellions of John Huss and Thomas Münzer; today it inspires the theologies of revolution. It has manifested itself especially in Latin America where it has taken three forms: (1) a movement of "conscientization," launched by the bishops beginning in 1962–63; (2) a movement of active nonviolence, led by Dom Helder Camara, whose chief merit has been to demystify the concept of violence and to show that the worst violence is not the active violence of revolutionaries but the institutional violence of those in possession; (3) a revolutionary movement under Camillo Torres who thought it possible in this way "to make real the love human beings should have for their neighbors."[21]

In its active elements the Church is today carrying on a political struggle which represents its opportunity for the future. The faith of Christians, which used to be a harmful "opium" and reflected a distorted social situation, is increasingly becoming "a leaven for the transformation of the world." Such a faith is not to be censured. On the contrary: "Every blow struck at such a faith is a blow struck at the revolution," says Garaudy.

A Rereading of Marx

With this new understanding of Christianity as his starting point Garaudy has set about reinterpreting Marx. In the past, religion too often showed itself as an ideology in the service of the bourgeoisie and a check on the development of socialism. Marx and Lenin rejected religion because this was the only side of it they saw. Instead of interpreting the resistance of Christianity to socialism as bound up with the established situation in the societies of the past, they took this resistance to be inherent in Christianity as a religion that turns people away from this earth and from action. If we are correctly to reread Marx and Lenin, we must first understand that their struggle was primarily not anti-religious but a struggle in behalf of human beings. They fought against religion, but they did so because it was opposed to the advent of man. Garaudy joins them in their struggle:

> Our struggle as Marxists is a struggle *for* man. . . . Our attitude is entirely positive: we struggle for man, and the logic of this struggle leads us to atheism when the answers the religions give to the questions raised by man are unworthy of these questions; when under the pretext of raising us above nature it offers what is in fact subhuman, for example, religions of irrationality or resignation.[22]

Garaudy's atheism—the atheism he accepted prior to his conversion—began, like that of Marx, not with a denial of God but with an affirmation: "the affirmation of human autonomy; this atheism has for its consequence a rejection of every attempt to deprive the human person of his creative power."[23] If a struggle against religion became necessary in some cases, this was solely because religion stripped man of this creative power. At bottom, however, atheism as a teaching is not the result of a denial of God but of a certain conception of the human person. This is true at least for Marx, and it distinguishes his atheism from that of the eighteenth century.

This granted, Garaudy believes that Marx and Lenin betray a one-sided vision of religion when they describe it as the opium of the people. For them as for Marxists today this formula has become "the cornerstone of all Marxist thinking on religion." The founders of Marxism could not help this. "Each person must be judged in the context of his times!" The founders' analyses reflect a historical situation; in the time of Marx and Lenin religion was indeed hardly more than a "balm" which the ruling class found useful and which helped the people bear up under their wretched conditions. But is religion in fact nothing but an opium?

> Marx summed up these irrefutable historical facts in a lapidary formula: "Religion is the opium of the people." But the element of reflection of social conditions is accompanied by the element of protest. I mean the aspect of religion that makes the latter not simply an ideology, a search for an explanation of misfortune and weakness, but also a search for a *way out* of misfortune; in other words, the aspect that makes it not only a way of thinking, but a way of confronting the world and acting in it.[24]

Religion is indeed an opium, but only from a certain viewpoint and not absolutely. From another point of view it is "protest" or "faith," and in certain situations "faith can play a positive and progressivist role,"[25] can become a revolutionary force. Garaudy recalls how on this point he found himself in agreement with a man like Togliatti:

> In analyzing the official positions of the French Communist Party on these points Togliatti said to me: "In France your Party is suffering the consequences of eighteenth-century materialism which led to the Soviet thesis: Religion will van-

ish once the social structure has been changed and a satisfactory effort at scientific propaganda has been made. Don't
you think history shows that religion has deep wellsprings
and that if we do not confuse faith itself with the ideologies
in which it has found expression at various times, it need
not be an opium but may be a leaven of protest and struggle?[26]

We must therefore carefully distinguish these two aspects of
religion, for it is not a matter of one simply replacing the other
and showing a different side of religion. Rather they continue to
coexist in religion. Religion is always both "reflection" and
"protest."

The most obvious thing about religion is that it is a reflection of real distress. But this reflection can become an "opium"
to the extent that religion lulls people to sleep and causes them
to lay down their arms. When religion locates human deliver-
ance on a different plane, it does not eliminate present distress
but does open itself to all sorts of political exploitation, since ty-
rants depend on it to secure the submission of their subjects.
This kind of religion certainly deserves criticism.

But religion has another face: that of "protest." As an opium of the people it helps those in power to maintain their position, but as protest it is a source of trouble for them. It is able to
call energies into play for a future that is progressive. In Garaudy's view, therefore, it is wrong to claim that "at all times and
in all places religion turns people away from action, work and
struggle." When properly understood, religion ceases to be a
"mythology of escape" and becomes a source of dynamic life.

Garaudy rejects religion insofar as it is an ideology in the
service of power, but welcomes it insofar as it is faith, that is, a
source of dynamic life. There is no opposition between faith and
socialism; on the contrary, they can only profit from dwelling together. There can even be a "reciprocal fertilization,"

faith giving socialism a transcendent, prophetic dimension,
keeping it from settling into complacency, and opening it to
a future of limitless renewal; socialism, on the other hand,
giving faith a historical dimension, keeping it from fleeing
the world of human struggles, and compelling it to give its

promise and hope a concrete embodiment in that world so
that it will be not an opium but a leaven.[27]

Could there be any happier marriage than this?

In the real order, of course, things are not so simple. Conflicts between socialism and religious faith continue to be nu-
merous, as recent history shows. But these conflicts are due not
so much to the ultimate nature of the one or the other as to the
injurious alliance of faith with capitalism. The reason why in
past history socialism has turned to materialism and atheism is
that faith has been too closely connected with the bourgeoisie
and has espoused their interests. Restore both socialism and
faith to their pure form, and not only dialogue but a fruitful alliance will become possible.

Both faith and socialism must be aware at each moment of
the standpoint from which they speak. Religious faith, for example, may express itself in terms of its own proper sphere (the
theological) or in terms of the political power that it supports.
As long as it remains in its own sphere, it is unchallengeable, but
when it leaves this sphere and enters into the political sphere, it
becomes suspect. Past history shows that it is not easy to keep
the two spheres clearly separate. Does not "theological" discourse often turn unwittingly into "ideological" discourse and
serve to justify political choices? "When the Encyclical *Quadrage-
simo anno* (1931) says that 'the capitalist system is not intrinsically evil,' and when, shortly afterward, the Encyclical *Divini
Redemptoris* (1937) asserts that 'communism is intrinsically evil,'
are the authorities speaking in the name of theology, that is, of
faith, or are they making a political option, and a class option at
that?"[28]

For Garaudy there can be no doubt about the answer. But
we also come to realize that the only side of religious faith that
interests him is not the theological but the relation to economics
and the class struggle. In his eyes faith has validity when it
serves the socialist ideology. Having said this, I must immediately add that Garaudy wants to do justice to religious faith, which
Marxists have overly disparaged, and that, far from regarding
religious faith as external and opposed to socialism, he concludes from what he sees that faith can become a dynamic element in socialism. He even finds it indispensable, because it

keeps socialism from hardening and becoming platitudinous and saves it from despotism and dogmatism.

I Am a Christian

The reason why Garaudy considers a dialogue between Christians and Marxists to be indispensable is that the destiny of each is at stake. The least to be expected from such a dialogue is a modification of positions and a reciprocal challenge:

> There is a clerical Stalinism just as there is a Marxist clericalism. The former leads to the inquisitions and the Syllabuses, the latter to bureaucratic and despotic forms of socialism. We will be able to rescue ourselves from our corruptions only through the abiding, mutual challenge issued by what is best in each of our two communities.[29]

Only dialogue can defend each side against its special demons and bring out what is best in it. In addition, Christians and Communists are condemned to build the future together, a future which cannot be built "despite believers or even without them," "despite the communists or even without them."[30] This dialogue is a necessity for the destiny of the human race.

But Garaudy does not stop there: he now shares the faith of Christians. He has not only acknowledged the objective contribution of Christians to the revolutionary struggle; he also thinks that the substance of faith can be retained, integrated into Marxism, and even personally accepted by a Marxist. In his workroom Garaudy has symbolized this non-exclusion by hanging, side by side, a picture of Karl Marx and a picture of the Virgin with the Christ-Child. Positivism is "not only a world without God but a world without man,"[31] and to it he therefore prefers the militant, creative faith he has found in Christians. But of what faith is he speaking? Christian faith or a simple human faith? Has the dialogue converted Garaudy to Christianity to the point that he accepts Christian teaching? Let me begin by listening to what he has to say.

A Profession of Faith

Garaudy himself has provided us with a sketch of his journey of conversion. In the conclusion of his book *The Alternative*

Future he still hesitates to call himself a Christian, although he has for practical purposes made the convictions of Christians his own: "It is an overwhelming experience when a man who has professed himself an atheist for many years discovers that there has always been a Christian inside him. It is overwhelming to accept responsibility for such a hope."[32]

Three years later, in 1975, Garaudy has taken the step; he ends *Parole d'homme* with the words "I am a Christian."

> My task as a communist is to give socialism that kind of face.
> The face of human plenitude in all its dimensions.
> To live according to the fundamental law of being: the law of love.
> The Cross has taught me the needed renunciations.
> The Resurrection has taught me to move ever further beyond.
> I am a Christian.[33]

Garaudy thus sees himself as having contributed to the internal development of Marxism and Christianity and to their closer relationship, while himself standing apart from one of these two. He believes that he has made this development a reality in his own life. What does such a development mean concretely? Garaudy felt obliged to offer an explanation so as to avoid all misunderstandings:

> This acceptance of faith has not meant that I now remove myself from the world of the political. On the contrary, the acceptance of faith is a way of giving the political its true dimensions. . . . We do not need faith in order to explain the world; we do need it in order to change the world. . . . The essential thing for me is to live in such a way that I no longer live by myself and for myself. And Jesus is the one who teaches us how to do this.[34]

On reading this confession of Christian faith some Christians voiced their quiet jubilation, others uttered a real cry of victory. But this enthusiasm is ambiguous and needs to be moderated. It is not at all clear that Garaudy's faith is quite the same as that of the Christians who acclaim it. Let me not mince words: Garaudy has not passed over to Christianity; he has made Christianity pass over to him. He has not achieved a synthesis, but has rather staked a claim, annexing God, Christ and a good number of theologians for his socialist project.

We need only look at how he reads the theologians who have led him to Christianity. He says that he has learned from Karl Barth that every statement about God is a human statement (whence the title of his own book: *Parole d'homme*). Here is how he interprets Barth: "I cannot set myself up as a civil servant of the Absolute. If I do, I immediately become either an inquisitor or a Stalinist."[35] The point is well taken. Theologians have tended too much to utter discourses based on the absolute, justifying themselves by saying they are depositaries of revealed truth. Garaudy urges a greater modesty, for it is truly an error to think that one can "enter into direct relations with the Absolute and be his spokesman or executor."[36] But, this granted, there is still ambiguity in Garaudy's talk of God. What does the word "God" mean to him? Is there any substance behind it?

From Blondel Garaudy has learned "to live the faith as a journeying, with the assurance that God is a dimension of man, that God is part of the definition of man as breaker of limits and boundaries and as abiding openness to the invention of the future."[37] There is no difficulty in accepting this interpretation. We do find in man an openness which only the infinite can satisfy, and this openness is ontologically constitutive of man. But is Garaudy ready to pass from immanence to transcendence, from the human dimension to the divine dimension? In other words would he utter the "It is!" which terminates *L'Action,* the book in which Blondel expresses his own faith?

The list of theologians goes on. From Teilhard de Chardin Garaudy has learned that creation is unfinished, from Chenu that man is responsible for finishing it, from Gutiérrez that salvation comes through political struggle, and so on. Surrounded by this prestigious council, Garaudy goes forth to the reconquest of the faith, but inspired more by modern attempts at demythologization than by these teachers whose names he displays.

Garaudy's Creed

Garaudy teaches us, and rightly so, that only a committed faith is an authentic faith; on the other hand, it seems that the

faith of which he speaks is simply an internal dimension of the
struggle for socialism. Is it possible to discern the shape of this
faith? It should be enough to offer some examples.

Let me begin with Garaudy's use of the adjective "divine."
Christ's life, he says, is "divine." What does he mean? Simply
that Christ "never acts routinely or rebelliously, but inventive-
ly. . . . He is a permanent centre from which creation springs up
ever new."[38] Garaudy speaks of art as "divine" in the same
sense. In other words, the dimension of "divine" is not a monopoly of Christ, but is found in every human being whose life is
"fully human," that is, "conscious of sharing in the creation."[39]
In its use, therefore, the term gets flattened out and is reduced
to a purely human meaning. To say that a life is divine is only to
praise it for its creativity.

What of God? The only God that counts is the incarnate
God, that is, the God who "acquires a human face."[40] Where is
this incarnate God to be encountered? In Christ? Doubtless, but
also in us and in others. What does the word "God" mean? "I
give the name 'God' to that inaccessible yet intimately present
source, that personal, loving presence, that thinks in me when I
think, that is, when I conceive new possibilities, new projects,
and so on."[41] Now this kind of immanence is not in itself suspect. Moreover we may be lulled by Garaudy's talk of a "personal presence." But the context obliges us to face facts. God is
"that which loves, that which creates," that is, something imper-
sonal. In other words, God has no substance independently of
the actions of human beings. The interior God, the "God-poet"
(or "God-maker"),[42] is man himself acting in the world, man the
creator, who refuses to settle for a closed world and constantly
opens himself to new possibilities.

The same is true of the God I encounter in others. While
seeming to say something orthodox Garaudy in fact reduces
God to an aspect of the human person.

> God has no face except the face of these other men and oth-
> er women. There is no other way of attaining to him except
> that of recognizing him in each of these other people. He *is
> not:* he *makes.* His action is not external to that of each of the
> other people I meet: in each of them he is their specifically
> human dimension.[43]

And even more clearly: "God has no existence apart, but has passed entirely into human beings: he reveals himself and continues his creative activity in them and through them."[44]

If the word "God" says nothing but these human realities, why bother retaining it? "The word calls for respect because for millennia human beings have given this name to the presence in the world of what transcends them and urges them forward."[45] In Garaudy's view God is not to be looked for above and outside of time; he is up ahead of us and within time. He is not a "being" that subsists in himself, but an "act" which symbolizes the limitless human dynamism. He is not a transcendence apart from the world but a transcendence within the world, an image of human beings in their perpetual moving beyond themselves to new possibilities. The idea of God is a symbolic, or even a mythical, expression of this human reality.

The resurrection of Christ is assigned the same meaning. It is turned into a utopia, that is, a dream which inspires revolutionary hope. This hope, however, is concerned not with "another world" but with a "different world," and the problem as Garaudy sees it "is not to integrate the resurrection into the historical perspective but rather to see history in the perspective of the resurrection,"[46] since "there is nothing beyond history. . . . The other world is this world after changing."[47] It is to this that the resurrection bears witness. Another example: the Eucharist. What is its meaning? It is simply a call to human sharing.[48]

Garaudy thus undertakes a horizontal flattening out of Christian truths that empties them of their substance while retaining the terminology. All differences of order disappear: the act of faith, revolution, works of art, are all one and the same action. It comes as no surprise, therefore, to hear him say that the opposition God/man is a false problem.[49] In his desire to do away with all destructive dualisms Garaudy ends up destroying what he wants to save.[50] No matter what he says, he remains a one-dimensional man. Faith opens the human person to no dimension save history; it is nothing but "a leaven of earth and history,"[51] because for Garaudy our world is the only world there is, and our history the only history.[52]

It also comes as no surprise that in speaking of death Garaudy abandons Christian perspectives and adopts the wisdoms of the East which do away with illusory individualities and prom-

ise a communion with the all.[53] Garaudy's faith is at the service
of socialism; apart from this context it has neither meaning nor
reality.

> The entire game is played out in our present history and
> our present life. Together we form but a single human enti-
> ty which does not die when we do. All of nature is my body.
> The total project of the human race—a project constantly
> being reborn, never completed either in execution or con-
> ception—constitutes my spirit. I am damned if I refuse to be
> responsible for it, saved if I contribute to its creation and
> fulfillment.[54]

As a brilliant disciple of Feuerbach, Garaudy is constantly
reducing theology to anthropology. He is sympathetic to modern efforts at demythologization. But can any Christian recognize himself in this truncated faith? No one can prevent Garaudy
from calling himself a Christian. After all, Christianity contains
many dwellings. But we must take him for what he is: a man of
undeniable sincerity and committed faith who believes in the future of the human race. On the other hand, no one achieves a
Christian identity simply by taking over Christian words and using and abusing them.

Esthetics and Religious Faith

In our effort to understand the meaning of "faith" in Garaudy I think it enlightening to compare his ideas on faith with
his esthetics. Religious faith and artistic creation have the same
function in his vision of the future: they preserve an openness to
the possible. In relation to society, their role is to challenge and
to anticipate. We can see here the interrelationship of the three
aspects which ultimately form but one in his mind: politics, art,
and faith.[55] A dialectical unity holds them together: politics has
to do with reality, while the other two embrace the as yet unreal-
ized possibilities and point them out to politics as its goal.

It is significant that Garaudy applies the same schemata to
the work of art that he uses for interpreting Christianity. In recent decades a profound revolution has taken place in art. We
have moved from an art that reproduces—the edifying art of the

ikons which called God to mind, then in the Renaissance the realistic art that explores this world—to an art that looks ahead, an art that expresses human creativity and openness to new possibilities. When Garaudy defines art as a "pointer to transcendence," he does not mean the phrase as the Middle Ages did when the ikon reminded human beings of the existence of a transcendent world; he understands it in the modern sense in which "transcendence" means moving beyond the present to the future and takes on a purely anthropological meaning. "A picture is no longer a pious image that serves in worship nor a reconstruction of nature according to a human plan. It is an object that has value in itself without reference to any mythical or natural reality distinct from it. It claims a status comparable to that of the technological product as a pure creation of man."[56]

As a pure creation of man that has no point of reference except the world of the imagination, modern art tends to substitute "the possible for the real." It no longer mirrors a pre-existent order, heavenly or earthly, but projects a possible order and creates a future that does not yet exist but is anticipated by the artist. Lacking any model, the work of art becomes itself a model, referring us to "a coming world." It is "a project or prospective projection of a world that does not yet exist. . . . The true artist thus has a prophetic function: he is beyond all others the one who helps his contemporaries invent the future."[57] The role of art, whether it be dance, painting or poetry, is "to make the invisible visible,"[58] but the invisible in question is not a reality hidden in the beyond, but a possibility buried in the recesses of the present and perceived only by the artist.

Art, like religion, can in fact have two functions: an ideological and a prophetic. It can serve merely to bind human beings hand and foot to the present order of things; it thus loses any sense of distance from the real and simply represents and celebrates what is. But then it also ceases to exercise its properly artistic function, which is to keep alive or create a tension between the given and the possible. The true vocation of art is prophetic (or utopian); that is, it should speak to human beings of "absent things." This is precisely the point of the *60 oeuvres qui annoncèrent le futur* [Sixty Works That Foretold the Future] which Garaudy selects from a four-centuries-long period. It is also the point of modern dance. Unlike mime, which represents an al-

ready existing reality, dance speaks what does not exist as yet
and is not even conceptualizable:

> The mime's gesture is *descriptive,* the dancer's is *projective:* it
> elicits in us an experience that is not conceptualizable and
> not reducible to words. If we were able to put it into words,
> we would have no need of dance. There is the same differ-
> ence between mime and dance as between the concept,
> which sums up what exists, and myth, which looks beyond
> what is and suggests what is possible.[59]

Here we can see the identity of structure and function in religious faith and in esthetic experience. The accompanying table
sums up the points in this identity.

Art and religion are essentially elements in a political project. From this point of view there is a minor art which is comparable to religion as ideology, for it imitates the given, idealizes
it, and offers it as a model; and there is a major art which is a
"parable" of the future and has the function, along with religious faith, of dynamizing the present.

> Its task is not simply to say what exists, but to express the
> movement and life in what exists and to move beyond the
> latter into a myth that prefigures the future. We are told in
> the Bible that after creating the heavens and the earth with
> the animals and man who dwell therein, God said: "It is
> good!" and granted himself rest on the seventh day. In
> painting, Picasso is the man of the eighth day of creation,
> the one who challenges the creation produced by gods too
> easily satisfied. For Picasso, nothing is finished, everything
> is beginning. . . .[60]

The words just quoted also describe the faith of Garaudy: it
is not an adherence to what is but a looking forward to what is
coming. It challenges the existing world but also the God who
can be defined as Being. It proclaims a coming world and acknowledges a God who is Act and reveals himself in human beings who are open to the future and responsible for its coming.
Garaudy's God, like that of Ernst Bloch, seems to be a symbol
for all the human possibilities not yet realized; apart from this
utopian function he seems to have no existence.

	Ideological function	Prophetic function
Religion	Constantinian era: Religion — reflection / opium	Post-conciliar era: Religion — protest / faith
Esthetics	Middle Ages—16th century: Imitative art (a reflection of reproduction)	Modern age: Prospective art, pointing to transcendence
Politics	Opium of the people: Art and religion in the service of the dominant class	Challenge to the present: •Anticipation of the future •Participation in "project hope"

Garaudy's faith is commitment in the world and is concret-
ized in political action. The dialogue with Christians that he has
undertaken is not without its value to them. He has retaught
them, or reminded them, that it is through involvement in the
world that we come to God; that we attain to heaven through
bringing the earth to its fulfillment, as Teilhard has said; that we
open ourselves to Jesus Christ through encounter with others;
that we can awaken the hope of salvation in human hearts by our
struggle for human liberation. Garaudy rightly emphasizes the
operative character, the prophetic dynamism, of faith. He reminds Christians of the role they must play in history.

But Garaudy also forgets an essential dimension of Christianity: the fullness of meaning and the freely bestowed salvation that Jesus Christ brought into the world. Faith then
includes the acknowledgment of this unexpected dimension
which is obscurely anticipated by human action but which human action cannot attain and can only receive as a gift. Garaudy
has found that faith is "practice" (something Christians have too
often forgotten), but does not understand that it is first and
foremost a free acceptance here and now of the God who is
coming. He has rightly attacked religious ideology as a compromise between faith and political interests, but he has not yet
grasped the real identity of faith.

8

Ernst Bloch
A Hope without God

For some years now theologians have once again been sing-
ing the song of hope. Is this just a passing fashion that has no
future but will soon be replaced by some other fashion? Perhaps. Theologians like to keep changing the vantage-point from
which they view the Christian landscape and to see it in a new
light. This changeableness, which at times is rather frenzied, dis-
concerts people who are used to a theology that is fixed, locked
into a set of immutable formulas, and therefore repetitive. If
theology is today discovering hitherto untrodden paths, this is
reason for rejoicing, because the Gospel is an inexhaustible
source.

But in venturing on to the terrain of hope, theology seems
to be following a different attraction than mere novelty. The
theology of hope has two important features:

• On the one hand, it shows us a side of God that we had to
some extent forgotten. The God whom Christians venerated
right down to our own day was a fixed, settled God who was
closely tied to an orderly system of fixed values. But we have
been realizing that such a God reflects not so much the Scriptures as a Greek philosophy of substances. Scripture talks rather
of the God of the promise, the God of hope, the God who "has
the future as an ontological property."

• On the other hand, this rejuvenated image of God is
matched by a new picture of the human person. The human person is a being that is in movement, a being that has been
launched on a journey by the God of the promise and that is always looking for new horizons. The theology of hope thus
brings home to us a dimension of Christian existence that strikes

a chord in each of us, even if the political conclusions drawn by this theology may frighten or shock some of us. The theologians of liberation and even of revolution have been inspired by this theology of hope.

For these various reasons I turn now to the thinking of the man who inspired the whole business: Ernst Bloch. Strangely enough, the kind of theological thinking that I have described has behind it the impetus given by a Marxist philosopher whose principal work bears the title *Das Prinzip Hoffnung*. It is a monumental work, and I can here give only a general outline of its contents.[1]

Nowadays Ernst Bloch is the subject both of commentary and critical challenge. The Marxists criticize his humanistic tendencies; they also attack him for his sharp criticisms of the Communist apparatus (these are independent of his work on hope). His stock is low among the Marxists. In France, Roger Garaudy embodies the kind of thinking represented by Bloch, but Garaudy too is an outcast. The theologians have also commented on Ernst Bloch, but until recently we had no translation of his great work and no good introduction to it. At present, French readers are in a somewhat better position to gauge his influence.[2] Jürgen Moltmann expressly appeals to his authority; without Ernst Bloch, he says, his book on the theology of hope would not have been written.[3]

Man in Search of His Identity

But first, who is Ernst Bloch? He was born in 1885 and throughout his life has been a non-conformist. He quickly became aware that capitalist society was not working, but he eventually came to see that Marxist society was likewise too cramped. As a young student he was already fighting the established order and, before Marcuse, was denouncing society's preoccupation with profit and its lack of human goals. During the First World War (1914–1918) he protested against German imperialism. The direction his thought was taking is clear even in his first book, *Der Geist der Utopie* [The Utopian Spirit] (1918). He assigns a very important role to music because in music the human person glimpses the identity to which he aspires: "Be one with yourself" is the dream every person should be trying to fulfill.

Work after work came from Bloch's pen, all of them developing the same basic themes. In his *Thomas Münzer als Theologe der Revolution* [Thomas Münzer as Theologian of Revolution] (1921)[4] he brought to public attention one of the most prominent utopians of all. Bloch was greatly attracted by this extraordinary man and saw him as a revolutionary who had the ability to electrify crowds, shake them out of their fatalism, and mobilize them for struggle. Thomas Münzer's venture was indeed a failure; his rebellion was more of a putsch than a revolution. But the reason why it did not succeed was that the situation was not ripe for it. The case of Thomas Münzer shows that "the underground waters of revolution" are never wholly calm except on the surface. Even in the most tranquil periods of history these waters are always ready to rise. We see them stirring in heretical movements, in the frenzied enthusiasm of the various illuminati, and in the rebellions that crop up from time to time. Thomas Münzer is but one witness to a utopian current that runs through history; it is usually suppressed, but the proletariat of our time has adopted it.

Ernst Bloch is a Jew and was forced to go into exile in 1933; he had been denouncing the dangers of Nazism since 1924. When he left Germany, he went to Prague, Vienna, Paris, and finally, in 1938, to Philadelphia where he started his principal work, *Das Prinzip Hoffnung*. After the war, in 1949, he accepted a call to Leipzig as a professor of philosophy. There he soon became at odds with the official doctrine of the Communist Party, which he accused of dogmatism and immobilism. In 1956, at the time of the invasion of Hungary, he was accused of revisionism; he lost his post, abandoned East Germany, and received an appointment as professor at Tübingen in West Germany. German publishers bestowed on him a literary prize for contributions to peace. He celebrated his ninetieth birthday on July 8, 1975, and has continued to write.[5]

In Search of a Homeland

It is not surprising that the key word in Bloch's work should be "homeland." What is a human being? A being in search of a homeland. In Bloch's view, the basic dynamism of this quest is supplied by hope. Hope is an urge to "happiness, freedom, disalienation, the golden age, the land of milk and honey, and so on."[6] Hope looks to a perpetual "elsewhere," a better existence which Bloch also speaks of as the "summum bonum," the "new heavens and new earth," but above all as the "homeland" (German: *Heimat*). This very concrete term is highly evocative for a German ear and expresses the "place" where the principle of hope finds rest: "Once human beings have taken control of their lives and have established themselves in a true democracy, where there is no exteriorization or alienation, something enters the world that has been a guiding star constantly shining for each individual since childhood but that no one has as yet reached: homeland."[7]

Childhood is not the only period to be haunted by this dream of a homeland, a place to be at home. The dream keeps coming back throughout life, taking different forms at different ages. The principle of hope begins its work by summoning up "the little day dreams" that human beings cultivate from childhood to old age. In children these are often pure fantasies, for childhood acknowledges nothing as being impossible. They become more modest in adults: dreams of business success or sexual happiness; they also become more bitter (dreams of revenge) or more matter-of-fact (private dreams with no collective dimension). But even when dreams do not soar as high, they nonetheless constantly slip in through the fissures of life and transfigure it.

The ability to dream does not die out. True enough, "as the years pass we learn to forget,"[8] but even the elderly dream. They may be content simply to embellish the past and to make it more beautiful than it really was, but they never stop dreaming: dreams of rest, happiness, peace. Bloch concludes that there is no age at which people are able to be satisfied with what is. They want something else; they look for an elsewhere and the goal of their journey can only be the "homeland," socialist style, that would satisfy all their longings. "Interruptions are an everyday experience. The significant thing is that we are glad to be interrupted by anything new and unexpected. It is as if nothing in life is so good that it cannot be set aside at any moment. The pleasure attendant on change leads us astray and often deludes us. But it always takes us outside our customary round."[9]

From these observations Bloch derives a definition of man that matches Heidegger's definition: man is a being of distances. He is nowhere "at home," at least in the world as it now exists. He is constantly on the move toward the place where he will find peace and satisfaction. But let us not delude ourselves. This "place," this "homeland," is not hidden somewhere outside of us, in some heavenly Jerusalem or some as yet unexplored part of the universe. The place is man himself, who is still hidden from his own eyes. Bloch therefore speaks, in more philosophical terms, of a search for identity. "I exist but I do not yet possess myself. This state of affairs is the origin of our becoming."[10] The tension toward the future or the elsewhere is the tension of man toward the revelation of himself in the future and toward the establishment of the "homeland" that welcomes all of his dreams.

It is true that the tension is not always keenly felt. Most of the time we live "mechanically," carried along by the certainties and habits we have acquired. But as long as his consciousness is not completely eliminated, the human person cannot surrender the desire to unite self with self. The need of dreams and escapes, which is a sign of this longing for identity, is a constitutive dimension of consciousness. Bloch never wearies of repeating that to think is to surpass, to cross boundaries, to move beyond (*Denken heisst überschreiten*). To think is to be in tension toward the place—which is ontological rather than geographical or temporal, although it must be translated into spatio-temporal reality—where human beings will achieve their fulfillment.

All-Conquering Hunger

What is the moving force behind this becoming? What is it that sets history in motion? The answer is not to be looked for outside of ourselves. The thing that gives rise to all becoming and launches revolutions is the desire that dwells in the human body. Desires are legion, of course, as experience shows. Neither as a society nor individually do human beings succeed in settling into a definitive satisfaction or a permanent way of life. One desire is hardly satisfied when other, even more demanding desires spring up. Desire is constantly reborn from its own ashes. A human being resembles a cascade of desires that are constantly finding new forms of satisfaction. Desires crisscross or exclude each other. Society interferes with them: capitalist society, for example, favors some and stirs others to fever pitch, as in the case of sexual desire and the desire for profit; it also stifles certain desires, such as religious feeling. Desires always function within a given society. Their ebb and flow reflects the values set on them by society. But no society has ever been able to satisfy all desires to the point of fully reconciling the individual to that society.

Bloch looks through this crowd of desires for the primary one, the one that keeps history going and is powerful enough to overturn the structures of society. The question is one that has elicited discordant answers from philosophers. Freud explains all becoming on the basis of sexual desire. Adler invokes will power, and Jung the vaguer need of "intoxication"; others appeal to the need of self-preservation, and so on. Bloch follows none of these leaders. He thinks that all these desires are secondary and do not explain either becoming or historical upheavals. If we give them priority, it is simply because we have been misled by the particular kind of society in which such desires occupy the center of the stage. Each of them may dominate a period, but it is a mistake to make it the first mover of all becoming. Freud is a clear example of such an error. When he gives central place to the sexual drive he shows himself to be a prisoner of lower middle-class Viennese society. After all, how can the whole of history be explained on such a narrow basis?

As a good Marxist Bloch falls back on an economic explanation. For him the strongest force is hunger; it explains the becoming of the world and the succession of economic structures. In hunger Bloch sees at work "the elementary energy of hope": hunger is the source of improvement; more than that, it is a revolutionary force that has changed the face of the world and may change it yet again. It is not surprising, of course, that the bourgeoisie, who have never experienced hunger, should neglect this instinct. But where is any more powerful moving force to be found? Unlike other desires, hunger is constantly renewed and therefore makes necessary a ceaseless search for new structures for satisfying it. As soon as it is impossible to satisfy hunger due to a given historical situation, the very hunger impels men to change the situation. In individuals with empty stomachs hunger can become a "concern for revolution":

> The concern always begins with hunger, but conscious hunger becomes an explosive that smashes out the prison-bars which we call "privation." Therefore the self does not seek merely to preserve itself; it becomes an explosive power: self-preservation becomes self-expansion. And this movement of expansion overturns everything opposed to the

class which is not on the rise, and, finally, everything opposed to classless man.[11]

For Bloch, then, hunger constitutes the first degree of anticipatory consciousness. If people dream, it is first of all because they are hungry, because they lack something and want a life in which desire is satisfied.[12] Many of these dreams are illusory and empty, but others that are anchored in the real world open up new horizons and make it possible to invent a different future.

What Future for Man?

Bloch thus takes as his starting point a certain conception of the human person. Human beings are separated from themselves and seek their own identity. The primitive instinct that explains historical becoming is hunger. It was because they were hungry that human beings began to organize chaos and to humanize the earth. What does it mean, then, to be a man? It means to reject the situation as it is and to move beyond it, initially in dreams. It is to look beyond what does exist and to glimpse what might exist. It is to discern in the present all the possibilities that are buried in it and that prophesy the future.

The basic characteristic of human beings is that they have utopias. Utopia has become a discredited category and Bloch seeks to restore it to good standing, for he regards it as the category proper to our century. Conservative concerns have led us to neglect it excessively or to surpass it. We must restore it to its proper place; we must begin to dream again.

But there are dreams and dreams. Bloch introduces a distinction between nocturnal dreams and day dreams. Freud was interested in dreams, but in the nocturnal kind that dip into the past of the dreamer and bring a part of the unconscious to the surface. Bloch turns instead to day dreams which feed on the possibilities of the present and look ahead to the future. Nocturnal dreams move back to a past that is no longer conscious, day dreams turn to the future that has not yet become a reality. The former cause us to breathe in "the smells of a cellar," the latter "the perfumes of the dawn."[13] The former are repetitive, bringing back from the unconscious what has already been; the latter are forward-looking, directing us to a "not yet." A day dream that reaches a structured stage sketches in the form of a utopia a picture of what is desirable and can be brought to pass. It is an intuition of the future.

Dreams of the Future

Day dreams can, however, be snares. As an activity of the imagination, a day dream invents utopias, that is, anticipations of the future, which may be either abstract or concrete. A dream can develop in an idle way and build castles in Spain; or it can lay hold of the real and with this as a starting point outline realizable plans for the future. Two factors play a part in a constructive day dream: a subjective factor, the human capacity for dreaming, and an objective factor, the discernment of the possibilities latent in the real. If these two factors are separated, the one ends in subjectivism, that is, the operation of imagination without connection with reality, and the other in objectivism, which is a rejection of imagination and the expectation that change will come about through the simple evolution of reality (to extol a kind of "objective automatism"[14] is simply to encourage defeatism). Imagination may, of course, ramble, but on the other hand it alone can break through into the future, provided it remains in contact with reality.

We must thus distinguish between a healthy and a pathological use of the utopian function. Bloch defines this function in terms of a dialectic of consciousness and knowledge: consciousness of the desire that is in us and seeks fulfillment, and knowledge of the objective reality that is around us and whose possibilities we must know how to explore. The utopian function anticipates the future in terms both of desire (the subjective factor) and of the real (the objective factor). If it spends its time among empty possibilities, it will end up building abstract utopias; if it bases itself on the possibilities written into reality, it will invent what Bloch calls, in a paradoxical phrase, concrete utopias. Hope overleaps the narrow bounds of the present and looks to the possibilities which the present contains in a germinal state and which are not yet actualized. A utopia is a vision of the future of human beings and the world as this future can be anticipated from the known real.

Not all utopias, therefore, have value. Only those have value which come into existence at the point of juncture between the real and the possible. A dream that has no contact with life is an illusion; on the other hand, life without dreaming is simply the flat world of the positivist. Here we have a criterion for distinguishing concrete utopias from abstract utopias. The latter are detached from reality, while the former prolong reality even while they move beyond it toward the future. Also to be mentioned here are anti-utopias which see reality as containing no possibilities for the future and therefore regard it as destined for annihilation.

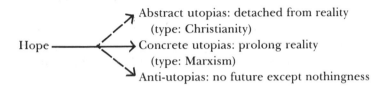

Hope
Abstract utopias: detached from reality (type: Christianity)
Concrete utopias: prolong reality (type: Marxism)
Anti-utopias: no future except nothingness

In Bloch's view, hope feeds on desire but is grounded in the real. It is a *docta spes:* not a foolish hope but a hope that is informed. It draws its information from contact with reality and is focused on what has now become really possible. People have always prolonged the real world in their attempts to find its fulfillment in a different world; most of the time they have done so in an idealist and abstract way, as in Christianity. Bloch does not see Christianity as being an effective response to the present. Only Marxism, because it is based on a scientific analysis of the real world, efficaciously prolongs the present world and offers it a utopia that can mobilize all its energies:

> It is here that the power and truth of Marxism is seen: it has dissipated the clouds which used to envelop dreams of the future, yet it has not extinguished the column of fire in these dreams but has on the contrary made it burn brighter with the help of reality. . . . As thus exercised, the utopian function deserves to remain: it is a transcending without transcendence.[15]

But why have utopias at all? A utopia is always revolutionary. Unlike an ideology, which is a set of ideas that strengthen and seek to stabilize the established order, a utopia prefigures the future and reacts against the present by challenging and overthrowing it. An ideology is produced by the dominant classes which want to retain a situation that is advantageous to them.

A utopia is produced by the disinherited, the dominated classes, which long for a different future. An ideology aims at reconciling subjectivity with present reality, and envelops this reality "in the smoke of incense";[16] a utopia protests against present reality and turns subjectivity toward a future which the utopia renders already possible.

Toward a New Society

At all times there have been men ready to indict a society gone awry and to imagine a new model of society. All these dreams that stand as landmarks along the road of history, from antiquity (Solon, Diogenes, Plato, St. Augustine, and so on) down to our own time (Fourier, Saint-Simon, Bakunin, Proudhon, Marx, and others) are more than curiosities. Ernst Bloch welcomes them with sympathy, for utopias throw into relief what is incised in the body of society; they reveal tendencies that have been repressed.

As I pointed out, utopias may be abstract or concrete. When the utopian spirit operates at the abstract level, independently of the social conditions of the age, it produces fantasies but is incapable of producing a social revolution. This describes the nineteenth century utopians before Marx:

> The utopians were wholehearted in their condemnation of injustice and their desire for justice; with their heads they tried, but at the abstract level, to rebuild a better world; they were also wholehearted in their hope that they might fire men's will for that world. . . . In these utopians who remained abstractionists the lamp of their dreams lit up an empty space; reality was being forced into the mould of ideas. As a result, it was in an ahistorical and undialectical, abstract and static way that the images elaborated by desire were connected with a reality that had nothing to do with them.[17]

What, in plain language, does Bloch have against the abstract utopians? He does not deny that they were magnanimous: they reacted to injustice with their hearts and called for change. Nor does he dispute the models of society that they constructed in their heads: the architecture of the society they dreamed of is perfect. But neither generous heart nor clear head is enough to change reality. Most of the utopians simply developed "private" fantasies that had no contact with social reality and no grasp of historical conditions. This is why the visions were abstract, moral, undialectical.

The weakness of these utopias is now clear: they do not provide a real lever with which to move history. We may ask why these utopians had no real influence on history. Essentially, there were two factors that militated against them.

First, there was their own situation: these utopians continued to think as bourgeois. They were doctrinaire thinkers who cultivated a rational ideal but had no sense of history and of the forces that confronted one another on the historical scene. They may not have expected "the heavenly Jerusalem to descend from on high," but neither did they expect it to rise up out of concrete history. They simply substituted in their heads "a social machine that worked perfectly for another that was defective."[18] The utopians were excellent "social engineers," but they paid no heed to the laws of social change.

The second factor was the objective situation of society: society was not ripe for change. Industrial development was inadequate as yet, the proletariat was non-existent as a social force, capital was too fragmented, and so on. Should we, then, be surprised that these utopias remained abstract and developed in the heaven of ideas?

These pre-Marxist utopians thus lacked an instrument of analysis and action, or, in other words, a lever capable of exerting effective pressure on society. The abstract utopians remained at the stage of desire, but desire alone has never altered reality. Their hope remained subjective, for it was not based on positive contents of the real world. And yet, though these abstract utopias were far removed from reality, they are not without interest. Three aspects of them are to their credit.

First, they show a real will to change. Without the utopias the will to change would have died out in society. The economists of whatever age have never done more than throw light on chaos; the utopians dreamed of emerging from chaos. It is true that in the abstract utopians this will was unsuccessful: it was generous but ineffective, impatient but unrealistic. But at least it bore witness to a dissatisfaction.

A further point to the credit of these utopians is their clarity of mind: they saw what had to be abandoned. They had the ability to rid themselves of that "idolatry of the objective" which can only encourage fatalism. Their utopias were so many protests against entrenched conditions. They may not have had any way of bringing the objective situation to the needed ripeness for revolution but they did show a possible way out and thus kept hope alive.

Here we have the third positive thing to their credit: their mental vision. Not only did they see what needed to be abandoned; they also glimpsed the goal to be striven for. These men were characterized by the "pathos of the fundamental goal."[19] The goal was sometimes awash in generous but vague ideas: liberty, brotherhood, justice, and so on, preferably written in capital letters. But the goal was nonetheless capable of energizing men and women. People do not risk their lives for an unbalanced budget, but they are indeed ready to die for freedom.

Such are the positive aspects of these utopias. Evidently their very source of strength is also their weakness. They represent the triumph of subjectivity over objectivity, freedom over fatalism, hope over defeatism. But they did not succeed in changing society.

Marxism as a Concrete Utopia

The history of abstract utopias "shows that socialism is as old as the West." They are signs of a magnanimous determination to bring about change, of a fiery protest against an inhuman world, and of a tenacious longing for a better world. And yet it took Marx to make this socialism "scientific." What does this mean? Marx introduced into it certain changes which made it really functional.

To begin with, he changed priorities. He was more concerned to criticize the present situation than to project models of the kind of society he wanted. He is more concerned to challenge the present than to imagine the future.

We do not find in him any detailed prefiguration of the future, such as we find in the older utopias. The abstract utopias devoted nine-tenths of their energy to a portrait of future state and only one-tenth to criticism of the negative aspects of present society. As a result, they painted a vivid picture of the goal, but the way to it remained hidden from them. Marx devotes nine-tenths of his work to a critical analysis of the present situation, and allows only limited space to a *description* of the future.[20]

Second, this reversal of priorities highlights the element of effectiveness. Marx dismisses moralizing appeals and devotes himself to a scientific analysis of the conditions required for the transformation of capitalism. "Marx's critique does not bring to light any 'fold of the heart,' as Hegel would say, but it does reveal the folds, faults, and contradictions of the economy."[21] Such a critique enables him to see within reality itself the dynamism leading to its destruction.

This dynamism is the result of a double contradiction, one objective and located at the economic level (accumulation and concentration of capital, monopolization, crisis due to overproduction, and so on), and the other subjective, located at the social level, and due to confrontation of two classes, the proletariat and the bourgeoisie (the first of these is engendered by the second as its antithesis). The destruction of capitalism will be due to the combined action of these two contradictions.

Third, we must add that Marx has only a minor interest in the future. He refuses to draw a detailed picture of the new society. This last remains quite vague: "a classless society" (Marx), "a realm of freedom" (Lenin); these are expressions that have no precise definition. Although his entire work is oriented toward the future, Marx is more concerned with the means of getting there than with foreseeing its organization and modeling its shape. He speaks of a realistic prefiguration: "Marxism is not a prefiguration of a utopian kind; it is the *novum* of a concrete prefiguration, the development of which begins in the present."[22]

But while Marx does not sin through excessive abstractionism, does he not go to the opposite extreme: a realism that lacks any definite horizon? He urges men to act "reasonably and as people without illusions," but he does not mean to discourage enthusiasm for the goal. He wants people to have no illusions, but he does not want them to have no horizons. Rather he urges them to combine rigorous knowledge of historical processes (therefore of the means) with a revolutionary enthusiasm for the goal.

The question is sometimes asked whether Bloch is really a Marxist. He has been accused of indulging in a spiritualism of evolution.[23] However, while he does assign an important place to subjectivity, he does not conceive the movements of this subjectivity as unconnected with the real world. On the other hand (and for this reason some do not regard him as a Marxist), he rejects the economism which is having its day among various anti-humanistic Marxists. Inasmuch as he makes his own certain categories such as the suppression of alienation, the return of the human person to himself, or the classless society (with the class struggle as the way to it) he is locating himself in the line of the younger Marx rather than of the mature Marx.

Error and Truth in the Religions

The hope which Ernst Bloch represents is of a future that will be socialist or will not exist at all. This future remains undefined, and we do not have its identity papers. At the end of *Das Prinzip Hoffnung* Bloch speaks of a homeland that will be a "true democracy." Thus far, however, neither East nor West has given us a model of such a homeland. In any event, it is an earthly homeland which human beings must create. It is useless to expect it as a gift from heaven.

Any escape into a world that is not our present world is thus automatically suspect to Ernst Bloch. The "homeland" of which man dreams signals to him through the real possibilities of our world. It proclaims itself to be "the homeland of identity," of a restored harmony, a homeland in which man will no longer be separated from nature and other persons and in which even the alienation of man from himself will be overcome. Such a hope, which looks to a future belonging solely to man himself and which calls all of his energies into play for its building, is evidently a direct rival of the Christian hope. It contains promises of an earthly fulfillment that leaves no room for the Christian promises. The latter are dismissed as illusory.

Confrontation is inevitable between two hopes that both claim to be absolute. Bloch is quite aware of this, and for this reason he does not dodge the confrontation in all its explicitness. He examines the Christian hope with sympathy but without making any concessions to it. He does not reject the fulfillment which Christianity sets before us, but he brings it from heaven down to earth. How does he attack this problem? How does he carry out his reductionist undertaking? This is the question to which I now turn.

Man Hidden from Himself

If we regard as an adequate biographical notice the few pages of *Spuren* in which Bloch describes the stages of his life, we can say that from the age of fifteen he had rid himself of all religious beliefs: "On the day of my confirmation, at the moment when I had to pronounce the formula before the altar, I added three times 'I believe in atheism,' or words to that effect."[24]

This was the age when the God of the Decalogue became intolerable to him and he gave his allegiance instead to the God of "Life." The former of these two Gods is a repressive God; the latter seethes with all the vitality of the human person.

This adolescent rejection of God, this fervent atheism of Bloch's early years, was gradually transformed into a clear and firm certainty. Bloch gradually came to the reflective conviction that God does not exist and that the religions are a form of error. The conviction was nourished by the thinking of Feuerbach and Marx. But Bloch also offers his own original explanation of the phenomenon of religion; it is drawn from his personal conception of man. What, then, is religion?

To begin with, it is an *illusion*. Bloch here simply takes over the peremptory judgment of his predecessors. As a motto for the pages in which he deals with religion he takes these words of William Butler Yeats: "If you peer into the darkness for a long time, you always end up seeing something there." He then makes his own the explanation given in this text of Feuerbach: "What man is not but dreams of being, he represents to himself as realized in his gods; a god is man's desire for happiness when set free by the imagination."[25]

The gods are products of human desire as supported and given shape by the imagination. But for Bloch, as for Feuerbach, such products are always illusions, for instead of submitting to control and instruction by reality, desire mistakes itself for the reality. It absorbs into itself an ontological substance that is in fact created solely by the imagination. The gods are human products that are to be explained in the light of the way desire works; the explanation is to be completed by an understanding of the way in which man splits himself in two and becomes alienated. When faced with his own limitations, man divides himself in two. He projects all his limitations outside himself, but in the

process inverts their meaning. What he experiences as an emptiness within him, he sees as a fulfillment outside of himself, and
instead of recognizing in this fulfillment an attribute or attributes of the human essence, he assigns it to another, namely,
God, whom he perceives as independent of himself. But all this
is simply playing with illusions. "Nothing exists besides nature
and man; the higher beings created by our fantasy are merely
the fantastic reflections of our own essence,"[26] says Bloch, following the lead of Feuerbach and Marx.

Second, religion is an *opium*. It is this only secondarily, but
to the extent that it is indeed an opium, it is deadly in its effects.
It deactivates the will, for the latter now leaves it to another to
do what it itself should be doing. Again following his predecessors, Bloch thinks of religion as an opium on two counts: it produces false consolations, and it exercises an oppressive power.

Marx had already said in a striking way that religion is a
consolation that enables human beings to support their wretchedness in this life. Bloch agrees with him: "In the great religions
of mankind the will that looks for a better world has often found
only a consolation that proves disastrous; for a long time this
will has made of this consolation the most elaborately decorated
part of its house, or has even made of it its only dwelling."[27]

Instead of energizing the will and making it concerned with
the earth, religion turns it toward heaven and causes it to hope
to receive in the next world that which is refused it in this. To
the extent that religion focuses the best of man's being and energies on this illusory place, it is destructive.

Above all, religion is an oppressive force that has always
served the current rulers. When Marx describes religion as an
opium, he has in mind a particular historical situation in which
religion served as a supplementary ideology for the dominant
class. When he indicts the Church, he does so because it is on
the side of the ruling powers. And when he declares war on the
Church—he likes to repeat Voltaire's exclamation: "Crush the
abomination!"—he does so not for rationalist reasons but for
social reasons: the Church has objectively taken sides with the
oppressors; the temple is in the hands of the tradesmen; the
Church is in the service of the bourgeoisie. The criticism of religion is thus a weapon in the struggle for man and the future of
the earth.

While Bloch accepts the explanations of his predecessors,

he also distances himself from them in certain ways. Feuerbach had analyzed the mechanism by which gods are made; he had taken the works apart. Marx had sought an explanation at the economic level: religion originates in the distress human beings feel in the midst of a world that is too harsh for them. Bloch for his part seems at times to adopt psychological explanations: man invents the gods, heaven, heavenly rewards, and, in short, the whole "tropical vegetation," either because he feels an "inordinate terror" or because he feels himself filled by a "joy that has no reason."[28] But in fact Bloch regards this approach as inadequate. There is a truth in religion which most of his predecessors have failed to see and which can be grasped only in terms of an ontology of the "not yet."

Bloch repeats after Kant that man possesses within himself "the organs for his higher destiny,"[29] but Bloch also sees that man does not use these in order really to explore the possibilities which the world offers him. Instead he invents all sorts of fantasies that are nothing but the fruits of his subjectivity and have no connection with reality. Bloch is not satisfied to point out the error of these fantasies (scientific rationalism has undertaken this task) nor to show their harmful effects (they hamper the revolutionary struggle, and the proletariat has rid itself of them). He looks for their positive meaning. This meaning is in fact quite simple: the hidden God of religion is nothing but man who is hidden from himself. God is the "abyssal" gap (the *Hohlraum*) which enables man to represent to himself what he has not yet succeeded in becoming.

This notion is in the logic of what we already know about man. Man's *Dasein*, his authentic existence, his real "core," has not yet been revealed. Man is living in ignorance of what he shall be; he does not know where his "ship" is taking him. He has a ticket which no one is able to read and which he has in fact now lost. What does all this mean? It means that man must invent the goal of his journey.[30] He has a presentiment of this future in music in which lurks "something of the gladness which the (possible) resurrection of all the dead brings,"[31] in joy, which is the "sign of the house," and even in death which, though destructive, also brings a revelation of man's real "core."[32] This is a point to which I will return.

What, then, is God? He is a projection into the beyond of man's future here below, a projection not of what man is but of what he will be and of what desire makes known to him. God is a utopia abstracted from what remains hidden to us regarding ourselves. God is the "form of the fullness" and of the "true kingdom" that will be made a reality in the future. In order then to recoup for ourselves what is true in religion it is enough to apply to the future what religion says about the next world. Religion simply proclaims in a utopian form "the unknown future of man."[33] "God is thus seen to be the ideal, hypostatized in the form of a utopia, of the as yet unfulfilled human essence."[34]

It is clear now that while the problematic of Ernst Bloch is identical with that of Feuerbach, he nonetheless introduces a manifest difference. Like Feuerbach, Bloch aims to reduce theology to anthropology, but the reduction is carried out no longer for the benefit of present-day man in his social dimension but for the benefit of man who is to come and who will be revealed in the future. Bloch distinguishes in man "his present manifestation and his not yet present nature,"[35] and by so doing is able to eliminate God as a hypostasis while still retaining the hope which energizes the religions. Bloch recoups this hope in its human dimension: it is the process which carries man on to his true completion, toward his still hidden essence.

Ambiguity of Christianity

Above and beyond these general reflections on the religions Bloch has a very special interest in Christianity. He has a very complete knowledge of it, and his interpretation of the Christian religion is based on very thorough study. By and large he puts Christianity into the same boat with the other religions, but he also discerns in it a tendency, very largely repressed, which has often turned it into a revolutionary leaven in the course of history. Christianity is a consolation but it can also become a protest, as Marx observed. Christ himself did not shrink from taking a whip and chasing the buyers and sellers from the temple. Bloch therefore sees Christianity as containing two currents which have not been brought into harmony.

Here is the most important judgment Bloch passes on Christianity:

Where there is hope, there is religion. If this statement be true, then it must be acknowledged that Christianity . . . embodies the true essence of religion. In other words, in

Christianity we are no longer dealing with a static myth and therefore with apologetics, but with an eschatological and human messianism, and therefore with something explosive. In it, the truly meaningful substratum of religion—stripped of the illusory hypostasis, God, and even of the taboos issued by teachers—is seen for the first time: hope that is all-embracing and really explosive. Either Caesar or Christ! With this battle-cry a kingdom different from the kingdom of power and oppression appears on the scene.[36]

This and other texts show that Bloch introduces a division into Christianity. He distinguishes two irreconcilable aspects. Authentic Christianity is the Christianity embodied in the prophetic and apocalyptic currents of thought. But this current is rivaled by another, a priestly current that is focused on cult. The two currents are constantly interacting, each trying to eliminate the other. Each is based on principles which contradict those of the other; the Bible tries to bring them into harmony after a fashion.

The priestly current predominates. It emphasizes the text in Genesis: "God saw that it was good." This statement is an ideological principle (a static myth) which the priestly current puts at the service of the established order and which gives it an authority that justifies any and every prohibition. The apocalyptic current has its focus not on what is but on what is coming. It wants to see the old world pass away, and it appeals for this to the God who "makes all things new." A utopian principle (eschatological messianism) dominates this current and energizes human beings to establish a new order.[37]

The first of these two currents takes as its point of reference the Creator God who has a vertical, static relation to the world: God is above the world, dominates it, and keeps it in submission. The second current takes as its point of reference the God of the exodus who revealed himself to Moses as the God of the future, who has "the future as an ontological property": "I will be who I will be."[38] He is the Redeemer God who goes before his people and leads them to the promised land and to freedom. What is the connection between these two currents?

The Creator God who has made a finished world that is very good and very perfect, and the God who is Hope and

whom Moses proclaimed to his people, are fully identified
only in rabbinical theology (and later on in the Creed of the
Christian Church). By contrast, the prophets, who are faithful to the God of the Exodus, rarely evoke the Creator
God.[39]

Bloch speaks in the name of this "other Bible," the Bible of
the disinherited and the rebellious. This Bible drew its inspiration from the exodus and found its true embodiment in Christ.

Bloch gives this opposition a universal application. He
shows that while all religions have had founders, some were simply products of the ruling class and invented religions (the
mythical religions) which were simply reflections of the ideology
of their class. Other founders, however, drew their support from
the oppressed and gave expression to the longings and secret
rebellions of this class (messianic religions). Moses belonged to
this second category of founders, as did Jesus who fulfills and
moves beyond all the prophets, including Moses. The threat
hanging over this second group is formidable: not only do they
risk being persecuted, but in addition, and above all, they are in
danger of being co-opted. They suffer this fate nearly every time
that the movements they initiate turn into Churches, which are
more disposed to bury freedom than to inspire it.[40]

This law is exemplified especially in the case of Jesus who,
according to Bloch, introduced a radical cleavage between God
and man and who, in his human dealings, put himself on the
side of the weak and in opposition to the priestly caste. But the
priests got their revenge! When he claimed the title Son of Man
Jesus located himself as a human being in the prophetic and
apocalyptic current. He came not to put an end to history but to
make known the unlimited openness of history, a truth to which
the resurrection bears witness. He gave other human beings a
glimpse of the possibility there is of their disclosing their true
selves and attaining fulfillment. But Jesus was soon co-opted. St.
Paul turned him into the *Kyrios,* the "Son of God" who is
clothed with all the attributes of the emperor: "The key-word
Man in Son of Man, along with the intentional element of *novelty*
and *mystery,* defines the expression as belonging to a line of tradition, to a Christ-*topos* that is different from the so to speak legitimate, dynastic title, *Son of God,* which has been far more
common."[41]

The title "Son of Man," which is at once new and obscure, unexpected and secretive, introduces a twofold novelty: (1) it implicitly contains a negation of the transcendence of God (emphasis on man); (2) it implies an unknown future, that of man himself. Jesus used it because of its eschatological significance. For the parousia of God, which the Jews expected, Jesus substituted the parousia of man.[42] But, Bloch observes, the title "Son of Man" quickly disappeared. From the very beginning Christians replaced it with the titles "Lord" and "Son of God," which had been invented by the Church for cultic and then political purposes: "The Kyrios-Christos God admirably suited the purposes of those who would reduce the Christian community to a sort of military service of their cultic hero, with the inevitable consequences in terms of allegiance to worldly rulers whose authority, according to Paul and others, is likewise 'from God.' "[43]

This shift was a victory of conservatism over eschatology. The early Church and especially the official theologians of Byzantium only widened the gap between these two perspectives. The revolutionary novelty that had found expression in the title "Son of Man" was eliminated in favor of a mythical title, "Son of God" (or "Pantocrator"), with its obvious ideological advantages for the ruling power.

Such interpretations as these are open to debate. Turning Christ into an atheist in disguise or a secret revolutionary can hardly be taken as serious exegesis and offends Christian sensibilities. On the other hand, is it really possible to deny the tendency to take control of the Gospel message and render it innocuous? The two currents which Bloch describes are perhaps not as irreconcilable as he says, but we do in fact see that in our time the second current, the clerical or, as Garaudy would say, the "Constantinian" current, has in fact effectively repressed the first, that is, the prophetic and apocalyptic current which enjoys only a peripheral life.

The Heritage of Christianity

But let me remain a little longer in the company of Bloch, who despite everything shows a sympathy toward the religions that is rather striking in a Marxist. He does, of course, make his own selection and acknowledges as truly meaningful and important only the apocalyptic current which, as he sees it, has been betrayed by the Churches. Moreover, he sees in religion only a subjective, abstract utopia that lacks any connection with reality. In addition, the Jesus of whom he speaks is not the Jesus we customarily recognize in the Gospels, or at least Bloch captures only part of the Gospel personality. For Bloch Jesus is a man and the most human of all human beings, but he has no divine dimensions to his being. Bloch accepts Christianity only after having first redrawn the picture of it and having eliminated its real essence. If we are to grasp the full import of his criticism we must go back to his definition of religion: Bloch understands religion as "hope of wholeness":

> Inherited religion (meta-religion) becomes a consciousness of the ultimate utopian function *in toto.* This function consists for man in surpassing himself, transcending himself (in close connection with the tendency of human history to transcend itself dialectically)—transcending himself without any heavenly transcendence. "Heavenly transcendence" is understandable, however: it is a hypostatized anticipation of the identity of the self with itself.[44]

Further on, Bloch adds:

> The anthropological criticism of religion does not do away with the hope on which Christianity is founded; it only removes from this hope that which would destroy it as hope and turn it into a superstitious trustfulness, that is, into a mythology of fulfillment, a mythology that is crazily unreal but that is nonetheless hypostatized as a reality. The criticism of religion reduces the contents of religion to human desire.[45]

These two texts can be taken as a summary. They express the essentials of the criticism Bloch levels at the religions and of the heritage he wants to retain from the religions.

To begin with, he eliminates the *hypostasis* we call *God.* "God" has no ontological substance; he is a utopia contrived out of all human desires and is therefore an illusion. Bloch urges us to do away with this transcendence as being a hypostatized personification, and to reject it as a mythological holdover.

He takes for his own use the definition of religion as *hope of wholeness!* He retains from religion the hope which is its ground and the wholeness which is its goal. In destroying the mythical and superstitious content of religion Bloch is careful not to suppress the hope which led to the invention of religion. This hope is indispensable for human beings. Without it they would be prisoners of a closed universe. Therefore, after objective transcendence (the hypostasis God) has been rejected, there remains the subjective transcendence found in religion, the dynamism that carries man ahead.

For Bloch, then, religion is reduced to a self-surpassing, a movement of transcendence without heavenly transcendence. All that he retains of religion is its formal expression: the idea of wholeness. But this wholeness is not defined in advance, as it is in religion, for it is identical with the "not yet" of man. Whereas religion offers an illusory anticipation of wholeness, Bloch identifies it with the concrete utopia of Marxism, the homeland which every human being yearns for.

Bloch fills the idea of wholeness with a *new content:* the identity of the self with itself, the "homeland." While he criticizes the hypostatized anticipation found in religion, he does away neither with the idea of an anticipation of wholeness nor with its content, but he does humanize these.

Once the God-hypostasis has been eliminated, what is left? An empty space.[46] This space is there before the religions and is the condition for their possibility. But it is also the condition for the possibility of man. The gods fill this empty space in the wrong way, and they must be driven from it. Bloch calls for giving this empty space a new and immanent content. The space is open to human beings as a real possibility that can be successfully actualized or that can fail to yield any fruit. It can be filled with a genuine reality in the future (a *totum*) or it can remain empty (a *nihil*). No guarantee is given in advance as it in the religions. Everything depends on the choices human beings make.

Rather paradoxically, Bloch concludes that atheism is the best guarantor of hope, for it opens up to hope a space for a fulfillment that is never determined in advance as it is in the religions. "Atheism liberates the messianism that precedes it."[47]

Death, Where Is Your Victory?

It seems, however, that Bloch's hope must sooner or later admit frustration. However far the human adventure may take

us, it eventually runs up against death, the wall against which all
utopias are shattered. Hope may emerge victorious from all human trials, but how can it confront death? Is it not condemned
in advance to failure? Bloch does not evade this question; he accepts the challenge.

At first sight, indeed, death looks like bankruptcy, the "ultimate fiasco," "the most terrible of all anti-utopias."[48] There is
no escaping the anguished experience of it. It signifies destruction and nothingness. How is it possible to go on hoping in the
face of this evident negation of hope? Here again Bloch advances by eliminating false answers and introducing us to new
perspectives. For a Marxist, hope is the stronger in the struggle:
it overcomes even death.

Strategies Against Death

At all times, hope has gone forth to challenge death. It is
even possible to maintain that the idea of death has caused the
vastest and most extravagant of utopias. At a very early date
mankind began to invent strategies for exorcising death and
stripping it of its power. Biblical man, for example, placed death
in the realm of appearances and saw man's true reality as being
attained on the other side of death. Because biblical man wanted
to prolong his life indefinitely and also because he longed to
have justice done him, he invented the world to come.[49] This escape to what is above relieves death of its scandalous aspect and
makes possible the hope of survival, because in the Jerusalem on
high there will no longer be even the memory of the ancient enemy. For Bloch, of course, there can be no question of following
this path to an "abstract" utopia. All these various hopes, which
were already cultivated by the Egyptians and the Greeks, are
simply fantasies, that is, pure products of the imagination.

Religious man strips death of its power by inventing the
myth of survival. How will secular man tackle the problem of
death, since escape into a world on high is impossible? Like religious man, secular man cannot live in continual anxiety about
death. How will he manage to give death a meaning that serves
him? Bloch first examines the strategies invented by capitalist
society. In this society everything possible is done to keep people from thinking about death. Forgetfulness of the coming of
death is aided, at the unconscious level, by an inherited vague

sense of survival. Or else death is accepted as the unavoidable debt the individual must pay to life and progress. But capitalist society also develops some more conscious attitudes. I shall mention two of these, which represent two extremes.

A flight into the future: in times of war or danger death enjoys an artificial and exaggerated esteem in capitalist societies. When these societies are under attack, they mobilize individuals in the service of the society's ideals and render them enthusiastic by exalting the shedding of one's blood. "Tomorrow we shall die!" was the song heard in Germany during the Nazi period. The young people who sang this refrain were not satisfied simply with conquest. They were willing to die because they were convinced that shed blood is not lost. What is capitalist society doing in such cases? What trick is it pulling off by means of this strategy? It is managing to transform the death instinct, which brings anxiety with it, into an exalting aggressive instinct which it causes the individual to direct toward others and toward himself as well. Society is attributing value to the loss of a life it can no longer protect; it is seeking to convince individuals that the blood they shed is not shed in vain.[50]

Nihilism: in times of peace capitalist society does not have the same resources to draw on. Death is then seen as an unavoidable fate, unless, of course, it is simply forgotten altogether. One whole school of thought openly speaks of death as the only outcome of life: man is "a being-for-death," says existentialist philosophy under the leadership of Heidegger. We can do nothing but bow to this brute necessity. Such is the attitude of the various "decadent" philosophers (Heidegger, Jaspers). But what unconscious tactic is being used here? What trick is being played? These philosophers identify the problem of the individual's death with that of the society in which the individual lives. Capitalist society is condemned. Does this therefore mean the end of hope for individuals, as they would have us believe? "They turn the simple nothingness in the capitalist future into an inevitable and absolute nothingness, so as to prevent men completely from seeing a transformed world, a socialist future."[51] The nihilism thus serves unwittingly as camouflage for a political strategy: By destroying hope in a future for man as an individual, nihilism kills the taste for a different future and severs the revolutionary nerve.

Overcoming Death

Ernst Bloch will have nothing to do with the illusions offered by religion, but he also rejects the absence of hope that
characterizes capitalist societies. When he speaks of death, he
sticks to materialist dogma which, he believes, offers the only
valid understanding of the world. Yet he does not surrender
hope. On the contrary: everything bids him hope in the future of
the world. But on what is such a hope based? It is based on the
real and as yet unactualized possibilities of the world: "The
world does not have a 'beyond' . . . but neither does it have limits here below or, better, its only limit and its only direction are
those set for it by the dialectical process. . . . No one can say
whether the process of life does not conceal and provide a basis
for a transformation that is still invisible."[52]

This conviction manifests the true scope of Bloch's optimism. The "no" which death utters is not decisive. Bloch
glimpses the possibility of man's transcending all limits, even
those set by death. But how, concretely, does he meet the challenge of death? What can he say to the men and women of our
day? He proposes two types of self-transcendence.

First, in proposing a moving beyond self toward the social
class, Bloch introduces the idea of a class consciousness. The
individual is not isolated but is part of a collectivity, and the collectivity saves him. A Marxist has no expectation of a resurrection, but he is not therefore without hope. The best part of
himself survives his death. His Good Friday is not eased by an
Easter Sunday that would restore him to his individual life. And
yet his death does issue into light, because as a Marxist he does
not live a life that is selfishly focused on his individual self; he
lives in solidarity with a class. He is conscious of being part of a
collective entity, and this entity survives his destruction as an individual: "And this certainty that class consciousness transcends
individual life is in fact a *novum* against death."[53]

This perspective may be a source of enthusiasm for the
"Red hero" but it does not have the same attraction for the ordinary person as he confronts natural death. What solution can he
be offered? There can be no question of falling back on the religious illusion as a way of overcoming his fear of death. The
means of doing so is rather to bring him to see the *historical project* which is bigger than he and is able to bring all his energies

into play; for death, though not yet conquered for the individual, will not have the final say about history. History is the triumph of life. In relation to the project of an integral humanization of nature that will, at its term, reconcile man with nature, death takes on a positive meaning.

If then the individual can die without losing hope, it is because he knows that his individual death is made up for in a global project which transcends him and has a meaning. Once again, who can say that the humanization of nature will not end in a victory over death itself? Nor is this an "abstract" utopia, for it is based on the real possibilities of matter. At present "nature provides no positive solution to our fate, but neither does it provide an utterly negative solution."[54]

Revelation of Human Identity

Is it possible to go a step further and say what form this complete mastery of death might take? Bloch introduces a final approach for exorcising death. He asks us to take a new look not only at the universe but at man himself. It is possible that death may have a meaning not only through self-transcendence toward class consciousness (the social perspective) or toward the project of humanizing nature (the cosmological perspective), but also in relation to the death of the individual as such (an anthropological perspective). What is death for an individual? The answer depends on one's conception of the human person.

Bloch here introduces into his conception of the human person an odd dichotomy that almost looks like a return to Platonic dualism. He distinguishes between "that which" (*Das-sein*) the person now is, and his "being there" (*Da-sein*) which, from Bloch's standpoint, is a "not yet there," i.e., the as yet unrevealed being of man or, again, the *novum* which is there in a potential state. In the human person, then, there is a non-essential part which is connected with the past, and an essential part which is connected with the future and which is waiting to be revealed. The meaning of death changes according as we relate it to the one or the other of these two parts.

If death is thought of in connection with the *Das-sein*, that is, with the human essence as actualized in the present, then death is seen as destructive. If, on the other hand, it is thought of in connection with the *Da-sein*, the existential core that has not yet been revealed, death shows itself to be revelatory of man's fu-

ture. For this existential core escapes death. Death simply cracks
the shell without harming the kernel within; the latter retains all
its potentialities with regard to the future. Bloch concludes:
"Death, then, is no longer the negation of the utopia . . . but on
the contrary the negation of that in the world which does not belong to the utopia. . . . The content of death is then no longer
death itself but the revelation of the new content that is achieved
by life, the content present in the core."[55]

Are we justified in speaking of an immortal core? This dualism that places a part of man out of death's reach is strangely
reminiscent of the Christian view. But while this "core" enjoys a
kind of "extra-territorial" status in relation to death, we must
not betray Bloch's thought by attributing to this core the privilege of personal survival. It represents the possibility not of personal survival but of the future of man; as such, its existence is
not fully revealed. The *Da-sein* is not an eternal dimension in
man; it is rather his dimension of "not yet thereness" which the
future will reveal. Is all this an illusion? No, it is a "concrete utopia," that is, a real possibility for man:·

> The utopia of the *non omnis confundar* (I shall not be totally
> put to shame) abandons this shell to the negation of death,
> so that death may crack it open. But it gives death the pow-
> er only to crack open the shell which surrounds the content
> of the subject who, if he were really liberated and fully de-
> fined, would no longer have the appearance of a shell. Once
> our existence approximates its core, there begins a duration
> that has nothing fixed about it but contains a *novum* from
> which everything transient and perishable is excluded.[56]

What is death, then? Where is its victory? If we consider it
no longer in relation to the past which it destroys, but in relation
to the future which it announces, death opens up the hope of *lux
luceat,* a light which will never cease to shine. For the paralyzing
sight of a past that has been destroyed Bloch substitutes a loving
passion for a future that is to be built. But what exactly does
such a statement mean? It is hard to say. Bloch tells us that music, "the most utopian of all the arts,"[57] affords the best presentiment of this unlimited duration in which man will attain his
identity. But if we move beyond this image, are we to suppose a
kind of limitless duration (a substitute for eternity), a kind of

restoration of the lost paradise, or, more simply, the absence of fear of death in a pacified universe in which death is no longer accompanied by violence and fear but is a natural occurrence inasmuch as man will have revealed and actuated all his possibilities, a feat impossible in society as it now is?

Bloch's thinking bears witness to an awesome hope that nothing can resist. It thrusts into the future and has no need of an illusory other world. From this point of view, Christianity has been discredited as one of the abstract utopias that should be eliminated. Does this mean that Bloch has succeeded in his venture? His aim was to show that Marxism is effective not only on the social level but also in existential questions, even in those in which we hardly find evidence of it. But the mere reading of Bloch's texts does not remove all questions. Of one thing Bloch is certain: A Marxist can look at death with eyes of hope. Death is not the unavoidable entrance into nothingness (*Nichts*); rather it is the negation of what is not authentically human (*nicht*), of the shell of the human, and, at the same time, a revelation of a core or nucleus that escapes death. Thus death is not the harshest of all anti-utopias; on the contrary, it is the most powerful of utopias, for it authentically reveals man to himself. Astonishing though this inversion may appear, it is very much in Bloch's style: "impossible" is a word that hope does not acknowledge.

For Ernst Bloch, the principle of hope is not a vague feeling, a "wrinkle of the soul," as Hegel would say. On the contrary, it is anchored in man and matter, both of which offer unsuspected and unexplored possibilities. It projects man toward a better future, but a future which he can already sense as in a gestation in the present. It forbids him to resign himself and let his hands drop.

Hope is therefore optimistic, but not with the complacent optimism that we find in those who expect capitalism to collapse simply from the pressure of its internal contradictions. That kind of optimism is due to a lack of any horizon; Bloch calls it a new "opium of the people."[58] Nor is hope's optimism the hotheaded kind found in "enthusiasts"; their optimism is due to ignorance. In this kind of optimism Bloch sees a failure to analyze the situation. Militant optimism is quite a different thing. It is neither passive expectation nor venturesome activism. It pursues a concrete ideal that is not the mere product of desire but emerges from reality through an analysis of reality's repressed elements.

This militant optimism characterizes the revolutionary. In the final struggle for their own liberation the proletariat must "bring into play the determination of the subjective factor together with the objective factor of the economic and material trend."[59] The revolutionary militant is not satisfied to be an economist whose mind is obscured by the real world, but neither is he a putschist who follows only his own dreams. The revolutionary militant keeps the spirit of rigorous analysis that characterizes the economist, and the enthusiasm for the future that marks the putschist. He is not a timid person, but is in the van of the fight.

> Militant optimism knows no other post than the one revealed by the category of "front." The philosophy behind this optimism, that is, behind hope understood *materially,* is itself—insofar as it is a science that focuses its attention on what has not been taken into consideration—concerned with the most advanced sector of history. This is so even when it concerns itself with the past, that is, with the future as inscribed, in all its vividness, in the past.[60]

The optimism that always puts the militant on the forward line (the "front") in the fight for the future (socialism) comprises attention to reality—but a reality which it does not accept in its present state—and openness to the future as this allows itself to be discerned in the ongoing process of history (the *novum*). This history is already big with possibilities that are about to emerge. The work of the militant is to hasten their emergence. In the daily struggle he does not lose sight of the final goal (the *ultimum*) which is the complete fulfillment of man. The category of *ultimum* is well known in all religions. What does it mean for a Marxist militant? Marx equated it with the "humanization of nature" and a "classless society." Speaking generally, Bloch sees it as "that which corresponds as an objective and real correlative to a precise anticipation, a concrete utopia."[61] It is the idea of this *novum* and the presentiment of this *ultimum* that sustain a militant optimism and inspire it to be always in the forefront of the struggle.

These analyses of Bloch are a challenge to Christian hope, a challenge which Moltmann has accepted. The reason why I have emphasized Bloch's dialectic of the "real" and the "possible" is that Moltmann has taken it over word for word, as he has the categories of "front," "*novum*," and "*ultimum*," making of these the channels for his own thinking. In thus accepting Bloch's challenge on its own terms, Moltmann maintains that Christian hope is in fact not an abstract utopia but a passion for the future that has become "really possible" thanks to the resurrection of Christ. By entering into history the resurrection of Christ introduces a *novum* which gives substance to hope and opens up to it a definitive horizon (an *ultimum*) that does not signal the end of history but is rather a real possibility for human life and for history itself.

But other questions arise in connection with the process of demythologization to which Bloch subjects Christianity. These questions are to some extent the same that I have raised in discussing Garaudy, who has been deeply inspired by Bloch. The distinction and selection of elements in Christianity which Bloch makes may be relevant to his purposes, but is it legitimate from the viewpoint of Christianity itself? Are the tendencies he detects within Christianity really as opposed and contradictory as he believes? Or do they not rather reflect a particular Marxist reading of history? Is our picture of Christ really a politically profitable clerical invention by the early Christians and one that canceled out messianism, or is it rather the expression of an experience which has no parallel? These questions still call for an answer.

There is no doubt that Bloch's sympathies are with the prophets and the apocalyptic currents in Christianity. He regards messianism as the salt of the earth.[62] Why? Because he thinks that by approaching Christianity from this angle he can effect a rapprochement between it and Marxism. But are Christian messianism and Marxist messianism really the same thing, as Bloch would have us believe? His attempt to harmonize the two is questionable; he harmonizes them by forcing them into a common mold, but without getting the consent of both sides. He makes Christian messianism his own in order to inject it, as it were, into Marxism, which is constantly running out of steam, but in the process he hardly respects the Christian identity. Messianism is first and foremost an inner necessity for Christianity, which draws from it its vitality and energy. Messianism is not opposed to Christianity, as Bloch claims.

No one would deny that there is a convergence of Christianity and Marxism on the points which Bloch indicates. Both protest against power that debases, against the state and wealth, against oppressive forces, and so on. They can work together to get a new movement underway and to inspire a revolutionary attitude and behavior. Bloch sees the same messianism at work in both. But how can a Christian recognize his own faith in a messianism that has eliminated the person of Christ? In the one case messianism has created an illusory utopia: the kingdom of God; on the other it creates the concrete utopia of a classless society. Bloch is convinced that in both cases the messianism rests on the same principle: the principle of hope, which antecedes all messianism and is the condition for their possibility. But he secures such a convergence only by depriving Christianity of its Messiah. With the help of Marxism he rids Christianity of all its fantastic elements; thanks to Christianity he is able to pump into Marxism the vital breath it is always in danger of losing because it lacks an adequate horizon. But is this sort of operation enough to do justice to Christianity?

9

Some Human Words
about God

In the presence of this pervasive atheism, which sometimes roils the waters, sometimes moves along peaceably, is it still possible to speak in a credible way about God? Admittedly, there is plenty of talk about him. Christians continue to speak of him as a being who is part of the spiritual capital and their concerns. But what real meaning can such talk have? When a Christian speaks of God, he is referring to a reality that is already present to him and that he has either discovered by way of personal reflection or inherited via familial tradition. The atheist is not in the same position. He challenges any and all talk of God, and his challenge is a radical one. He hears people talk of God, but whence does such talk derive its legitimacy? Suppose all talk of God is nothing but empty words?

In dealing with an atheist it is not enough to talk about God; the need is to re-establish the validity of such discourse. One must therefore begin by presupposing the absence of God, or at least the absence of any grasp of the meaning of "God." God is at best a notion that is part of the atheist's cultural field, but it is an empty notion or one that carries with it all sorts of prejudgments. No doubt, each person who talks about God has his personal pre-understanding of the term. But the idea must still be justified. Any talk about God must take into consideration the two classical questions (which are connected and call for one another): Does God exist (*an sit*)? What is his nature (*quid sit*)?

In view of the contemporary distrust of all rational discourse, many Christians do not move beyond the first kind of talk: they talk about God, but do not make any effort to prove his existence. Demonstration, as a tool of logic, seems to them unsuited when applied to God. Do you ever demonstrate the existence of a person? No, you accept the person and live with him or her. A demonstration involves the manipulation of concepts. But is it thinkable that we should "manipulate" God as though he were an object for us to reason about? This would be to overlook the fact that he is free and surrounded by mystery. As a personal being, he makes himself available for encounter in an interpersonal relationship, but not as the conclusion of a reasoning process. You do not demonstrate his presence; you bear witness to it.

This kind of thinking seems dominant nowadays, even outside of fundamentalist or charismatic movements. I do not challenge the value of this approach; I simply observe that these Christians have remained sheltered from atheism or at least are not familiar with the questions it asks. They distrust the God of the philosophers and the scholars and fall back, essentially, on the God of Jesus Christ, refusing to get involved in intellectual fights. God has "given proof" of himself in his word. The Christian can bear witness to this word, and the atheist has no real choice but to accept it. If, as the Christian is convinced, God is already present in every human heart even before he is recognized, his presence can be "experienced." Acceptance of God comes through meditation, not through the construction of elaborate intellectual scaffolding. There is no "proof" or test for the existence of God; God, on the other hand, is a "test" for every human being.

It does seem that witness rather than rational argument is the preferred contemporary way of speaking about God. But is witness enough? Human beings can accept only what they understand. In dealing with an atheist should we not come down a peg from our lofty position and join him in asking the radical question of whether God exists? Should we not take a stand at the level of human discourse that is based on reason? But at this point we find ourselves in a very difficult situation. How are we to proceed? Are we to return to the classical proofs of God's existence? Are we to explain them yet again and patch up the holes which atheism has made in them? Well-informed atheists are not unaware of these proofs. They are simply not moved by them. The proofs seem completely ineffective.

As seen through the eyes of an atheist the proofs are reducible to a tricky and barren intellectual game. They often have the very opposite effect to the one intended. According to François Jeanson they are the best means of turning the atheist away from belief in God.

> If God is dead in our present world, we should not blame the libertines, the Marxists, the existentialists, and other infidels, for the Catholic thinkers had already done him in. If God were alive, truly alive, in the hearts of human beings, we would see the anarchic and scandalous reign of simplicity of spirit. But proper order (let us render to Caesar what is Caesar's . . .) demands a God who is a concept, a God who is a mummy, a splendid corpse on which the initiated wise men can indefinitely carry out their pious autopsies. God is dead; long live theology![1]

Are we then caught on the wheel? If witness is not enough and if rational discourses about God have for their only effect to hasten the turn to atheism, what more can we say? Is there today an acknowledged ground on which the question of God can be raised? This is a preliminary question of which we should be conscious, even if it is not possible to answer it here. The atheist's refusal of the question of God does not spring from a passing mood, but is due to the bankruptcy of an entire system of thought which has been routed by Nietzsche and his modern imitators.

In speaking of the contemporary crisis, we find ourselves using such expressions as the "discontent" of our civilization (Freud), the death of traditions, the decline of absolutes, the loss of values, and so on. These, however, are surface phenomena which point to a deeper dislocation in the realm of thought. The real crisis is a crisis of "principle," since the modern mind no longer has any universally accepted organizing principle.[2] It has neither hearth nor home. Every kind of discourse is allowed, provided only that it be coherent and yield meaning. Therefore there arises the radical question which I mentioned a moment ago: Is there a ground common to atheist and Christian on which the question of God can be raised? Well, at least the question has now been asked.

In Western tradition, the question of God has arisen on two different grounds, which Christianity has tried to bring into harmony: reason and Scripture. Reason proposes an ascending process: starting with the existence of the world or of the structures proper to the spirit, it concludes to the existence of God. In the name of the principle of sufficient reason, for example, the world calls for a Creator; or, to take another example, in the name of the coherence of truth, thought requires a reference to a stable truth, which can be identified with God. Scripture proceeds differently. It often challenges the pretensions of reason and claims that the latter is incapable of laying hold of God or saying anything true about him. Only God can speak in an authentic way about God. Scripture is the place where this revelation of God is to be found. It demands that the revelation be accepted in faith. Are these two grounds or locuses mutually exclusive or can they be brought into harmony?

The Exclusive Word of God

In Christian tradition there is a current of thought that rejects any knowledge of God except that given us by God himself through biblical revelation. God is hidden and must take the initiative in manifesting himself. He is accessible only if he makes himself accessible. No valid knowledge of God can bypass this revelation. This approach to the subject can be traced back to the very origins of Christianity and is adumbrated in the Gospel: "I thank thee, Father, Lord of heaven and earth, that thou hast hidden these things from the wise and understanding and revealed them to babes" (Lk 10:21). Paul goes a step further when he writes to the Corinthians that God prefers the foolishness of the cross to the wisdom of the Greeks (1 Cor 1:17–25).

The Scandal of the Christian Fact

Soren Kierkegaard formulated this same position in philosophical terms. In the course of his philosophical inquiries he came across people who were eminently "religious." The most attractive of these was Socrates, the very model of a religious person, with a distaste for objective knowledge and a passionate concern for subjective inwardness and for the absolute. In Socrates Kierkegaard finds the characteristic mark of all religion and therefore of Christianity: an absolute passion for the absolute.

But Kierkegaard immediately introduces a distinction between religion A and religion B. Religious man A finds eternity and God through his own speculative study and in spiritual interiority. Religious man B encounters God in Jesus Christ; he lives in time and relates himself to "the eternal in time." Socrates, who belongs to the former of these two types, is not a Christian. He trusts in his own logic, but Christianity requires something more.

The two characteristics which forever distinguish Christianity from pagan religion are, on man's side, a consciousness of sin and, on God's side, the gift in Jesus Christ of a state or condition that makes salvation possible. Socrates correctly located himself in the sphere of the existential but did not understand that sin is constitutive of the human situation and that man is not in the necessary condition for entering into a relationship with the absolute. Socrates was not aware of the real distance that separates man from the absolute, and he thought that man could establish himself in a correct relation to the absolute by his own powers. He was also ignorant of the condition that is really needed for entering into this relation. He fell into the error of thinking that every human being is already in contact with the truth and possesses in himself the a priori condition for the encounter.

Here is precisely where the scandal of Christianity intervenes. Christianity calls upon man to build his eternal happiness not after the manner of Socrates, who symbolizes reason, but through adherence to Jesus Christ, "the eternal in time," and thus to a historical truth that presents itself as the absolute within history. Kierkegaard formulates his question here in terms apparently derived from pure logic: Is it possible to pass from history to the absolute, from a fact located in time to eternal beatitude, from Jesus Christ to God?[3] Reason can only return a negative answer, for it maintains that there is discontinuity between history and the absolute, the former being the domain of an authoritative "approximately," and the latter the realm of necessity. To attempt to base one's happiness on an event located in time is the height of absurdity. Feuerbach was right in pointing out this scandal of Christianity.

It seems, then, that reason is forever divorced from faith. Nineteenth century rationalism understood this and overcame the separation by reducing revelation to a temporary form taken by truth, a kind of push that helps reason enter into its own domain. Kierkegaard, too, believes we will always lack the link that would make it possible to connect the two domains dialectically. But faith succeeds where reason left to itself fails. What logic prohibits, the concrete existence of Jesus Christ makes possible, for his existence effects a "synthesis" of the eternal and time. Adherence to this historical truth thus makes possible man's entrance into eternal happiness. But the adherence means an existential choice, accepting the risks of a faith which though difficult is not absurd. The Christian paradox cannot be explained, but it can be understood. "We can live within its sphere."

The Christian fact is admittedly not capable of being proved. For what, after all, can historical reason establish? "At most that Jesus Christ was a great man, perhaps the greatest of all human beings. But that he was God? No! Stop there! God willing, this conclusion will not be drawn!" What Kierkegaard, a Danish Lutheran, means is that there is no way of gaining oneself except by the surrender of oneself in faith. It is not through reason but in faith that one appropriates the condition for access to the eternal. Two decisive moments mark the course of time: the moment of the incarnation at the level of universal history, and the moment of personal choice in the history of each individual.

Christianity is the sphere in which Kierkegaard's thought usually moves. He had been formed in the school of Hegel but, like Marx, he had rejected the master's facile syntheses. He does not think it possible to build bridges or walkways between reason and faith. He rejects the easy kind of apologetics that would assure people of entrance into the realm of faith without experiencing any kind of a break. But whereas Marx follows Feuerbach and disqualifies faith in the name of reason, Kierkegaard takes the opposite course: he uses faith to reduce the stature of reason, intending in this way to safeguard the originality of Christianity. In his view faith is the only way to God, and it is a way that demands a decision, a leap, a commitment. The road to God is forever blocked by the cross which renders it "scandalously difficult to become a Christian." Kierkegaard thinks of intellectual activity as an irresponsible game, a pile of knowledge that can be adapted to any life-style whatever. He maintains the primacy of the ethical and the religious, and, in the question of God, insists on the importance of personal commitment. No one is ever a Christian unless he has made the effort to become one;

no one ever commits himself to God "except by inflicting wounds on himself."

We Know God Through God and Only Through God

The same intellectual outlook recurs in the Protestant theologian Karl Barth. His central thesis is clear and unchallengeable: "The Bible sets aside as an idol any God other than the God of revelation. It proclaims that there is no other access to the true God than faith in the Word."[4] Barth recognizes in the various religions and pagan philosophies a call to the God who reveals himself in Jesus Christ, but he radically rejects any other way to him except his own word. "God is known through God and only through God."[4a] Natural theology, which tries to open a way to God by means of reason, is in Barth's view a slur (a "criminal attack," he says) on the Christian idea of God:

> "God" in the meaning of the symbol—of the symbol which aims at giving again the testimony of the prophets and apostles—"God" is not a magnitude with which the believer is already acquainted before he is a believer, so that as a believer he merely experiences an improvement and enrichment of knowledge that he already has. When Paul says (Rom. i, 19) that what can be known of God is manifest to them, for God manifested it unto them, the whole context as well as the immediately preceding statement (Rom. i, 18) shows that Paul sees the truth about God "held down" among men, made ineffective, unfruitful. What comes of it in their hands is idolatry. . . . Only God's revelation, not our reason despairing of itself, can carry us over from God's incomprehensibility.[5]

An objection immediately comes to mind: Why, then, do believers, even after accepting revelation, always insist on developing rational proofs for the existence of God? Barth's answer is a theological one: even after conversion, man remains a sinner. He refuses to admit that he has been conquered by grace, and he does not easily renounce his will to self-justification. Constructing proofs is one way he has of bringing the Gospel over to his side, when he should in fact be surrendering himself without reserve to the obedience of faith. As Barth sees it, then, natural theology is simply the activity of a sinner who refuses to submit to the word of God. Barth shares the entire Reformation's distrust of reason, a distrust for which the way had been prepared by Occam at the end of the Middle Ages and which was intensified by Kant. Luther expressed his pessimism about reason by calling it a "whore."

The triumph (a sham one) of reason in the form of natural theology thus shows the sinfulness of the believer and the failure of the Gospel in his life. On the other hand, the failure of reason to which atheism bears witness reveals the profound truth of the Gospel. From this point of view, atheism makes a considerable contribution to the Gospel by showing that the God of reason is nothing but a projection of man: "Theology is anthropology; i.e., in the object of religion, which we call . . . God, there expresses itself nothing other than the . . . deified nature of man."[6] Any God who emerges from the mind of man and not from the Gospel is an idol, as Feuerbach showed. We must renounce all such gods and allow ourselves to be remade by God in his image. Atheism has a purifying role to play. As Marx said, Feuerbach is the "fiery brook" through which we must pass; he helps tear down the idols.

For Barth, then, atheism has its beneficent side. On the one hand, it indirectly makes clear the failure of reason: reason is incapable of reaching God by its own power. Atheism thus provides the theologian with proof of his thesis that we attain to God only through obedience to the Gospel. On the other hand, there is another theological insight which atheists confirm. For when the atheist says that the content of the word "God" is a pure product of the imagination, he is simply discovering a truth which is everywhere clear in the Gospel. Atheism thus indirectly supports two theological theses. What a splendid surprise! The conclusion is clearer than ever: if we are to speak truly about God, our starting point must be Jesus Christ.

But have these thinkers grasped all the implications of their position? They make shrewd use of atheism to support their theological views, but it is not at all sure that they have come to grips with the questions atheism raises. For in fact there is here a whole series of questions which neither Kierkegaard nor Barth has really taken into consideration. To begin with, in their approach revelation is in danger of appearing to be a requirement imposed on man purely from without, as something he must accept in blind obedience whether or not he understands it. But does not such a radical division between reason and faith jeopardize the very Gospel itself? How can we discern the "true" God in the face which he presents to us in Christ unless we already have some kind of basic comprehension of God?

> How could we see in them [the "works" of God] an action of God, if we did not possess in the very heart of our spiritual activity the power of knowing God . . . ? Without positing an original apprehension of God (implicit though it might be), we would have no judgmental principle which would permit us to base our recognition of divine revelation on history.[7]

If we bracket reason we come dangerously close to fideism and risk asking human beings for a blind faith. And do we not at the same time put an end to any dialogue with atheism? If we wish to clear the way for a return to the "repressed God" who we may think dwells in even the most rascally of atheists, we shall not do so by tearing down the "citadel" of metaphysics and removing every "natural support" from the God of faith.[8] Like every human being, the atheist has a right to expect a discourse about God that carries some sort of justification with it.

A Human Discourse about Man

Where do we stand at this point? The conclusion which this only too brief survey yields seems slight indeed and even negative, namely, that no word or message, even the word of God, can demand obedience of man as long as it has no connection with the questions he is asking. But this seemingly negative conclusion implies a new demand of its own: to show that human life is fully intelligible only when located within the sphere of God. But for such a claim to have a meaning, it must arise out of reflection on the experience of man. In other words, the only discourse on which atheist and believer can reach an agreement is a human discourse about man.

If we want to start a dialogue about God with the atheist of our day the only chance we have of getting on the same wavelength with him is to focus on the human person. Together with the atheist we must rediscover what human existence means and implies. The God question will emerge from oblivion only if we first dispel our forgetfulness regarding our own existential questions. The only thinking about God that will be valid is thinking that springs from the human depths. Therefore we are faced with a crucial question: is it possible in our day to formulate "a discourse about God that will also, and inseparably, be a discourse about man and by man"?[9] The task is not an easy one, and successes are few. A few stammerings may be the best we can achieve.

Proofs That Have Been Challenged

Thinkers have not waited for our day to undertake the task just defined. After all, what is "natural theology" but the effort, undertaken repeatedly through the centuries, to put the existence of God on a solid basis by taking the human person as a starting point? The procedure in every case involves beginning with a radical question about the world and man. There can be no question here of my displaying all the "proofs" for the existence of God, of inventorying this treasure in which old and new are stored up. I can, however, indicate a few lines of thought, those that are the most classical. The proofs that have been excogitated are essentially of two types. Some are a priori, that is, they avoid the roundabout way that leads through the world of experience; the others are a posteriori, that is, they start from human experience in the world.

The a priori proofs pass immediately from the simple concept of God ("a being than which no greater can be conceived"; "absolute plenitude"; the "infinite"; and so on) to the assertion that he exists. This argument was invented by St. Anselm who used it in a theological context in order to establish the validity of the idea of God which is already possessed through faith. The rigorous logic of the argument was then developed by Descartes, Leibniz, and Malebranche in the seventeenth century, although the argument is given a different place in each of these philosophers. But as far as the atheist is concerned the structure of the argument is always the same: the idea of the infinite, of which the human mind has interior experience, inasmuch as without this notion it would not grasp its own finitude (it grasps its finiteness as a lack by comparison with the infinite), necessarily implies the existence of this infinite, for if it did not exist it would be defective and thus automatically cease to be infinite. This form of reasoning has been attacked by philosophers, atheists and believers alike, and especially by Kant. It supposes a realism of concepts that is difficult to establish and that all moderns reject. According to Kant, the existence which is attributed to the idea of God is at most a "potential" existence; that the existence is also real remains to be proved, and this proof can be obtained only by way of experience.[10]

Other thinkers accept this objection and construct a posteriori arguments, that is, arguments which have for their starting point the experience of the self or the world. It is this kind of proof that yields Voltaire's well-known God the clockmaker: "The more I think of this clock [the world], the less conceivable it is that it should run and not have a clockmaker."

The most famous of these a posteriori "proofs" are those of St. Thomas. The latter also call for careful attention and discerning application. St. Thomas takes as his starting point the existence of the world. He observes that in the things that make up the world (all "beings") there is a tension between what they are (their "essence") and the fact that they are (their "existence"). He concludes that their essence does not account for their existence; it is not self-sufficient. We must therefore look beyond the world to a cause that is responsible for the existence of the world as a whole. This cause, however, can only be a being whose very essence it is to exist, or, in other words, which has in itself the reason for its existence. Such a being he calls "God."

This argument claims to be more solid than the a priori arguments. And to a certain extent it is, since its point of departure is not an idea but existing reality; the passage from world to God takes place in the realm of being. But is the argument without any weaknesses? As a matter of fact, it supposes several principles which are open to question. Two of these deserve a brief word. The first is the principle of sufficient reason. But Monod thinks he can do justice to this principle while appealing not to God but to chance and to the necessity inherent in nature.[11] He thinks he can provide a coherent explanation without leaving the world at all. He has not, of course, answered the question of the existence of the world: Why is there something rather than nothing? (Heidegger). But he continues to hope that scientific reason (the only kind of reason that counts) will succeed in finding the answer to this. A further consideration: Why this demand for a principle of sufficient reason? Nietzsche and Sartre see this principle as simply a manifestation of the human will's desire to justify itself at any cost and its refusal to admit error. And Brunschvicg challenged the principle by saying: "We shall not explain the why of being simply by imagining a being without a why."

The second principle open to question is the principle of causality. Ever since Kant, it has been maintained that the notion of cause can be of use in coordinating human experience but that using it as a way of moving beyond the boundaries of experience is illegitimate. "Pure" reason is thus deprived of the essential tool it had been using in order to reach God.

To all this I must add that the God reached by these "proofs," whether a priori or a posteriori, is himself very much open to question. Whether he be a "First Mover," a "First Cause," a "Necessary Being," "Infinite Perfection," or "God who consoles" (and this list is far from exhaustive), he is always a God who is required as a response to a human need, a satisfaction of human aspirations, a necessary condition for human reasoning, a fulfillment of human exigences, and so on. This God who satisfies human needs and exigences is difficult to reconcile with a God who is free and generous. He is an abstract God, a conceptual God, one whose portrait we try to touch up and modify by subjecting it to the surgical operations of a Christian esthetics—but without any great success. Heidegger made quick work of this bastardized God in his well-known criticism of ontotheology.

I shall not develop further the criticism of these "proofs," the limitations of which St. Thomas himself emphasizes by speaking modestly of them as simple "ways." Atheists have piled up complaints against them. They regard the "proofs" as tricks and snares, and claim that the appearance of strict logic in fact conceals inconsistencies and a misuse of principles that betray a put-up job. No one will be convinced of the conclusion yielded by these proofs unless he has already settled for God.

Whatever be the validity of this attack, it must be admitted that the proofs for the existence of God are not compelling or universally accepted. Are we therefore at an impasse? Are we to throw them out on the grounds that they have never convinced anyone? Are we, as Gabriel Marcel puts it, to "discard" them like "postmarked stamps"?[12]

While granting that "many unbelievers ... have been

brought to know an invisible God through visible nature,"[13] Pascal is impressed above all by the fact that the universe is mute and filled with an "eternal silence" and that man is "left to himself with no light, as though lost in this corner of the universe."[14] Of what use are "proofs"?

> The metaphysical proofs for the existence of God are so remote from human reasoning and so involved that they make little impact, and, even if they did help some people, it would only be for the the moment during which they watched the demonstration, because an hour later they would be afraid they had made a mistake. . . . That is the result of knowing God without Christ.[15]

As a result of the attack by the "teachers of suspicion," this pessimism is very widespread today. Some follow Pascal's lead and are content with the God of Jesus Christ, while others, unimpressed by all the criticisms, either tirelessly repeat the traditional proofs out of mental routine or, at best, try to give them a modern form.

The Implications of Experience

Is it possible to go a step further? How are we to escape the dilemma of either cleaving to the word of God and thus closing off any dialogue with atheists, or repeating the "traditional proofs" and thus getting ourselves involved in a dialogue of the deaf, as the arguments pro and con cancel each other out? There is in fact another way that can be tried: the way of experience. If we develop the implications of experience we will perhaps reach a more solidly based affirmation of God that in addition will satisfy the demand formulated earlier: that our discourse about God should be a discourse by man and about man.

We may note that the traditional proofs fall short of meeting this requirement. For they are in fact neither a discourse by man nor a discourse about man. They are a discourse carried on by the rational mind; they are of the same kind as scientific discourse, less rigorous indeed in character but no more self-involving. At best, they produce a tissue of abstractions that is anything but a discourse about man that might be a challenge to the way he lives his life. Once again, then, we must change the locus of our thinking and substitute for discursive reason a more

existential style of thought and for dialectical victories a more
tentative approach. Despite appearances, contemporary thinkers
have not ceased to look for the ultimate foundation of existence;
they simply set about the task in a different way.

Is there a human datum, a solid and unchallenged experience, that is such as to reveal the existence of God when we are
willing to face up to all its implications? Many attempts have
been made to pursue this line of thought. Some are inadequate:
they are based on feeling, interior emotion, the experience of
joy, the spiritual attraction of the absolute, the intuition of
values, the reciprocity that characterizes love, desire, and so
on. These feelings are not unimportant, of course, but in
themselves they can at best provide only a starting point for
philosophical reflection. They develop into proofs only if philosophical analysis is able to discern in them the working of a basic
dynamism of the spirit and to elicit from their structure an affirmation of God.

Other attempts are on more solid ground, for they subject
the human datum directly to reflective analysis. I shall focus
here on three basic data which have served philosophers as the
foundation for an affirmation of God. The three are: the structure of the spirit, moral experience, and action.

First, then, there is the argument from the *structure of the
spirit.* Rather than look for God "outside," in the world, some
philosophers have chosen to follow the path of interiority. Recall Socrates and his constant admonition, "Know yourself!"
The kind of knowledge meant is not a narcissistic preoccupation
with the self but rather an approach to one "older" than the self,
a contact with the eternal, an entering into the realm of the
gods. Within Christianity St. Augustine has been the greatest
explorer of the ways of the heart. Like Socrates, he gives priority
to intuition and the mystical thrust of the soul over the processes of the rational mind. On the basis of his own rich experience
he constantly reminds his hearers and readers that God is not to
be found outside (*foris*) in the sensible world, at the end of a
journey through that world. We must enter into ourselves (*intus*)
and set out on a spiritual journey. God wills that "we should return to our heart and find him there,"[16] "for he was within."[17]
"You were closer to me than the closest part of myself, and
higher than the highest part of myself."[18]

If there were question in all this simply of Augustine's personal interior experience it would be of interest to the historian who wanted to understand Augustine's life, but it would hardly be of concern to a philosopher. However, Augustine believed that in his own experience he could discern a universal logic, a structure peculiar to every spirit. He observes, first of all, that there is in every spirit a tension which is explicable only by the alienation of the spirit from its unifying center. The interior division of the spirit is the sign of its separation from the truth but also of its contact with the truth, which is present in the call it issues. St. Augustine then tries to decipher the structure of the spirit in a more methodical way. He observes that all spirits seek the truth. But if the truth did not exist independently of the various subjects who speak of it, it would be impossible for them to pass a judgment on truth (there would simply be divergent cascades of successive impressions), nor would agreement between minds be possible (they would simply be juxtaposed monads).

Augustine thus makes a philosophical attempt to submit his own interior experience to a test. He believes that he discovers in spiritual activity the presence of a reality that transcends the spirit. He does not hesitate to identify this "truth," which is the norm for our judgments and the basis of agreement among minds, with the Word, a personal being who enters into an interior dialogue with each individual prior to any of the dialogues in which the individual engages with other human beings in time.

It is at this point that questions arise. What is Augustine doing when he asserts this identification? Is he simply asserting the merger of different experiences, one mystical, another Christian, the third philosophical? In this case there is reason to suspect a reciprocal influence and to question the really philosophical status of the structure of the spirit which he describes to us. Or else Augustine means to assert an equality between experiences each of which has its autonomous value. But, if this be the sense, how can the passage from the idea of truth to its identification with God escape the criticisms leveled at the ontological argument?

It is precisely the passage from immanence to transcendence that remains unresolved in most of the philosophies that are influenced by Augustine: those of Gabriel Marcel, Lavelle, Nabert. Each has tried in his own way to solve the problem of the passage. Each is convinced that the thought process is not complete in itself, and tries to pass beyond it, relying on an interior certainty rather than on apodictic arguments. Aimé Forest, for example, writes:

> Reflection always shows us both our own limitations and our thrust toward the unlimited. In this experience we grasp the idea of the absolute. We cannot deny this absolute because without it there would be neither thinking nor willing; nor can we locate this absolute within the confines of our own nature. . . . The idea of mere self-possession would always carry with it an aspect of incompleteness. With this new consciousness of all that is implied in our initial project we enter into the realm of religious experience.[19]

For Forest the consent to the absolute is the supreme act of the spirit. Such a consent depends on the internal dynamism of the spirit more than on rational logic. Thus Forest assigns only a secondary role to discursive reason, which has for its function not to "conclude" but to examine and check the spiritual intuition that has its supreme climax in the mystical élan.

In thus opposing intuition to discursive reason and interior experience to formal logic, the philosopher chooses an approach that will hardly satisfy the modern mind any more than the older "ways" did. Nowadays people have become distrustful of any procedure that would have the spirit blindly cross the boundaries of the verifiable. What, after all, is the value of interior experience? For a long time now, psychoanalysts have been discovering in this experience the unconscious strategies adopted by desire, and they assign it little credibility. In addition, despite all the justifications given for it after the fact, this kind of experience is difficult to share with others.

Human Action

Is there more to be hoped for from the other two experiences I mentioned, namely, moral experience and action? Let me go into them briefly in order to see whether they really lead to the affirmation of God. Both are concerned with human action, but with different aspects of it. In turning to action as compared with the interior experience of the spirit we are once again shifting focus: from thought to action, "theory" to "practice," saying to doing. The field of human action, on the other hand, is a vast one. Kant turned his attention to a privileged area of it: moral action.

It may seem paradoxical to go back to Kant for a way out of our impasse. After all, was not Kant the one who closed off all the roads which used to lead men to God? He limited human reason to the function of explaining the world, and he denounced as illegitimate the use made of reason in the classical proofs for God's existence. In his *Critique of Pure Reason* he says that knowledge tends toward the intuition of its object, but he goes on to add that "intuition occurs only to the extent that the object is given to us."[20] Ideas that are constructed a priori and are not given in experience are beyond rational justification. As a matter of fact, in the case of the idea of God, reason can neither affirm nor deny; it is incapable of passing judgment.

But Kant does not stop there. If God cannot be "known," he can nonetheless be "thought," just as freedom and the immortality of the soul (two other ideas which cannot be known) can be thought. What is the point of this distinction between "knowing" and "thinking"? It means that the God hypothesis is excluded from the field of science but also that it cannot be excluded totally. One can do science without having recourse to it, but while science can do without it, it cannot eliminate it. One can think the idea of God without thereby introducing a contradiction with science and without automatically having an idea that is internally contradictory. But in order legitimately to assert that which is thinkable without contradiction, there must be a reason for doing so. Such a reason exists in this case: the reason is moral action. This is the human basis on which Kant grounds the idea of God.

How does he proceed? As he sees it, the moral conscience is an undeniable fact, no less evident than the starry sky over our heads. As a fact, it is observable and stands in no need of justification. What does, however, need justification is its character as "categorical." To each individual conscience dictates duty in an unconditional manner, in the form of the "categorical imperative ("You shall!"). If moral conscience ("practical reason") can speak in this fashion, it can only do so on condition that the person is free. Freedom is a postulate required by the existence of moral conscience. This first postulate is accompanied by two others: immortality and God. The human person demands that virtue be rewarded and vice punished. Yet virtue and happiness do not go together in this world. Immortality and God are both required in order to ensure that virtue and happiness will be conjoined in another life. These are the postulates which in the final analysis justify the categorical imperative. Thus that which "pure" reason cannot know and can only think without being able to affirm it as true is posited by "practical" reason as a postulate, i.e., as the ultimate justification of morality.

The rigor of Kant's argument is seductive. But what, in fact, is the value of his argument? It involves presuppositions which threaten to bring the whole house of cards down in ruin. To begin with, by what right can he demand that virtue and happiness go together? May we not suspect that this demand is an expression of that will to meaning at any cost of which Nietzsche spoke? What justifies the unconditional will to the union of virtue and happiness? Secondly—now Freud comes on the scene— what is the real status of the supposedly unquestionable "fact" of moral conscience? What if this conscience were simply the introjection of social imperatives? At least in its Kantian form, the rigid, unqualified "You shall!" has all the earmarks of the "super-ego" and reflects a particular kind of society rather than an authentic demand of conscience.

I have not gone back to Kant simply for the pleasure of immediately putting him on the spot. On the contrary, he opens the way to a new type of reflection. Unfortunately, the basis of his thinking is too narrow and too uncertain. Our contemporaries no longer share his firm convictions on the moral conscience and therefore no longer recognize their own experience in his arguments. And yet if moral action is beset with pitfalls, what is left? What is left is activity as such or, to use Blondel's term, "action."[21] Blondel endeavors to embrace the entire range of action and to grasp fully the dynamism at work in it; he tries then to make it the basis for a new way of affirming God. He shows that action involves necessity after necessity and ultimately the "one thing necessary."

It is impossible for me here to follow his procedure through all its stages; the procedure is at once very concrete and very rigorous. Blondel accepts the two challenges of his day, the positivist and the Neo-Kantian, and seeks to develop a "science of action." In other words, he intends to take as his basis a fact that cannot be denied, and to submit this to a careful explanation.

The *fact* is action in all its dimensions: everyone acts, wills, commits himself, and chooses; this is true even of the dilettante, since not to will is to will, and even of the pessimist, since to "will nothing" is to make a choice. Blondel then traces the unfolding of action, first in the individual, then in the group. His *method* is meant to be on the same footing as that of the positive sciences of his day; it is a method of "ex-plication" that is meant to show what action implies and to bring to light the ultimate consequences of these implications. He shows that no human action ends within itself.

His reflection begins from the gap found in human action between aspiration and accomplishment. At the very time when it is carrying out its successive projects, the will contains a demand for outstripping or going further which no accomplishment can satisfy. The disproportion between accomplishment and aspiration is the source of new projects, increasingly extensive accomplishments, especially at the collective level. But the gap persists and can never be completely closed, at least on man's side. After surveying all the circles of human action, from the lowest degree of action to the action of even the largest collectivities (family, nation, human race), Blondel concludes that in all his accomplishments man wills himself; he knows he is finite and wants to be infinite. He wills the infinite.

Action thus implies a will to totality which nothing can satisfy. This is the term to which the philosophical journey leads. The existence of the One Thing Necessary, though implied in all the necessities inherent in action, has not been demonstrated. We do, however, see it looming up on the human horizon. As he reflects on human destiny, Blondel shows what man is, the exigences he carries within him, the demand for the One Thing Necessary. He also shows that man cannot bestow this infinite on himself. The very thing he requires is therefore impossible; more accurately, it is possible only in the hypothesis that this infinite freely gives itself to him. In other words, the condition for the fulfillment of man's desire rests with God. Is not the verification of this condition precisely what the Christian religion asserts?

Blondel's conclusion has an obvious apologetic aspect. But we must be sure to understand the conclusion aright. Like Kierkegaard, Blondel is convinced that only the "supernatural" can bring man his completion. But he offers a philosophical way of drawing near to it, by showing that man is led to the *supernatural* "fact" by the *natural* movement of action. However, when he reaches the end of his philosophical journey Blondel does not enter the promised land; he does not assert the existence of the "supernatural," this One Thing Necessary that gratuitously bestows itself on man. He simply offers a hypothesis, suggests the possibility. And if *L'action* does end with an assertion ("It is"), Blondel is aware that at this moment he is going beyond the possibilities opened up by reason and making the leap of faith.

What does all this mean for our purpose here? In Blondel's work we certainly have a discourse by man, for he does not leave the level of what man can know. We also have a discourse on man, since he deals with man in his basic dynamism. But the discourse leads to a threshold which man cannot cross, to the evocation of a hypothesis regarding which man, left to his own powers, cannot say whether or not it corresponds to reality. The answer to this last question comes from a discourse of God himself. Blondel certainly has in mind the response given by the Christian religion (God freely gives himself to us), but he knows that the passage from the hypothesis, which is required by the implications of action, to the reality, which depends on God, requires on man's part an act of faith and not a further reasoning process.

We have reached the end of the Blondelian journey, but it has now been made clear to us that the discourse of man about God is vulnerable as long as it has not been met by God's discourse about himself: a discourse of God which is in fact always a discourse about man as well, if it be true, as Blondel's argument implies, that man fully understands himself only through God.[22] The circle seems to be closed. But is this conclusion satisfying? Can an atheist make the whole argument his own? He can certainly grasp its organization and thrust, but Blondel does not provide him with an apodictic response. He opens a way for him which is not neutral and which safeguards both God's freedom and man's freedom. At this point the atheist is left on his own and faced with a choice.

In Dialogue with the Atheist

We sometimes get the feeling today that all the strategies have become threadbare, including dialogue. Christians often feel vexed by this. We find them giving a wide range of responses to the atheist's refusal to play the game: from scandalized fright ("How can anyone be an unbeliever!") to sympathetic benevolence ("What a sad state you are in!"). Such attitudes on the part of believers are not always conscious; it takes the sharp eye of the atheist to spot them.[23] Francis Jeanson echoes some of them when he writes: "As for believers, they are, if I may say so, very nice to me. In all likelihood they have in mind, for example, Pascal's advice: 'Begin by pitying unbelievers; after all, their state makes them an unhappy lot. We must not be abusive to them unless it will help.' "[24]

Is it surprising that atheists should regard such an attitude as insulting? When they reject the Christian creed, they are not displaying an absence of faith. They are pursuing a different goal and occupying themselves with different questions; when all is said and done, they live by a human faith that has power to elicit complete dedication and to give their lives a very full meaning.

The difficulty of a dialogue with atheists arises from the fact that the problem of God no longer brings intellectual resources into play. Atheists seem to have abandoned the ground on which they used to meet with Christians, even if only to do battle with them. They seem no longer interested in fighting over the idea of God, especially since, as Jean Rostand writes, "the idea of God is difficult to define and so I find it difficult to oppose it."[25] Atheists have better things to do! What then do they expect? Not that Christians should enlighten them but that they should rather join them in the struggle, not the struggle over God but the struggle in behalf of man. If contemporary atheism is thus to be described as more agnostic than militant, more practical than theoretical, how are we to approach the question of God?

The discussion thus far has shown that there is no compelling proof of the existence of God. As a result each individual seems to be left with his own questions and his own personal options, without it being possible to say where the truth lies. And in fact the affirmation of God's existence does call into play a personal factor that is not unimportant. Does this mean that the alternatives are equally valid and that it is a matter of indifference whether we choose for or against the existence of God? The answer seems to be No, because what is really at stake is not the existence of God but the meaning of man. This is the final point to be explained.

The Personal Factor

But first let me analyze this personal factor which plays a part in the acceptance of the "proofs" for the existence of God and is so often encountered during the journey. In speaking earlier of various classical approaches I distinguished two grounds on which the affirmation of God has been based; neither proved tenable to the end. In Blondel we saw a different approach which included both grounds but which also made clear the importance of the personal factor.

Why is it that an atheist will reject the proofs while a believer finds them acceptable? Can the atheist accuse believers of a simple error in logic? This is unlikely in view of the number of persons who are satisfied with them and find them coherent. Must believers therefore accuse the atheist of bad will? This too is unlikely when we realize the sincerity which inspires many atheists in their search. If the atheist does not accept the proofs, no matter of what kind they are, it is because the proofs are not a matter of logic alone and therefore do not force themselves upon the mind with mathematical evidentiality. If the believer, on the other hand, is satisfied with them, it is because he already possesses faith and finds in the proofs a way of solidifying the intellectual basis of his faith. In other words, the validity of the proofs depends in good measure on an antecedent subjective conviction. This must be kept in mind in any dialogue with atheists. The proofs are not independent of the situation of the person speaking or listening.

> The fact of *proving to* implies the existence of a communication between oneself and the other which is possible only on the basis of a concrete situation which philosophy—or theology—must take into account if it wants to avoid being isolated in a zone of a false or at least indifferent abstraction. . . . One of the most serious mistakes made by a certain philosophical view . . . seems to involve the postulation of *natural man* as a transhistorical constant.[26]

In other words, every proof depends on the cultural context in which it was excogitated and on the personal situation of the person to whom it is being offered.

The reasoning person presupposed by the classical proofs ("natural man" in full possession of his reason, lacking any history, wounded indeed but at bottom *capax Dei,* "with a capacity for God") does not exist. Human beings are always concretely situated, and Christian revelation or the positive religions are factors in this situation. Human beings think on the basis of their existence in its entirety, and their thinking is affected by their attractions and repulsions, their reason and their imagination. In the final analysis, the only real proofs are proofs geared to an individual. We may therefore agree with Etienne Borne that by reason of the particular existential situation of each person there is an infinity of proofs, with "each individual in his concrete situation being challenged by the One in a unique way and having to find his personal response which will contain belief and proof indivisibly conjoined."[27] Borne's point is not that the only access to God is through sensible experience, after the manner of "God exists, because I have met him!" He is only suggesting that the personal factor is not without influence on the acknowledgment of God.

It is therefore not enough to carry on a dialogue with the atheist on a purely intellectual level. Theoretically speaking, it is always possible to show the coherence of the "proofs" and to refute atheism. However, the converse is also true. But the God question does not arise solely on the rational plane. It is a question that is as practical as it is theoretical. Despite his extreme positions, Kierkegaard was right on this point, and so was Blondel. The approach to God requires both proof and belief, intellectual argument and trusting commitment. "Without proof belief would be blind, and without belief proof would be empty and useless."[28]

The relation between faith and reason has often been taken to be one of mutual exclusion, and has even been turned into a dilemma: Either you can demonstrate the existence of God—but then how do you safeguard faith?—or you cannot demonstrate the existence of God—but then is faith still reasonable? Francis Jeanson presents this dilemma in all its rigor, but he also resolves it in his own way. His opening move is to disqualify rational discourse about God by opposing to it the Scriptures which, according to the Protestants whom he calls on as witnesses, alone lead us to knowledge of the true God. In a second step, he gives reason back its rights and opposes it to the discourse of the Scriptures, in order to show the absurdity of the latter and disqualify them in turn. Thus the circle is closed, and atheism has been proved true. Jeanson has carried off the trick of discrediting reason by means of faith and then discrediting faith by means of reason. But the dilemma can be resolved in another way as well.

If it be true that there is interaction between proofs developed by reason and faith (at least the human faith which chooses meaning against absurdity), then the two terms are not mutually exclusive but control one another. Reason provides a framework for faith by way of a preliminary process that opens the way for faith, and by way of subsequent elucidation in which the validity of the leap of faith is shown and its coherence ensured. If faith without proof leads to fideism, which is unworthy of faith, proof without faith turns into a gratuitous game that may satisfy the intellect but does not involve the person and that can lead to the God hypothesis but without getting outside the world of concepts.

In former ages Christian philosophers were bolder than they are today and believed that the proofs were enough to generate conviction. The Christian philosophers of our own time are more attentive to the real movement of life. Individuals confront existential problems according to their situation, with their minds but also with the whole weight of their experience behind them. No one faces any question, even one so essential as the God question, with "pure reason." This does not mean that after having removed the excesses of intellectualism, we are to impose silence on reason and rely solely on the word of God. Were we to do this, we would be falling back to a position already judged untenable. You do not correct one form of excess by falling into another. Truth is undoubtedly to be sought by a path that runs between purely rational proofs and an authoritarian assertion of God—along the kind of path Blondel opens up for us.

The Alternatives at Issue

Is it not possible to go further? Is it not possible to reach a point of decision at which the God question can be answered with a Yes or a No? There are no irrefutable arguments which can compel the atheist's assent, but perhaps we can tackle the problem from another side, by asking: What is the existential weight of each of the alternatives? Does one have more weight than the other? In beginning a dialogue with an atheist in this way, we suppose that the question of God remains an open one for him and that he has an existential interest in it. We also suppose that he has a particular idea of God, namely, that if God does exist, he is reality as such, the center for man, the ultimate foundation of the world, the one thing necessary, and so on. What, then, is the value of the God hypothesis?

If in the final analysis both the affirmation and the negation of God depend on a personal choice, the choice is nonetheless not completely subjective. It must have an objective basis. Since atheism and faith are equally possible choices, what is there in the real order that can supply an objective justification?[29]

Two traits seem to characterize our present world. On the one hand, it exists and reveals some meaning. On the other hand, it is problematic and raises questions. A spontaneous movement leads human beings to put their trust in the world and to find a positive meaning for their lives therein. But the world also raises many questions for them. They do not know where they come from or where they are going. They realize that they themselves are a mixture of being and non-being, and that non-being wins the victory in their lives. They perceive their own frailty and know that they must inevitably suffer and die. These experiences cause doubts. Though the world contains much that is positive, isn't it ultimately a place of absurdity? Despite the trust it inspires, does it not in the final analysis lack all meaning?

If God did exist, would we be any better off? Yes, for his existence would enable us to understand the coherence of the world but also why the world is shot through with questions. If God existed, the *reality* of the world would be intelligible. He would be its source of coherence and its ultimate meaning; he would be the foundation of all foundations, the meaning of all meanings, and, in short, the being of all beings. But then the *problematic* aspect of the world would likewise leap to the eye. There is nothing absolute in the world; nothing in it can provide an ultimate foundation or an ultimate meaning for itself or for others. Neither the self nor society nor the world has such coherence and meaning as to keep man from asking questions and spare him from looking elsewhere: "If you listen to them, all things say: 'We did not make ourselves; he made us who remains for ever.' "[30]

But in this type of approach God is still only a hypothesis that would allow us to answer certain human questions; he is not an evident and compelling reality. The world no longer speaks as clearly to modern man as Augustine supposes. The existence of God does not force itself upon us as a necessity, as the contradictory answers of atheist and believer show. The world as it now is can justify the denial as well as the affirmation of God.

Atheism is not impossible. We must grant atheists that a No to the God question is possible precisely by reason of the *problematic* character of reality. When faced with all these questions, an atheist refuses to take a position, saying that we can have no certain knowledge (agnosticism), or he gives a negative answer, saying that all things end in absurdity and nothingness (nihilism). The experience of the problematic character of reality gives the atheist a reason for maintaining that there is no ultimate foundation or ultimate meaning. Atheism is therefore a possibility that is based on one aspect of reality, but a possibility that only a decision can turn into a firmly held position. At the same time, if atheism is a position that cannot be proved, it is also a position that cannot be refuted. It is a choice.

The same must be said of faith in God. This too is a choice based on an aspect of reality. The affirmation of God is possible by reason of the existence of a *reality* which, despite all that is problematic about it, offers a basis for believing in the existence of God. Without God this reality would have no ultimate foundation or ultimate meaning. Reality justifies a Yes to the originating foundation of things and of human life. Just as it is not possible to refute an atheist, neither is it possible to refute one who asserts the existence of God. If a believer cannot be proved right against the atheist, since it is impossible for the believer to do away with the *problematic* character of reality, neither is it possible for the atheist to be proved right against the believer, since he cannot do away with the basic confidence in *reality* as existent and revelatory of meaning. Like atheism, faith in God is based on a decision which is at once irrefutable, because based on reality, and not completely provable.

Here, then, are the two positions at issue; each is able to offer "good" reasons in its behalf. The alternatives are clear. It remains to make a decision. Is it possible to answer the God question otherwise than with an "if"? There can be agreement at the conditional level: If God exists, he is the answer to the problematic character of reality and he is the foundation of meaning. But is it possible to say, with Blondel, "It is!"? How can we pass to "God is," except by an act of faith? The existence of God does not follow necessarily from rational "proofs." But is it not basically implied in the act of trust in the reality of the world? Is not the "faith in God" (in the broad sense of the phrase) which is a confident assent to an ultimate foundation and meaning—is it not a "logical" prolongation of the fundamental trust we give to reality? And yet this prolongation is a leap, justified indeed but not necessary. There is room in it for freedom and risk.

Positions of Unequal Value

But if Yes and No are alike possible, it does not follow that the two are of equal value in our eyes. In the final analysis, faith and atheism both represent a choice, but we must evaluate the consistency and consequences of this choice for the existential situation of man. Up to this point, I have tried to show what the basis of the choice, positive or negative, is; now I must speak of what the choice implies for the meaning of life. A "No," unless it is spoken idly, means that the basic trust I have in reality is unfounded, while a "Yes" means that this trust does indeed have a foundation. One who asserts the existence of God knows why he has this trust in reality. Thus the two choices are not to be put on the same level.

The trust which an atheist has in the world and in life is in fact without a foundation. In refusing to assign an ultimate foundation and an ultimate meaning he prevents himself from satisfactorily explaining reality. Unless it represents an unthinking superficiality or a fad of the moment, atheism must admit that reality lacks coherence and that life is inevitably absurd. It is difficult for a thinking atheist to avoid anxiety and a sense of abandonment. He may give his life a partial meaning by a heroic effort to make it bear fruit in time, but sooner or later he is compelled to acknowledge the absence of meaning. As long as the ultimate questions, those having to do with the meaning of life and death, are left in the shadows, the partial meanings which an atheist can bestow on his life are themselves rendered absurd, because they are enveloped in the global absurdity afflicting human destiny.

Belief in God, on the other hand, ultimately justifies the trust which reality inspires and the meaning which reveals itself there or which man draws from it. When connected with a reality more real than the real, the world in its becoming and life in its temporal unfolding are given an ultimate foundation, coherence and meaning that redeem them from absurdity. The Yes to God by which human beings decide for an ultimate foundation and meaning bestows in return a radical rationality on the world and gives life its unity, value, and meaning. While faith in a foundation does not totally remove all the non-meaning that is due to the contingency of the world and to human fallibility, it does give the certainty that the non-meaning or the perverted meaning does not have the final say in human destiny. Faith in God thus justifies trust in reality, despite the absurdity which shows itself in reality and often seems to triumph there.

The human decision to say Yes or No is not unaffected by the chances of life. Each person makes a decision in a particular existential situation. In each, believer or atheist, there is a basic desire to understand the universe and to understand himself. Apart from complete thoughtlessness, there is no one who does not do his utmost to answer the question of reality's meaning and thus to eliminate its problematic character. People would like to know more about the ultimate meaning of things and beings and to attain to the ultimate foundation where all questions are answered. But the response does not come at the end of a clear reasoning process. For not only can the question of meaning be stifled, but its answer depends on a personal commitment. Whatever the position taken, the affirmation of God is not possible unless trust in the meaning of reality triumphs over suspicion and doubt. This trust does not necessarily lead to the assertion of an ultimate meaning and foundation, but it at least makes such an assertion possible, on the understanding that the ultimate foundation and meaning do not reveal themselves to man except to the extent that man opens himself to them.

Let me define further the connection we have recognized to exist between basic trust in *reality* and faith in the existence of God as ultimate foundation and meaning. The trust in question is related to reality as such, while faith relates to an invisible reality. But the two attitudes display the same structure. Neither one is simply a matter of reasoning; each involves the whole person, the concrete person who lives, is bound by traditions and mental habits, and is motivated by interests and values. Each is therefore an existential affair, an affair in which the person cannot succeed unless he involves himself. The relation to God, like the relation to the world, is a relation of trust. Neither is reducible to pure rationality; each does involve rationality, but a rationality affected by inwardness, a rationality that is never completely transparent to itself and yet is neither blind nor empty since it is supported by the objectivity of the real.

A dialogue with an atheist can advance only on the basis of reflection that is closely tied to the world and to the human person. The atheist may be shaken in his views by the witness of a faith that is also a "practice"; he may be aware of the risks which this faith can involve. But he will be really convinced only at the end of a process in which he discovers that the issue is the meaning of the human person and the world. Trust in the real is a condition for such a dialogue. The outcome of the dialogue depends on a choice: either to remain in uncertainty and limit oneself to the world, or to leap over doubts and connect all the little islands of meaning that we see in the world by recognizing God as the meaning of all meanings.

The results of the preceding analysis are far from satisfactory and do not escape all criticism. Some readers will regard them as overly optimistic. Others will think that they concede too much to atheism. Yet my reflections have had no other purpose than to call attention to a truth which by its very obviousness may escape us: that neither faith nor atheism is self-evident. Each depends on basic options which are justified up to a certain point; each is justified precisely up to the point where the other takes over. Consequently there always remains within faith a space where atheism can grow; conversely it has to be said that within even the most thoughtful atheism there remain islands of faith—faith in reality, in the human person, in meaning—which can be the jumping-off point for a radical leap of faith in God. Consequently, too, neither the atheist nor the believer can claim a monopoly of truth.

The atheist has given up the idea of establishing an absolute foundation. He settles for an existence that is limited in time and that runs its course on this earth. It is this single existence, so insignificant when compared with the immensity of time, that he must actuate, fill with value, and saturate with a maximum of meaning. As for the tragedy and absurdity that are inherent in human existence, he must be able to accept these stoically. But these aspects do not diminish the value of life, for this comes from what the human person makes of life; whatever the outcome, this value remains. Even if, like Sartre, an atheist is convinced that man is "a foundation without a foundation," he often endeavors to give his life a serious quality and a fullness of meaning that rival those of the best believers and that have nothing to do with hedonism, at least among the noblest.

The believer, for his part, has become more modest. Having lost his intellectual certainties, which were often only the social habits of an age, he has become more sensitive to the doubts and negative aspects of human existence. He is no longer a man filled with ready-made answers and he no longer feels completely protected against atheism. His situation closely resembles that described by Anne Philipe in another context: an alternation of doubt and certainty, of unbelief and faith, in which neither alternative gains a complete victory over the other:

> I move from shadow to clarity
> from clarity to shadow
> and in turn
> each of these
> lays hold of me so fully
> that when I am in the one
> I can hardly imagine
> that the other exists.[31]

One thing sure, in any case, is that the old proofs, no matter how refined, have lost their cutting edge. Despite their rigorous logic they cannot convince the mind that the ultimate foundation it is seeking is called God. And yet if these "proofs" are not listened to, can we hope that the Gospel will be? This is hardly likely. True enough, the encounter with God rarely comes on well-marked, logical paths. But if the "proofs" fail—and have they ever succeeded?—should we stake everything on the bare word of the Gospel? There is little chance that an atheist who refuses to bow to logic will be more open to testimony.

The word of God, moreover, is far from working its effects

by violating consciences. The word is a free initiative on God's part and is addressed to the freedom and initiative of man. This is why I have been able to maintain that any approach to God supposes as an indivisible pair both belief and proof, decision and explanation, the coming of God and the appeal from man. There is a reciprocal connection between reason and faith, with each calling for the other. Only one who is already on the road and who retains an unshakable trust in meaning can attain to enlightenment.

Conclusion

In celebrating the obsequies of God the nineteenth century went all out and multiplied its Requiem Masses. The liturgy of this burial had been somewhat uncertain of itself throughout the eighteenth century but with Feuerbach it suddenly acquired its full form and appropriate style. Before him, atheists had muttered their Low Masses, and these were rather artificial. After him they possessed first-class, increasingly learned tunes, which our age repeats with little modification. All this detailed and rather brassy ritual seems threadbare and antiquated today, even though many continue to find their own thinking reflected in it.

As he has made the acquaintance of the great tenor voices of modern atheism, the reader has had the opportunity of familiarizing himself with this somewhat outdated liturgy. He has also been able to discern its capacity for adaptation to new situations and the way the melodies have been modulated according to the temperament and philosophy of each individual. He will also have succeeded, or so I hope, in discerning the currents that run underground through our present cultural world, emerging into visibility here and there in a personal confession or a political declaration, and that have left their impress on contemporary unbelief and given it its shape.

As the twentieth century draws to a close, other liturgies, seemingly more modern, are already being improvised. But they are preparing not for the burial of God—this is regarded as over and done with and no one even remembers God anymore at the Memento of the Dead—but for the burial of man. It is a sign of the times that those who mourn for God are becoming ever fewer, while they are legion who dance around the coffin of man, of the subject, of everything that after God's death took his place and moved busily on the stage of history. Today we see that all those heirs who regarded themselves as the makers of history were in fact only its products, its innocent and ridiculous playthings. The real powers exist elsewhere, in other places and in other seats of authority. But that is another story, though one not wholly lacking in significance for our purpose here. May not the whole development be seen as heaven's just vengeance, with the gravedigger following God into the grave?

In any case, now, after this double Good Friday, some voices are already proclaiming the dawn of an Easter Sunday; the rumor of the resurrection both of God and of man is spreading. "God is not dead!" "God cannot die!" Sometimes the cries are more triumphant: "God is coming back!" As far as man's return goes, the rumor is more cautious, but already prophetic voices are heard exclaiming: *Ecce homo!* Man is taking his place again! The assaults of the structuralists have merely succeeded in shaking him a bit and putting him one rung further down the ladder, but not in getting rid of him. He is returning invigorated, rejuvenated, ready for the waters of a new baptism.

Has atheism failed? Has the hour come for God's counteroffensive and, in its train, man's return to the stage? They tell us that all our experiences of recent years are about to end in a commonplace swing of the pendulum: God was not really dead but only repressed. Man is beginning to be aware of this, and the awareness signals the start of his liberation. Neurotic, smothered, exhausted by his unequal struggle against this repressed God whom he was unwilling to acknowledge, man is surfacing again, thanks to reconciliation with his God. He is getting ready to renew with God the covenant he had broken.

All's well that ends well! But this bill of health may be too optimistic. Are we to say that atheism was only a parenthesis, an insignificant wrinkle, and will leave no lasting mark? A slight twist in the linear web of history? Has the "tremendous event" of the death of God, which Nietzsche said had hardly begun, already reached the end of its journey, exhausted itself, started into a decline? This is quite unlikely. If we are indeed witnessing a renewal, it is certainly not to be compared with the great rush homeward at the end of the summer vacation period.

At the level of philosophical reflection, first of all, it seems that notice has been given to both God and man for an indefinite period, and it is hardly possible to offer a prognosis regarding the future, despite some encouraging signs. People don't feel too ill at ease in the present no-man's-land to which both God and man are forbidden entry. God and the human subject have alike become useless hypotheses. The philosophers are reducing the number of seats of authority or centers where the decisions of history are made, and neither God nor man has any place in their calculations. There is meaning to be had without making any appeal to God or man; this meaning is to be attained through learned analyses and is not to be dictated by heaven or by man.

As for what is going on around us and is more directly discernible, it is clear that unbelief is winning ground. It is no longer an exception but has become the portion of the majority. In many cases this unbelief is even ceasing to be the result of a personal conviction and is experienced rather as a simple indifference. The great and sometimes violent battles over atheism that have been waged during the past hundred years are now over and done with and are even unintelligible to many. Unbelief is an atheism at peace. It is neither for nor against. In living their lives, exciting or dull, with their successes and failures, people either try to derive as much meaning as possible from them, or else they simply live them out as best they can; in neither case do they involve God in their lives. The sphere of man is no longer geared to that of God.

May we hope that this situation will be reversed? Is the return of God imminent? Sometimes people are tempted to accept this diagnosis, but only at exceptional moments. Most of the time, people believe in "something" but avoid any clearer position than this. Apart from a few dynamic or quixotic souls the majority prefer to remain silent. Is this so surprising? God after all shares the lot of all things that cannot be proved. In a world like ours, in which the only truth that compels recognition is truth that is verifiable, God, like the human subject, is in a difficult position. Who is responsible for this situation? Christians, who have not been able to bear witness with sufficient conviction and commitment? Of course. Men themselves, who bustle about and forget what is essential? Certainly. Pollution is also a spiritual phenomenon. But why not God himself?

God has never been an evident reality, even if in other historical periods, when the web of society was not so loose, he had a better chance of success and a more assured place in men's lives. He has progressively lost his place in society. Here is perhaps the real cause of atheism: men would no longer tolerate the invasion of the entire social space by anyone but man himself. However, here too is the real opportunity for faith, because once it ceases to be an apprehension of God through the prism of society, it can once again become a free choice of his free offer of himself. Atheism will at least have caused us to recover this obvious truth which the Muslims constantly repeat: God is hidden, and he makes nothing evident to anyone, not even his absence.

What are we to do? Go about hawking God? True enough, every age needs prophets who will shake unbelievers and believers alike from their lethargy. But how are we to set about it? Can we hope to restore the "rights of God" by banging the table with our fist? We would be forgetting that his entrance into a life is an act of absolute freedom which appeals to free beings. The freedom of God generates a personal relationship that manifests itself throughout the person's history. External interventions may have a role to play, but they are always left outside when there is question of existential decisions involving God and the free human person.

However, I must also repeat with Duméry: "Faith is not a cry!" This means that the believer cannot be satisfied with proclaiming faith as a heritage that is beyond question, nor can the atheist be satisfied with approaching it as something foreign that is making a claim upon his intelligence. Faith seeks understanding; it presents itself for justification. It does not fear confrontation. In the dialogue with atheism faith is open to its objections, criticisms, and rejections. It does not present itself to the atheist as something unrelated to the requirements of reason. If its object is at bottom the God of love, then it must situate itself at the level of this object. God, however, is not unreason, even if he is beyond measure.

Notes

Preface
1. Samuel Beckett, *Endgame: A Play in One Act* (New York: Grove, 1958), pp. 54–55.

Chapter 1
1. Jean-Paul Sartre, *The Words,* tr. by B. Frechtman (New York: Braziller, 1964), p. 99.
2. Cf. Christian Chabanis, *Dieu existe-t-il Non* (Paris: Fayard, 1973).
3. Michel Foucault, *Histoire de la folie à l'âge classique* (new ed.; Paris: Gallimard, 1972), pp. 110–11.
4. Cited by Benigo Caérès, *Loisirs et travail du moyen âge à nos jours* (Paris: Seuil, 1973), p. 56.
5. *Caractères* XVI, 11; cf. Foucault, *op. cit.,* p. 133.
6. Michel de Certeau, *L'écriture de l'histoire* (Paris: Gallimard, 1975), p. 133.
7. *Ibid.,* p. 143.
8. Jean-Marc Gabaude, *Liberté et raison* (Toulouse: Université de Toulouse–Le Mirail) 3 (1974), p. 24.
9. J. -P. Migne (ed.), *Collection intégrale et universelle des orateurs sacrés* 24:216–17.
10. Foucault, *op. cit.,* p. 114.
11. Pascal, *Pensées,* tr. by A. J. Krailsheimer (Baltimore: Penguin, 1966), p. 81, no. 157 (Brunschvicg no. 225).
12. In Leibniz, *Philosophical Papers and Letters,* ed. by L. E. Loemker (2 vols.; Chicago: University of Chicago Press, 1956), 1:168.
13. Yves Belaval (ed.), *Histoire de la philosophie* 2 (Paris: Gallimard, 1973), p. 677.
14. *Ibid.,* p. 676.
15. Cf. *Philosophie et religion* (Paris: Editions sociales, 1974), p. 33. On atheism in the eighteenth century cf. also Jacques-J. Natanson, *La*

mort de Dieu (Paris: Presses universitaires de France, 1975). Some of my citations here are from Natanson's book.

16. *Collection intégrale* . . . (n. 9), 49:956. Ballet: 1702–1762.
17. *Ibid.,* 65:1034. Cambacérès: 1721–1802.
18. *Philosophical Dictionary,* tr. by P. Gay (New York: Basic Books, 1962), 1:103, article "Atheists, Atheism."
19. *Philosophie et religion* (n. 15), pp. 27–28.
20. De Certeau, *op. cit.,* p. 188.
21. Karl Rahner, "What Does Vatican II Teach About Atheism?" in K. Rahner (ed.), *The Pastoral Approach to Atheism* (Concilium 23; New York: Paulist Press, 1967), p. 9.
22. Letter to Feuerbach, August 11, 1844.
23. Fragment 14, tr. in Kathleen Freeman, *Ancilla to the Pre-Socratic Philosophers* (Cambridge, Mass.: Harvard University Press, 1962), p. 22.
24. Fragment 16, in Freeman, *ibid.*
25. *Thus Spoke Zarathustra,* tr. by W. Kaufmann (New York: Viking, 1954, 1966), "Zarathustra's Prologue," no. 3, p. 13.
26. *Theses on Feuerbach,* no. XI, in Karl Marx and Friedrich Engels, *On Religion* (Moscow: Foreign Languages Publishing House, 1957; reprinted New York: Schocken, 1964), p. 72.
27. *Contribution to the Critique of Hegel's Philosophy of Right,* in *ibid.,* p. 42.
28. *Croire ou le feu de la vie* (Paris: Editions ouvrières, 1974).
29. *Pastoral Constitution on the Church in the Modern World,* no. 21, in A. Flannery (ed.), *Vatican II: The Conciliar and Postconciliar Documents* (Collegeville, Minn.: Liturgical Press, 1975), p. 921.
30. Paul Ricoeur, "The Atheism of Freudian Psychoanalysis," in J. B. Metz (ed.), *Is God Dead?* (Concilium 16; New York: Paulist, 1966), p. 60 [translation slightly modified].
31. Johann B. Metz, "Preface," *ibid.,* p. 2.
32. Ricoeur, *art. cit.,* p. 61 [translation slightly modified].
33. Peter Berger, *The Sacred Canopy: Elements of a Sociological Theory of Religion* (Garden City, N.Y.: Doubleday, 1967); W. H. van de Pol, *The End of Conventional Christianity,* tr. by T. Zuydwijk (New York: Newman, 1968).
34. Cf. Pierre Thibault, *Savoir et pouvoir. Philosophie thomiste et politique cléricale au XIXᵉ siècle* (Quebec: Université de Laval, 1972).
35. Cf. Jean Lacroix, *The Meaning of Modern Atheism,* tr. by G. Barden (New York: Macmillan, 1956).
36. Cf. Etienne Borne, *Atheism,* tr. by S. J. Tester (New York: Hawthorn Books, 1961); Claude Tresmontant, *Les problèmes de l'athéisme* (Paris: Seuil, 1972).
37. Cf. Maurice Clavel, *Ce que je crois* (Paris: Grasset, 1975); Viktor Frankl, *The Unconcious God: Psychotherapy and Theology* (New York: Simon and Schuster, 1975).

38. Maurice Merleau-Ponty, *In Praise of Philosophy*, tr. by J. Wild and J. M. Edie (Evanston: Northwestern University Press, 1964), pp. 42–43.

Chapter 2

1. Cf. S. Rawidowicz, *Ludwig Feuerbachs Philosophie. Ursprung und Schicksal* (Berlin: De Gruyter, 1931; reprinted 1964).
2. Cf. Marcel Xhaufflaire, *Feuerbach et la théologie de la sécularisation* (Cogitatio fidei 45; Paris: Cerf, 1970).
3. Letter of 1825, in *The Fiery Brook: Selected Writings of Ludwig Feuerbach*, tr. by Z. Hanfi (Garden City, N.Y.: Doubleday, 1972), p. 268.
4. Friedrich Engels, *Ludwig Feuerbach and the Outcome of Classical German Philosophy*, ed. by C. P. Dutt (New York: International Publishers, 1941), p. 42.
5. *Ibid.*, p. 19.
6. Hanfi (ed.), *The Fiery Brook*, p. 177.
7. *Preliminary Theses on the Reform of Philosophy*, in *ibid.*, p. 159.
8. *Principles of Philosophy*, in *ibid.*, p. 292.
9. *Ludwig Feuerbachs Religionsphilosophie* (Paderborn: Schöningh, 1936; reprinted 1961).
10. *The Essence of Christianity*, tr. by George Eliot (New York: Harper Torchbooks, 1957). References will be by *EC* and page number.
11. Nüdling, *op. cit.*, p. 3.
12. Cf. the introduction of J. -P. Osier to the French translation: *L'Essence du christianisme* (Paris: Maspero, 1968), p. 29.
13. There is a lengthy presentation of *The Essence of Religion* in Nüdling, *op. cit.*; cf. also Xhaufflaire, *op. cit.*, pp. 230–31.
14. Xhaufflaire, *op. cit.*, p. 255.
15. *Ibid.*, pp. 249, 254.
16. *Ibid.*, p. 255.
17. *Ibid.*, pp. 260–66.
18. L. D. Easton and K. H. Guddat (eds.), *Writings of the Young Marx on Philosophy and Society* (Garden City, N.Y.: Doubleday, 1967), p. 95.
19. Georges M. M. Cottier, *L'athéisme du jeune Marx. Ses origines hégéliennes* (Paris: Vrin, 1959), p. 135.
20. [The bracketed sentence is in the French version of this passage, but not in the English.—Tr.]
21. Nüdling, *op. cit.*, p. 64.
22. Cited in Xhaufflaire, *op. cit.*, p. 259.
23. Jürgen Moltmann, *The Crucified God*, tr. by R. A. Wilson and J. Bowden (New York: Harper & Row, 1974), pp. 251–52.
24. Soren Kierkegaard, *Journals and Papers*, ed. and tr. by H. V. Hong

and E. H. Hong, vol. 6 (Bloomington: Indiana University Press, 1978), p. 244.

25. Xhaufflaire, *op. cit.*, p. 320. Some studies of Feuerbach: Henri Arvon, *Ludwig Feuerbach ou la transformation du sacré* (Paris: Presses universitaires de France, 1957); Joseph de Finance, "Le sujet et l'attribut: A propos d'un texte de Feuerbach," in *De Deo in philosophia S. Thomae et in hodierna philosophia* (Acta VI. Congressus Thomistici Universalis) 2 (Rome: Officium Libri Catholici, 1966), pp. 149–53; S. Decloux, "Théologie et anthropologie," *Nouvelle revue théologique* 91 (1969), 6–22.

Chapter 3

1. Maurice Clavel, *Ce que je crois* (Paris: Grasset, 1975), pp. 96–97.
2. Michel Henry, *Marx* 1. *Une philosophie de la réalité;* 2. *Une philosophie de l'économie* (Paris: Gallimard, 1976).
3. Friedrich Engels, *Ludwig Feuerbach and the Outcome of Classical German Philosophy*, ed. by C. P. Dutt (New York: International Publishers, 1941), p. 18. For Marx's life and development cf. especially Auguste Cornu, *Karl Marx et Friedrich Engels* (Paris: Presses universitaires de France, 1955).
4. Here are some studies to which the reader may turn. First, some by Christians: Charles Wackenheim, *La faillite de la religion d'après Karl Marx* (Paris: Presses universitaires de France, 1963), a book to which I shall be referring frequently; Nguyen Ngoc Vu, *Idéologie et religion d'après Marx et Engels* (Paris: Aubier, 1975); Georges M. M. Cottier, *L'athéisme du jeune Marx. Ses origines hégéliennes* (Paris: Vrin, 1959), a basic work; Gustav A. Wetter, *Dialectical Materialism: A Historical and Systematic Survey of Philosophy in the Soviet Union*, tr. by P. Heath (New York: Wagner, 1959); Giulio Girardi, *Marxism and Christianity*, tr. by K. Traynor (New York: Macmillan, 1968). Some works by Marxists: Henri Lefebvre, *Pour connaître la pensée de Karl Marx* (Paris: Bordas, 1966); Michel Verret, *Les marxistes et la religion. Essai sur l'athéisme moderne* (Paris: Editions sociales, 1965); André Casanova, *Vatican II et l'évolution de l'Eglise* (Paris: Editions sociales, 1969); Centre d'Etudes et Recherches Marxistes, *Philosophie et religion* (Paris: Editions sociales, 1974).
5. Cf. Cottier, *op. cit., passim.*
6. Text in Karl Marx and Friedrich Engels, *On Religion* (Moscow: Foreign Languages Publishing House, 1957; reprinted, New York: Schocken, 1964), p. 14. The texts of Marx and Engels which I shall be citing in this chapter are taken mainly from this volume.
7. *Ibid.*, p. 15.

8. Wackenheim, *op. cit.*, pp. 100–1.

9. *On Religion*, p. 13.

10. *Ibid.*, pp. 16–40. The citations are from pp. 18, 19, 37, 38, 39.

11. *Ibid.*, p. 50.

12. *Ibid.*, pp. 41, 42.

13. *Capital* (1867), in Karl Marx, *Oeuvres* (Pléiade edition; Paris: Nouvelle Revue Française, I, p. 613.

14. Karl Marx, *The Jewish Question*, tr. in L. D. Easton and K. H. Guddat (eds.,), *Writings of the Young Marx on Philosophy and Society* (Garden City, N.Y.: Doubleday, 1967), pp. 216–48.

15. *Ibid.*, pp. 222–23.

16. Cf. my two articles on freedom in *Vivante Eglise*, January 15 and February 15, 1976.

17. Cf. Henri Lefebvre, *Hegel, Marx, Nietzsche et le royaume des ombres* (Tournai: Casterman, 1975).

18. *On Religion*, p. 71, Thesis VII.

19. *Ibid.*, p. 70. Thesis IV.

20. *Ibid.*, p. 71, Thesis VI.

21. *Ibid.*, p. 72, Thesis XI.

22. *Ibid.*, pp. 74–75 [translation slightly modified].

23. *Ibid.*, pp. 80–81.

24. Cf. *Capital*, in *Oeuvres*, Pléiade edition, I, p. 915, note a: "If this material basis is ignored, the history of religion lacks any criterion. It is in fact much easier to analyze the content, the earthly nucleus, of the cloudy conceptions of religion than it is to follow the opposite course and show how the real conditions of life gradually take on an ethereal form. The first way is the only materialist and therefore scientific way." Cf. Louis Althusser's reflections on the materialist thesis that "in the final analysis" the infrastructure determines the superstructure: *Positions* (Paris: Editions Sociales, 1976), pp. 138ff.

25. Cited in Nguyen Ngoc Vu, *op. cit.*, p. 29.

26. Cf. Jacques Milhau, *Le marxisme au mouvement* (Paris: Presses universitaires de France, 1975), p. 124.

27. Cf. *ibid.*, p. 113. See also Louis Althusser, *Eléments d'autocritique* (Paris: Hachette, 1974), p. 42, and his *Positions* (Paris: Editions sociales, 1976), pp. 67–125.

28. *On Religion*, p. 81.

29. *Capital*, in *Oeuvres*, Pléiade edition, I, pp. 550–51.

30. Moscow: Foreign Languages Publishing House, 1956.

31. Cf. *Capital*, in *Oeuvres*, Pléiade edition, I, p. 581.

32. *Manifesto of the Communist Party*, in *On Religion*, p. 89.

33. "The Communism of the Paper *Rheinischer Beobachter*," *ibid.*, pp. 83–84.

34. Cf. Wackenheim, *op. cit.*, p. 315.

35. On Engels, cf. Georges M. M. Cottier, "Engels," in *L'athéisme dans la philosophie contemporaine* (Paris: Desclée, 1970), 2:200ff.; Jacques Bidet, "Engels et la religion," in *Philosophie et religion* (n. 4, above).
36. Cottier, *art. cit.*, p. 212.
37. *Anti-Dühring*, in *On Religion*, pp. 147, 149.
38. *Dialectics of Nature*, in *ibid.*, p. 192.
39. Gustav A. Wetter, "Le marxisme-léninisme," in *L'athéisme dans la philosophie contemporaine*, 2:230.
40. Jean-Pierre Osier, "Lénine et la religion," *Cahiers de l'université nouvelle*, no. 730, p. 21.
41. Wetter, *art. cit.*, 2:230.
42. *The Gulag Archipelago (1918–1956): An Experiment in Literary Investigation* I–II, tr. by T. P. Whitney (New York: Harper & Row, 1973–74), p. 37.
43. G. Marchais, in *La Croix*, November 19, 1970.
44. *Ibid.*
45. Nicholas Berdiaev, *Christianisme Marxisme* (Paris: Le Centurion, 1975), p. 38.

Chapter 4

1. Ernest Jones, *The Life and Work of Sigmund Freud* 3 (New York: Basic Books, 1957), p. 351.
2. *Civilization and Its Discontents* (published in 1930), tr. by J. Strachey (New York: Norton, 1961), p. 11. The other works of Freud to which I will be making frequent reference are: *Totem and Taboo: Resemblances between the Psychic Lives of Primitives and Neurotics* (1913), tr. by A. A. Brill (New York: Modern Library, 1938; Vintage Books, 1945); *The Future of an Illusion* (1927), tr. by W. D. Robson-Scott, rev. by J. Strachey (Garden City, N.Y.: Doubleday Anchor Books, 1964); *Moses and Monotheism* (1938–39), tr. by K. Jones (New York: Vintage Books, 1939). Cf. also the impressive list of Freud's writings on religion from 1907 to 1939 either in Jones who analyzes them in chronological order or in Paul Ricoeur, *The Conflict of Interpretations: Essays in Hermeneutics*, ed. and tr. by D. Ihde (Evanston: Northwestern University Press, 1974), p. 122.
3. Letter of February 9, 1909, in Sigmund Freud and Oskar Pfister, *Psychoanalysis and Faith: The Letters of Sigmund Freud and Oskar Pfister*, tr. by E. Mosbacher (New York: Basic Books, 1963), p. 17.
4. "A Religious Experience" (1928), in Sigmund Freud, *Collected Papers* (5 vols.; New York: Basic Books, 1959), 5:244. [Henceforth: *CP*, with volume and page number.]
5. Cf. Ricoeur, *op. cit.*
6. Cf. Jones, *op. cit.*, 3:367.
7. *Moses and Monotheism*, p. 156.

8. *CP* 2:25.
9. *CP* 2:28.
10. *CP* 2:27.
11. *CP 2:34.*
12. Freud, of course, rejects the idea that it is a "fiction." Cf. *Civiliza-tion and Its Discontents,* p. 78. The reconstruction is to be found in *Totem and Taboo* and in *Moses and Monotheism,* pp. 167ff.
13. *Moses and Monotheism,* p. 168.
14. *Totem and Taboo,* p. 183.
15. *Moses and Monotheism,* p. 168.
16. *Totem and Taboo,* p. 185.
17. *Ibid.,* p. 184.
18. *Civilization and Its Discontents,* p. 78.
19. *Ibid.,* pp. 76–77.
20. *Totem and Taboo,* p. 187.
21. *Ibid.,* pp. 188–89.
22. *Moses and Monotheism,* p. 168.
23. Jones, *op. cit.,* 3:354, citing Freud himself.
24. Cf. *The Future of an Illusion,* p. 27.
25. *Civilization and Its Discontents,* p. 22.
26. *The Future of an Illusion,* p. 24.
27. *Ibid.,* pp. 60–61.
28. *Ibid.,* p. 71.
29. *Ibid.,* p. 80.
30. *Totem and Taboo,* p. 115.
31. *The Future of an Illusion,* p. 82.
32. Cf. Max Schur, *Freud: Living and Dying* (New York: International Universities Press, 1972).
33. *Civilization and Its Discontents,* p. 21.
34. *The Future of an Illusion,* p. 53.
35. *Ibid.,* p. 92.
36. Cf. Viktor Frankl, *The Unconscious God* (New York: Simon and Schuster, 1975).
37. Cited in Frankl, *La psychothérapie et son image de l'homme,* tr. by J. Feisthauer (Paris: Resma, 1970), p. 138.
38. Paul Ricoeur, *Freud and Philosophy: An Essay on Interpretation,* tr. by D. Savage (New Haven: Yale University Press, 1970), pp. 535–36.
39. *Ibid.,* p. 536.
40. *Moses and Monotheism,* p. 157.

Chapter 5

1. The reader may consult, among others, Jean Granier, *Le problème de la vérité dans la philosophie de Nietzsche* (Paris: Seuil, 1966); Georges

Morel, *Nietzsche* (3 vols.; Paris: Aubier, 1970–71); Martin Heidegger, *Chemins qui ne mènent nulle part* (Paris: Gallimard, 1962) (all of Heidegger's writings on Nietzsche have been published more recently by Gallimard); P. Valadier, *Nietzsche et la critique du Christianisme* (Paris: Cerf, 1974).

2. Cf. Valadier, *op. cit.,* who provides the evidence for this statement.
3. *The Gay Science,* tr. by W. Kaufmann (New York: Random House Vintage Books, 1974), no. 377, p. 340.
4. *Ecce homo,* tr. by W. Kaufmann and published with *On the Genealogy of Morals,* tr. by W. Kaufmann and R. J. Hollingdale (New York: Random House Vintage Books, 1967), Part I, no. 3, p. 226.
5. *The Gay Science,* no. 131, p. 185.
6. Letter of June 11, 1865, in *Selected Letters of Friedrich Nietzsche,* ed. and tr. by C. Middleton (Chicago: University of Chicago Press, 1969), p. 7.
7. *The Gay Science,* no. 377, p. 338.
8. *Thus Spoke Zarathustra,* tr. by W. Kaufmann (New York, Viking, 1966), Part IV, ch. 12, "On Old and New Tablets," p. 196.
9. *The Gay Science,* no. 377, p. 340.
10. *Beyond Good and Evil,* tr. by W. Kaufmann (New York: Random House Vintage Books, 1966), no. 216, p. 146.
11. *The Will to Power,* tr. by W. Kaufmann and R. J. Hollingdale (New York: Random House, 1967), no. 168, p. 101.
12. *La volonté de puissance,* tr. by G. Bianquis (2 vols.; Paris: Gallimard, 1932, 1, no. 420, p. 192. [The order of entries and, it seems, even the overall content is different in the French translation and in the Kaufmann-Hollingdale version. I have not been able to find all the cited passages in the English version and have therefore had to translate them from the French text.—Tr.]
13. *The Will to Power,* no. 200, p. 117.
14. *Ecce homo,* Part III, no. 1, p. 259.
15. *Thus Spoke Zarathustra,* Part I, ch. 1, "On the Three Metamorphoses," p. 25.
16. *La volonté de puissance,* II, no. 426, pp. 133–34.
17. *The Gay Science,* no. 346, p. 298.
18. Nietzsche, "Cahiers de Royaumont," *Philosophie* 6 (Paris: Minuit, 1967), p. 280.
19. Cf. Valadier, *op. cit.,* p. 435.
20. *Thus Spoke Zarathustra,* Part IV, ch. 6, "Retired," pp. 258–63.
21. *La volonté de puissance,* II, no. 426, p. 133.
22. *Thus Spoke Zarathustra,* Part I, ch. 1, "On the Three Metamorphoses," pp. 26–27.
23. *La volonté de puissance,* II, no. 426, p. 134.

24. *Thus Spoke Zarathustra*, Part IV, ch. 17, "The Awakening," pp. 312–13.
25. *Ibid.*, Part II, ch. 12, "On Old and New Tablets," p. 196.
26. *The Gay Science*, no. 346, p. 286.
27. *Thus Spoke Zarathustra*, Part III, ch. 12, "On Old and New Tablets," p. 196.
28. Valadier, *op. cit.*, p. 168.
29. *Thus Spoke Zarathustra*, Part I, ch. 1, "On the Three Metamorphoses," p. 27.
30. *La volonté de puissance*, II, no. 426, p. 134.
31. *Thus Spoke Zarathustra*, Part III, ch. 8, "On Apostates," pp. 180–81.
32. *Ibid.*, p. 180.
33. *The Gay Science*, no. 132, p. 186.
34. *Ibid.*, no. 125, pp. 181–82.
35. Valadier, *op. cit.*, p. 485.
36. *The Gay Science*, no. 343, p. 279.
37. *Ibid.*
38. Heidegger, *op. cit.*, p. 177.
39. *Thus Spoke Zarathustra*, Part IV, ch. 6, "Retired," p. 259.
40. *The Gay Science*, no. 347, p. 287.
41. *The Dawn of Day*, tr. by J. M. Kennedy, in *The Complete Works of Friedrich Nietzsche*, ed. by O. Levy (reprinted: New York: Russell and Russell, 1964), IX:91, no. 91.
42. *The Will to Power*, no. 135, pp. 85–86.
43. *Human, All-Too-Human*, tr. by H. Zimmern, in *The Complete Works of Friedrich Nietzsche*, VI/1:119, no. 111.
44. *The Will to Power*, no. 136, pp. 86–87.
45. *The Gay Science*, no. 360. p. 315.
46. *Ibid.*, no. 353, pp. 296–97.
47. *Thus Spoke Zarathustra*, Part IV, ch. 7, "The Ugliest Man," pp. 266–67.
48. This theme has been extensively developed by Sartre, especially in his play *No Exit*.
49. *Thus Spoke Zarathustra*, Part IV, ch. 9, "The Shadow," p. 274.
50. *The Gay Science*, no. 343, p. 280.
51. *La volonté de puissance*, II, no. 420, p. 133.
52. *Ibid.*, no. 421.
53. *Ibid.*, no. 422.
54. *Thus Spoke Zarathustra*, Part I, ch. 22, "On the Gift-Giving Virtue," p. 79.
55. *La volonté de puissance*, II, no. 427, p. 134.
56. *The Gay Science*, no. 320, p. 254.
57. *La volonté de puissance*, II, no. 582, p. 380.
58. *The Gay Science*, no. 1, p. 73.

59. *Ibid.,* no. 377, p. 340.
60. *Ecce homo,* Part III, no. 1, p. 261,
61. Valadier, *op. cit.,* p. 503.
62. Cf. Morel, *op. cit.,* 3:274.
63. *La volonté de puissance,* II, no. 440, 137.
64. Granier, *op. cit.,* p. 410.
65. Nietzsche, "Cahiers de Royaumont" (n. 15), p. 280.
66. Jean Granier, "La critique nietszchéenne du Dieu de la métaphysi-que," in *Procès de l'objectivité de Dieu* (Paris: Cerf, 1969), p. 92.
67. *The Will to Power,* no. 209, p. 123.
68. *Ibid.,* no. 215, p. 126.
69. Granier, *art. cit.,* p. 71.
70. *Ibid.,* pp. 73–74. Reference might be made here to other very good studies, e.g., Gilles Deleuze, *Nietzsche et la philosophie* (Paris: Presses universitaires de France, 1962).
71. *La volonté de puissance,* II, no. 437, p. 136.
72. Nietzsche, "Cahiers de Royaumont," p. 285.
73. *The Will to Power,* no. 252, p. 145.
74. *Human, All-Too-Human,* no. 113, tr. in W. Kaufmann, *The Portable Nietzsche* (New York: Viking, 1954), p. 52.
75. *Thus Spoke Zarathustra,* Part III, ch. 11, "On the Spirit of Gravity," p. 195.
76. Cf. *ibid.,* "Zarathustra's Prologue," no. 3, p. 13.
77. *The Will to Power,* no. 159, p. 98.

Chapter 6

1. Cf. *The Flies,* tr. by S. Gilbert, in *No Exit and Three Other Plays* (New York: Vintage Books, n.d.); *The Devil and the Good Lord and Two Oth-er Plays,* tr. by K. Black (New York: Vintage Books, 1960); *Being and Nothingness,* tr. by H. E. Barnes (New York: Philosophical Library, 1956); *The Words,* tr. by B. Frechtman (New York: Braziller, 1964).

   On Sartre, cf. Francis Jeanson, *Sartre par lui-même* (Paris: Seuil, 1971); *idem, Sartre* (Paris: Desclée De Brouwer, 1966); Régis Jolivet, *Sartre ou la théologie de l'absurde* (Paris: Fayard, 1965); Laurent Gag-nebin, *Connaître Sartre* (Paris: Resma, 1972).

   Sartre has often roused the indignation of Catholics. His works contain "extremely pernicious teachings," says Gabriel Marcel, who accuses Sartre of being an "inveterate disparager" and a "sys-tematic blasphemer." The passage of time has led to more moder-ate judgments on Sartre.
2. Sartre, *Nausea,* tr. by L. Alexander (New York: New Directions, 1964), p. 131. [I have modified the translation slightly, substituting

"deduce them" (*les deduire*) for "deduce anything from them."—Tr.]

3. *The Condemned of Altona*, tr. by S. and G. Leeson (New York: Vintage Books, 1963), pp. 7–8.

4. Cf. Michel Cantat and Michel Rybalka, *Les écrits de Sartre* (Paris: Gallimard, 1970), especially p. 240.

5. *Ibid.* Why take offense at the blunt statements in this play? Sartre tells us that most of the shocking phrases for which people rebuke him are taken from Christian writers: "The Church is a strumpet" is from Savonarola; Christ is a "bastard" is from Clement VII; and so on. Cf. Cantat and Rybalka, *op. cit.*, pp. 239–40.

6. *Existentialism Is a Humanism*, tr. in Walter Kaufmann (ed.), *Existentialism from Dostoevsky to Sartre* (New York: World, 1956), p. 309.

7. Preface to a staging of *No Exit* by Michel Vitot, Christiane Lenier, Gaby Silva, and R. -J. Chauffard.

8. *L'enfance d'un chef*, published with *Mur* (Paris: Gallimard, 1972), p. 167.

9. "François Mauriac and Freedom," in *Literary and Philosophical Essays*, tr. by A. Michelson (New York: Criterion, 1955), p. 18.

10. *Existentialism Is a Humanism*, p. 290.

11. [But the final passage cited is not where Neusch indicates it to be, and I have translated it directly from the French text provided by Neusch.—Tr.]

12. [Again, I cannot find the passage where Neusch indicates it to be, and I have translated from his French text.—Tr.]

13. Henry Dumery, *Foi et interrogation* (Paris: Téqui, 1963), p. 96.

14. *Situation I* (Paris: Gallimard, 1947), p. 142.

15. *Existentialism Is a Humanism*, p. 311.

Chapter 7

1. *Parole d'homme* (Paris: Laffont, 1975), p. 22.

2. French title: *Le grand tournant du socialisme* (Paris: Gallimard, 1969). English: *The Crisis in Communism: The Turning-Point of Socialism*, tr. by P. Ross and B. Ross (New York: Grove, 1970), Cf. also *Garaudy par Garaudy* (Paris: La Table Ronde, 1970).

3. For this cf. my article in *Vivante Eglise*, October 15, 1974.

4. *The Crisis in Communism*, p. 52.

5. *Alternatives sociales*, a journal edited by Roger Garaudy (Paris: Stock, 1974). Only two issues have appeared: 1. *Socialisme et liberté;* 2. *Foi et socialisme.*

6. Cited in Garaudy, *The Alternative Future: A Vision of Christian Marxism*, tr. by L. Mayhew (New York: Simon and Schuster, 1974), p. 30.

7. *The Crisis in Communism*, p. 156.

8. *Le projet espérance* (Paris: Laffont, 1976).

9. *Parole d'homme,* pp. 26 and 141.

10. *Ibid.,* p. 41.

11. *Alternatives socialistes,* p. 85.

12. *Parole d'homme,* p. 37.

13. *Ibid.,* p. 265.

14. *The Alternative Future,* pp. 178–79.

15. *La Croix,* Tuesday, April 27, 1976.

16. *From Anathema to Dialogue: A Marxist Challenge to the Christian Churches,* tr. by L. O'Neill (New York: Herder and Herder, 1966).

17. *Parole d'homme,* p. 118.

18. *From Anathema to Dialogue,* p. 56.

19. *Alternatives socialistes,* no. 2.

20. *Ibid.,* p. 12.

21. *Ibid.,* p. 17.

22. *Marxistes et Chrétiens: Entretiens de Salzbourg* (Paris: Mame, 1968), pp. 83–84.

23. *Marxisme au XXe siècle* (Paris: La Palatine, 1966), p. 117.

24. *Ibid.,* p. 118.

25. *Ibid.,* p. 119.

26. *Parole d'homme,* p. 112.

27. *Alternatives socialistes* 2:19.

28. *Marxisme au XXe siècle,* p. 177.

29. *Reconquête de l'espoir* (Paris: Grasset, 1971), p. 141.

30. *Alternatives socialistes* 2:12.

31. *The Alternative Future,* p. 83.

32. *Ibid.,* p. 177. The French original of this book appeared in 1972.

33. *Parole d'homme,* p. 265.

34. *La Croix,* April 27, 1976.

35. *Parole d'homme,* p. 233.

36. *Ibid.,* p. 238.

37. *Ibid.,* p. 250.

38. *Ibid.,* p. 14.

39. *Ibid.,* pp. 24 and 50.

40. *Ibid.,* p. 33.

41. *Ibid.,* p. 55.

42. *Ibid.,* p. 222.

43. *Ibid.,* p. 150.

44. *Ibid.,* p. 236.

45. Interview given to *Le Monde* and reprinted in C. Chabanis, *Dieu existe-t-il?* (Paris: Fayard, 1973), p. 399.

46. *Ibid.,* p. 398. Cf. *Parole d'homme,* pp. 242–44.

47. *La Croix,* April 27, 1976.

48. *Ibid.*

49. *Parole d'homme,* p. 225.
50. *Ibid.,* p. 77.
51. *Ibid.,* p. 241.
52. *Ibid.,* p. 50.
53. *Ibid.,* p. 77.
54. *Ibid.,* p. 58.
55. *Ibid.,* p. 268.
56. *60 oeuvres qui annocèrent le futur: 7 siècles de peinture occidentale* (Geneva: Skira, 1974), p. 290.
57. *Ibid.,* p. 292.
58. *Danser sa vie* (Paris: Seuil, 1973), p. 23.
59. *Ibid.,* p. 22.
60. *60 oeuvres qui annocèrent le futur,* p. 287.

Chapter 8

1. *Das Prinzip Hoffnung* (Frankfurt: Suhrkamp, 1974). Not translated into English. There is a French translation of the first part of the book: *Le Principe-Espérance* (Paris: Gallimard, 1976).
2. Cf. the little book of Laennec Hurbon, *Ernst Bloch: Utopie et espérance* (Paris: Cerf, 1974). A collection of essays has recently appeared: Gérard Raulet (ed.), *Utopie marxiste selon Ernst Bloch* (Paris: Payot, 1976). I have not been able to take this volume into account, although it is of interest for the question I am discussing here (my essay appeared in its initial form in *Vivante Eglise,* January to March, 1976).
3. Jürgen Moltmann, *Theology of Hope: On the Ground and the Implications of a Christian Eschatology,* tr. by J. W. Leitch (New York: Harper & Row, 1967).
4. The book has been translated into French as *Thomas Münzer, théologien de l'espérance* (Paris: Julliard, 1964).
5. Some of his books: *Spuren* [Footprints] (new and enlarged ed.; Frankfurt: Suhrkamp, 1967); there is a French translation, *Traces* (Paris: Gallimard, 1968). *Vorlesungen zur Philosophie der Renaissance* [Lectures on Renaissance Philosophy] (Frankfurt: Suhrkamp, 1972); French tr., *Philosophie de la Renaissance* (Paris: Payot, 1974). *Atheismus im Christentum: Zur Religion des Exodus und des Reichs* (Frankfurt: Suhrkamp, 1968); English tr. by J. T. Swann, *Atheism in Christianity: The Religion of the Exodus and the Kingdom* (New York: Herder & Herder, 1972).
6. *Das Prinzip Hoffnung* [henceforth: *PH*], p. 1627.
7. *Ibid.,* p. 1628.
8. *Ibid.,* p. 37.
9. *Ibid.,* p. 44.

10. *Traces* (n. 5), p. 7.
11. *PH*, p. 84.
12. *Ibid.*, p. 85.
13. *Ibid.*, p. 132.
14. *Ibid.*, p. 168.
15. *Ibid.*, p. 166.
16. *Ibid.*, p. 169.
17. *Ibid.*, p. 675.
18. *Ibid.*, p. 676.
19. *Ibid.*, p. 678.
20. *Ibid.*, p. 724.
21. *Ibid.*
22. *Ibid.*, p. 726.
23. Cf. Christoph Ertel, "Der Marxismus bei Ernst Bloch," *Lebendiges Zeugnis*, March 1972, pp. 76–82.
24. *Traces*, p. 71.
25. Cited in *PH*, p. 1392.
26. *Atheism in Christianity* (n. 5), p. 59.
27. *PH*, p. 1390.
28. *Traces*, p. 142.
29. *Ibid.*
30. *Ibid.*, p. 116.
31. *Ibid.*, p. 139.
32. *Ibid.*, p. 140.
33. *PH*, p. 1515.
34. *Ibid.*, p. 1523.
35. *Ibid.*, p. 1521.
36. *Ibid.*, p. 1404.
37. *Atheism in Christianity*, pp. 29–34.
38. Ex 3:14.
39. *PH*, p. 1458.
40. *Ibid.*, p. 1403.
41. *Atheism in Christianity*, pp. 160–61.
42. *Ibid.*, pp. 162–63.
43. *Ibid.*, p. 164.
44. *PH*, p. 1404.
45. *Ibid.*, pp. 1522–23.
46. *Ibid.*, p. 1529.
47. *Ibid.*, p. 1533.
48. *Ibid.*, pp. 1301 and 1297.
49. *Ibid.*, p. 1320.
50. *Ibid.*, p. 1362.
51. *Ibid.*, p. 1365.
52. *Ibid.*, p. 1303.

53. *Ibid.*, p. 1380.
54. *Ibid.*, p. 1383.
55. *Ibid.*, p. 1389.
56. *Ibid.*, p. 1391.
57. *Ibid.*, p. 1290.
58. *Ibid.*, p. 228.
59. *Ibid.*, p. 229.
60. *Ibid.*, p. 230.
61. *Ibid.*, p. 235.
62. *Ibid.*, p. 1415.

Chapter 9

1. Francis Jeanson, *La foi d'un incroyant* (Paris: Seuil, 1965), p. 21.
2. Stanislas Breton, *Du principe* (Paris and Neuchâtel: Aubier, Cerf, Delachaux et Niestlé, and Desclée De Brouwer, 1971).
3. Jacques Colette, *Histoire et absolu. Essai sur Kierkegaard* (Collection "L'athéisme interrogé"; Paris: Desclée, 1972).
4. Henri Bouillard, *The Knowledge of God,* tr. by S. D. Femiano (New York: Herder & Herder, 1968), p. 7. Cf. *idem,* "Le refus de la théologie naturelle dans la théologie protestante," in the joint work, *Existence de Dieu* (Tournai: Casterman, 1961), pp. 95–108; *idem, Karl Barth* (Théologie 39; Paris: Aubier, 1957).
4a. Bouillard, *The Knowledge of God,* p. 13.
5. *Ibid.*, pp. 11–12, citing Barth, *Credo* (New York, 1962).
6. *Ibid.*, p. 19, citing Feuerbach, *Das Wesen der Religion.*
7. *Ibid.*, p. 27.
8. Cf. Jacques-J. Natanson, *La mort de Dieu. Essai sur l'athéisme moderne* (Paris: Presses Universitaires de France, 1975), p. 267.
9. Cf. P. Fruchon, *Existence humaine et révélation. Essais d'herméneutique* (Cogitatio fidei 86, Paris: Cerf, 1976), p. 41.
10. *Critique de la raison pure* (Paris: Presses Universitaires de France, 1950), pp. 429ff.
11. Cf. my article, "Jacques Monod: Le hasard et la nécessité," *Prêtre et apôtre,* October 15, 1971, pp. 229–33.
12. Gabriel Marcel, *Creative Fidelity,* tr. by R. Rosthal (New York: Farrar Straus, 1964), p. 178.
13. Letter IV to Mlle de Ronnez, cited in A. -M. Dubarle, "Allusions scripturaires de Pascal," *Revue des sciences philosophiques et théologiques* 45 (1961), 644, n. 9.
14. *Pensées,* Brunschvicg 693 (Krailsheimer, p. 88, no. 198).
15. *Ibid.*, Brunschvicg 543 (Krailsheimer, p. 86, no. 190).
16. St. Augustine, *Confessions* IV, 12, 19.
17. *Ibid.*, VII, 7, 11: "Intus enim erat."

18. *Ibid.,* III, 6, 11: "Tu autem era intimior intimo meo et superior summo meo." Augustine sums up this transcendence-in-immanence in a compact formula: *internum aeternum,* "the eternal within" (IX, 4, 10).
19. Aimé Forest, *La vocation de l'espirt* (Paris: Aubier, 1953), p. 129.
20. Kant, *op. cit.* (n. 10), p. 53.
21. Maurice Blondel, *L'Action* (1893). Many reprintings.
22. This would also be Kant's conclusion; cf. Fruchon, *op cit.,* p. 41.
23. Cf. *Incroyance et Foi.* Dossiers du Secrétariat Français pour les Non-Croyants, no. 31 (Winter 1974–75, pp. 8–9.
24. Jeanson, *op. cit.,* p. 9.
25. "Dieu, croyants et non-croyants," *Echanges,* no. 83 (reprinted from *Combat,* September 29, 1967).
26. Marcel, *op. cit.,* pp. 179–80.
27. Etienne Borne, in *L'homme devant Dieu. Mélanges offerts au Père de Lubac* (Théologie 58; Paris: Aubier, 1964), p. 88.
28. *Ibid.*
29. Cf. Hans Küng, *On Becoming a Christian,* tr. by E. Quinn (Garden City, N.Y.: Doubleday, 1976). I am greatly indebted to this book for the approach suggested in the following pages. Cf. especially Küng, pp. 64–88.
30. St. Augustine, *Confessions* IX, 10, 25; also X, 6, 9.
31. Anne Philipe, *Ici, Là-bas, Ailleurs* (Paris: Gallimard, 1974), p. 74.

Bibliography

This bibliography makes no claim to completeness. It intentionally omits books and articles listed for the varous thinkers in the chapters devoted to them and gives only a few general works on the subject.

Arvon, Henri. *L'athéisme.* Que sais-je? no. 1291. Paris: Presses Universitaires de France, 1967.

L'athéisme dans la philosophie contemporaine. Vol. II/1 of Giulio Girardi and J.-François Six (eds.,), *Des Chrétiens interrogent l'athéisme.* Paris: Desclée, 1970.

Borne, Etienne, *Atheism.* Translated by S. J. Tester. New York: Hawthorn Books, 1961.

Breton, Stanislas. *Du principe.* Paris and Neuchâtel: Aubier, Cerf, Delachaux et Niestlé, and Desclée de Brouwer, 1971.

Bruaire, Claude. *Le droit de Dieu.* Paris. Aubier, 1974.

Dartigues, André. *Le croyant devant la critique contemporaine.* Paris: Le Centurion, 1975.

Humanism and Christianity. Edited by C. Geffré. Concilium 86. New York: Herder and Herder, 1973.

Lacroix, Jean. *The Meaning of Modern Atheism.* Translated by G. Barden. New York: Macmillan, 1956.

Lubac, Henri de. *The Drama of Atheist Humanism.* Translated by E. M. Riley. New York: Sheed & Ward, 1950.

Morel, Jean. *Problèmes actuels de la religion.* Paris: Aubier, 1968.

Murray, John Courtney. *The Problem of God Yesterday and Today.* New Haven: Yale University Press, 1964.

Natanson, Jacques-J. *La mort de Dieu. Essai sur l'athéisme moderne.* Paris: Presses Universitaires de France, 1975.

Schillebeeckx, Edward. *Dieu en revision.* Foi vivante 122. Paris: Cerf, 1970.

Tresmontant, Claude. *Les problèmes de l'athéisme.* Paris: Seuil, 1972.

Van de Pol, W. H. *The End of Conventional Christianity.* Translated by T. Zuydwijk. New York: Newman, 1968.

Zahrnt, Heinz. *Dieu ne peut pas mourir.* Paris: Cerf, 1971.